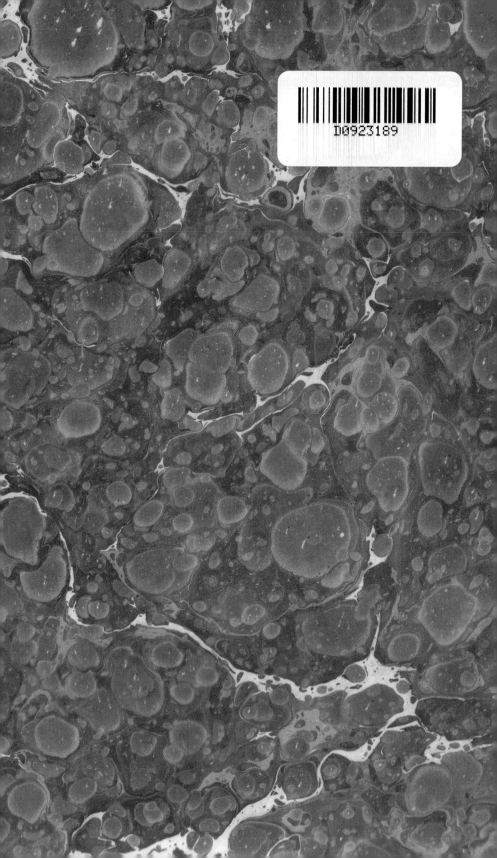
D0923189

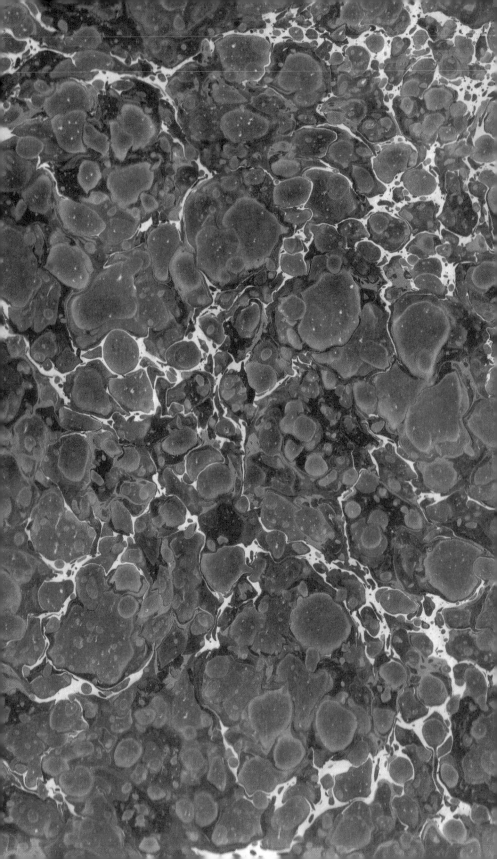

TRUTH MATTERS

TRUTH MATTERS

Landmark Chapters from the
Teaching Ministry of

JOHN MacARTHUR

35th anniversary anthology

1969–2004

THOMAS NELSON PUBLISHERS®
Nashville

A Division of Thomas Nelson, Inc.
www.ThomasNelson.com

CONTENTS

FOREWORD

This special volume has been compiled to commemorate the thirty-fifth anniversary of John MacArthur's entry into full-time pastoral ministry. For all those years he has devoted himself to shepherding one flock, the congregation of Grace Community Church in Sun Valley, California. So this occasion marks a landmark anniversary for the church as well.

The elders and pastoral staff of Grace Church collaborated to assemble this volume without John MacArthur's knowledge. We wanted to surprise him and honor him on his anniversary with a gift that we know will edify and bless thousands who read it.

So we selected our favorite chapters from some of our pastor's most important published works. Then we narrowed our choices down enough to make a manageable single volume. The result is the cream of a very select crop. These are complete and unabridged chapters, all compiled in this anthology—which we unveiled and presented to John MacArthur on his thirty-fifth anniversary celebration in February 2004. This book epitomizes what John has devoted his life to: clear, in-depth biblical exposition that makes the truth accessible to lay men and women.

John MacArthur's diligence as a student of Scripture is well known. He doesn't employ researchers to compile material or writers to help draft his sermons. In the privacy of his own study he has faithfully, tirelessly, steadfastly—for the past thirty-five years—prepared fresh material for at least two sermons each week. John's writing ministry is the outgrowth of that labor, as John has distilled his teaching into more than a hundred major books and commentaries. Perhaps no other single author since the Puritan era has produced so many doctrinal studies with such widespread popular appeal. This commemorative volume brings together chapters from several best-selling books. Our only regret is that space did not permit us to include more chapters.

Since 1989 (when the classic *The Gospel According to Jesus* was published and became an overnight bestseller) John MacArthur has produced at least two trade books per year—all of them substantial, serious, provocative, biblical, and hard-hitting. That style reflects John's preaching. He is nothing if not clear, straightforward, uncompromising, and passionate for the truth.

Several of the books excerpted here have been highly controversial. It may surprise those who know John only from his books to learn that he is not fond of debate. In fact, he despises confrontation and argumentation. But he loves truth more than he hates conflict, so his plain teaching has often put him in the position of having to defend unpopular truth. And he has always done that skillfully, persuasively, courageously, and above all, biblically.

In fact, the one passion John has tried to inculcate in those of us who sit under his teaching is an earnest conviction that *truth matters*. God is not glorified where the truth is stifled, watered down, or adjusted to fit human preferences. Sadly, in our generation, even the mainstream evangelical movement has all too frequently been guilty of trying to soften and tame the truth. John MacArthur has often been a singular prophetic voice calling evangelicals to embrace and stand for the hard truths of Scripture. He has in effect been the conscience of evangelicalism in our generation.

John is usually embarrassed by accolades and uncomfortable with any kind of acclaim. Those of us who have the privilege of sitting under his preaching each week will all testify that his life is consistent with what he teaches, and his humility is genuine. But Hebrews 13:7 commands us: "*Remember* those who led you, who spoke the word of God to you; and considering the result of their conduct, *imitate their faith*" (NASB, emphasis added).

Human words fail to convey the depth of our gratitude for John MacArthur's labor as our pastor. There is no way we can honor him in the way he deserves. That is something only God can do in the glory of eternity. But we want to express our heartfelt love to him and our profound appreciation for thirty-five years of faithful, fruitful ministry. Few churches have been blessed as Grace Church has with such a rich heritage of careful, faithful, verse-by-verse exposition over so long a period of time. We know that we are collectively and individually accountable for what we do with all we have learned from our pastor-teacher, because to whom much has been given, much shall be required.

To John MacArthur, we want to say thank you for your consistent, faithful, diligent study and teaching. We rejoice in God's goodness to us these past thirty-five years—only the *first* years of a ministry that we pray will continue for many more years. May God bless you, John, as you continue to teach us and challenge us with the truth of His Word. Be steadfast and unmovable, always abounding in the work of the Lord; you know that your labor in Him is not in vain (1 Cor. 15:58).

—PHIL JOHNSON

1

TRUTH IN A WORLD OF THEORY[1]

Sanctify them in the truth; Thy word is truth.

JOHN 17:17

It is significant that one of the biblical names of Christ is Wonderful Counselor. He is the highest and ultimate one to whom we may turn for counsel, and His Word is the well from which we may draw divine wisdom. What could be more wonderful than that? In fact, one of the most glorious aspects of Christ's perfect sufficiency is the wonderful counsel and great wisdom He supplies in our times of despair, confusion, fear, anxiety, and sorrow. He is the quintessential Counselor.

Now, that is not to denigrate the importance of Christians counseling each other. There certainly is a crucial need for biblically sound counseling ministries within the body of Christ. I would not for a moment dispute the important role of those who are spiritually gifted to offer encouragement, discernment, comfort, advice, compassion, and help to others. In fact, one of the very problems that has led to the current plague of bad counsel is that churches have not done as well as they could in enabling people with those kinds of spiritual gifts to minister excellently. The complexities of this modern age make it more difficult than ever to take the time necessary to listen well, serve others through compassionate personal involvement, and otherwise provide the close fellowship necessary for the church body to enjoy health and vitality.

Churches have looked to psychology to fill the gap, but it isn't going to work. Professional psychologists are no substitute for spiritually gifted people, and the counsel psychology offers cannot replace biblical wisdom and divine power. Moreover, psychology tends to make people dependent on a therapist, whereas those exercising true spiritual gifts always turn people back to an all-sufficient Savior and His all-sufficient Word.

A PSALM ON THE SUFFICIENCY OF GOD'S WORD

King David was an example of someone who occasionally sought advice from human counselors but always ultimately turned to God for answers. As many of the psalms reveal, he was especially dependent on God alone when he struggled with personal problems or emotions. When hit with depression or inner turmoil, he turned to God and wrestled in prayer. When the problem was his own sin, he was repentant, broken, and contrite. He prayed, "Examine me, O LORD, and try me; test my mind and my heart" (Ps. 26:2). The spiritually mature always turn to God for help in times of anxiety, distress, confusion, or unrest in the soul, and they are assured of wise counsel and deliverance.

That's because every need of the human soul is ultimately spiritual. There is no such thing as a "psychological problem" unrelated to spiritual or physical causes. God supplies divine resources sufficient to meet all those needs completely. David understood that. His writings reflect the depth of human experience, emotion, and spiritual insight of one who had fully experienced the extremities of life. He knew the exhilaration of going from shepherd to king. He wrote of everything from absolute triumph to bitter discouragement. He wrestled with pain so deep he could hardly bear to live. His own son Absalom tried to kill him and was then killed. He suffered from horrible guilt because of immorality and murder. His children brought him constant grief. He struggled to understand both the nature of God and his own heart. Of God he said, "Holy and awesome is His name" (Ps. 111:9), while of himself he said, "Wash me thoroughly from my iniquity, and cleanse me from my sin" (Ps. 51:2). He told God what he felt and cried out for relief—though he admitted God had every right to punish him.

At the end of some of David's psalms he looked out a window of hope; sometimes he didn't. But David always went to God because he understood God's sovereignty and his own depravity. He knew that his all-sufficient Savior alone had the answers to his needs and the power to apply those answers (Ps. 119:24). And he knew that those answers were to be found in the truth about God revealed in His Word, which is itself perfectly sufficient. The sufficient God revealed Himself in His sufficient Word.

Psalm 19:7–14 is the most monumental statement on the sufficiency of Scripture ever made in concise terms. Penned by David under the inspiration of the Holy Spirit, it offers an unwavering testimony from God Himself about the sufficiency of His Word for every situation. It counters the teaching of those who believe we must augment God's Word with truth gleaned from modern psychology:

The law of the LORD is perfect, restoring the soul;
The testimony of the LORD is sure, making wise the simple.
The precepts of the LORD are right, rejoicing the heart;
The commandment of the LORD is pure, enlightening the eyes.
The fear of the LORD is clean, enduring forever;
The judgments of the LORD are true; they are righteous altogether.
They are more desirable than gold, yes, than much fine gold;
Sweeter also than honey and the drippings of the honeycomb.
Moreover, by them Thy servant is warned;
In keeping them there is great reward.
Who can discern his errors? Acquit me of hidden faults.
Also keep back Thy servant from presumptuous sins;
Let them not rule over me;
Then I shall be blameless,
And I shall be acquitted of great transgression.
Let the words of my mouth and the meditation of my heart
Be acceptable in Thy sight,
O LORD, my rock and my Redeemer.

With an economy of words the Holy Spirit gives us a comprehensive catalog of the characteristics and benefits of Scripture, each of which merits our close investigation.

In verses 7–9 David makes six statements about Scripture. Each title for Scripture includes the phrase "of the LORD." In revealing the many-faceted general purpose of God's Word, he calls Scripture "the law of the LORD," "the testimony of the LORD," "the precepts of the LORD," "the commandment of the LORD," "the fear of the LORD," and "the judgments of the LORD." In each case "LORD" translates the Hebrew word *Yahweh*, which is the covenant name of God. Clearly David wanted us to know that Scripture proceeds from God Himself.

Each of the six statements highlights a characteristic of God's Word and describes its effect in the life of one who embraces it.

SCRIPTURE IS PERFECT, RESTORING THE SOUL

In the first statement (v. 7), he says, "The law of the LORD is perfect, restoring the soul." The Hebrew word translated "law" is *torah*, which emphasizes the didactic nature of Scripture. Here David uses it to refer to Scripture as the sum of what God has revealed for our instruction, whether it be creed (what we believe), character (what we are), or conduct (what we do).

"Perfect" is the translation of a common Hebrew word meaning "whole," "complete," or "sufficient." It conveys the idea of something that is comprehensive, so as to cover all aspects of an issue. Commentator Albert Barnes wrote,

> The meaning [of "perfect"] is that [Scripture] lacks nothing [for] its completeness; nothing in order that it might be what it should be. It is complete as a revelation of Divine truth; it is complete as a rule of conduct . . . It is absolutely true; it is adapted with consummate wisdom to the [needs] of man; it is an unerring guide of conduct. There is nothing there which would lead men into error or sin; there is nothing essential for man to know which may not be found there.[2]

Scripture is comprehensive, embodying all that is necessary to one's spiritual life. David's implied contrast is with the imperfect, insufficient, flawed reasoning of men.

God's perfect law, David said, affects people by "restoring the soul" (v. 7). The Hebrew word translated "restoring" can mean "converting," "reviving," or "refreshing," but my favorite synonym is "transforming." The word "soul" (in Hebrew, *nephesh*) refers to one's person, self, or heart. It is translated all those ways (and many more) in the Old Testament. The essence of it is the inner person, the whole person, the real you. To paraphrase David's words, Scripture is so powerful and comprehensive that it can convert or transform the entire person, changing someone into precisely the person God wants him to be. God's Word is sufficient to restore through salvation even the most broken life—a fact to which David himself gave abundant testimony.

SCRIPTURE IS TRUSTWORTHY, IMPARTING WISDOM

David, further expanding the sweep of scriptural sufficiency, writes in Psalm 19:7, "The testimony of the LORD is sure, making wise the simple." "Testimony" speaks of Scripture as a divine witness. Scripture is God's sure testimony to who He is and what He requires of us. "Sure" means His testimony is unwavering, immovable, unmistakable, reliable, and worthy to be trusted. It provides a foundation on which to build our lives and eternal destinies.

In 2 Peter 1:16–18 Peter reflects back to his time on the Mount of Transfiguration with all the supernatural events of that marvelous occasion (the majestic glory of Christ, the voice from heaven, and the appearance of Moses and Elijah). But despite all he had experienced, he says in verse 19, "We have more sure—the prophetic word" (literal translation).

In that statement Peter affirmed that the testimony of God's written Word is a surer and more convincing confirmation of God's truth than what he had personally seen and heard at the transfiguration of Christ. Unlike many today who cite spurious mystical experiences, Peter had a verifiable real-life encounter with Christ in His full glory on the mount. And in contrast with those today who advocate miracles as the necessary proof of God's power and presence, Peter looked to Scripture as a higher and more trustworthy authority than even such a dramatic experience. Commentator Samuel Cox has written,

> Peter knew a sounder basis for faith than that of signs and wonders. He had seen our Lord Jesus Christ receive honor and glory from God the Father in the holy mount; he had been dazzled and carried out of himself by visions and voices from heaven; but, nevertheless, even when his memory and heart are throbbing with recollections of that sublime scene, he says, "we have something surer still in the prophetic word." . . . It was not the miracles of Christ by which he came to know Jesus, but the word of Christ as interpreted by the spirit of Christ.[3]

Scripture is the product of God's Spirit moving upon its human authors to produce His Word in written form (2 Peter 1:20–21). As such, it supersedes even apostolic experiences with Jesus Himself. Perhaps that is why Jesus prevented the disciples on the Emmaus Road from recognizing Him as He "explained to them the things concerning Himself in all the Scriptures" (Luke 24:27). He wanted their faith and preaching to be based on Scripture, not merely on their own personal experience—no matter how moving or memorable that experience might be. If that was true of the apostles, how much more should believers today seek to know God's Word rather than seeking supernatural or ecstatic experiences. Experience can be counterfeited easily, but not Scripture. It is once-for-all delivered!

God's sure Word makes the simple wise (v. 7). The Hebrew word translated "simple" comes from an expression meaning "an open door." It evokes the image of a naive person who doesn't know when to shut his mind to false or impure teaching. He is undiscerning, ignorant, and gullible. But God's Word makes him wise. "Wise" speaks not of one who merely knows some fact, but of one who is skilled in the art of godly living. He submits to Scripture and knows how to apply it to his circumstances. The Word of God thus takes a simple mind with no discernment and makes it skilled in all the issues of life. This, too, is in contrast to the wisdom of men, which in reality is foolishness (1 Cor. 1:20).

SCRIPTURE IS RIGHT, CAUSING JOY

David adds a third statement about the Scripture's sufficiency. He writes, "The precepts of the LORD are right, rejoicing the heart." Precepts are divine principles and guidelines for character and conduct. Since God created us and knows how we must live to be productive for His glory, He has placed in Scripture every principle we need for godly living.

God's precepts, David said, are "right." Rather than simply indicating what is right as opposed to wrong, that word has the sense of showing someone the true path. The truths of Scripture lay out the proper path through the difficult maze of life. That's a wonderful confidence. So many people today are distressed or despondent because they lack direction and purpose. Most seek answers from the wrong sources. God's Word not only provides the light to our path (Ps. 119:105), but it also sets the route before us.

Because it steers us through the right course of life, God's Word brings great joy. If you're depressed, anxious, fearful, or doubting, learn to obey God's counsel and share in the resulting delight. Don't turn to self-indulgent pursuits such as self-esteem and self-fulfillment. Focus on divine truth. Therein you will find true and lasting joy. All other sources are shallow and fleeting.

David himself went to Scripture for help when he was discouraged or depressed. In Psalm 119:50 he wrote, "This is my comfort in my affliction, that Thy word has revived me." Again, David speaks against the futility of the joyless paths men follow, pursuing happiness but never finding it to last.

Even the "weeping prophet," Jeremiah, experienced joy amid tremendous human stress because God's Word was his joy and the delight of his heart (Jer. 15:16).

SCRIPTURE IS PURE, ENLIGHTENING THE EYES

Psalm 19:8 gives a fourth characteristic of Scripture's utter sufficiency: "The commandment of the LORD is pure, enlightening the eyes." "Commandment" stresses the Bible's nonoptional nature. It is not a book of suggestions. Its divine mandates are authoritative and binding. Those who treat it lightly place themselves in eternal peril. Those who take it seriously find eternal blessing.

"Pure" could better be translated "lucid"—Scripture is not mystifying, confusing, or puzzling. The synonym "clear" is best. God's Word is a revelation—a revealing of truth to make the dark things light, bringing eternity into bright focus. Granted, there are things in Scripture that are hard to understand (2 Peter 3:16). But taken as a whole, the Bible is not a bewildering book.

Scripture, because of its absolute clarity, brings understanding where there is ignorance, order where there is confusion, and light where there is spiritual and moral darkness. It stands in stark contrast to the muddled musings of unredeemed men, who themselves are blind and unable to discern truth or live righteously. God's Word clearly reveals the blessed, hopeful truths they can never see.

SCRIPTURE IS CLEAN, ENDURING FOREVER

In Psalm 19:9 David uses the term "fear" as a synonym for God's Word: "The fear of the LORD is clean, enduring forever." "Fear" speaks of the reverential awe for God that compels us to worship Him. Scripture, in this sense, is God's manual on how to worship Him.

The Hebrew word translated "clean" speaks of the absence of impurity, filthiness, defilement, or imperfection. Scripture is without sin, evil, corruption, or error. The truth it conveys is therefore absolutely undefiled and without blemish. That truth is pictured in Psalm 12:6, where David calls the Word "flawless, like silver refined in a furnace of clay, purified seven times" (NIV).

Because it is flawless, Scripture endures forever (Ps. 19:9). Any change or modification could only introduce imperfection. Scripture is eternally and unalterably perfect. Jesus said, "Heaven and earth will pass away, but My words will not pass away" (Mark 13:31). That guarantees that the Bible is permanent, unchanging, and therefore relevant to everyone in every age of history. It has always been and will always be sufficient.

I once agreed to debate a man who led an "evangelical" homosexual denomination. I asked, "What do you do with the Bible's condemnations of homosexuality as sin?"

"Oh, come on!" he said. "Everybody knows that the Bible is psychologically unsophisticated, reflecting the views of primitive thinking. The Bible is antiquated in its sociological theory. You can't go to an ancient document like this and expect to deal with twentieth-century social problems. The Bible ought to stay in its own environment. It needs to be updated with a contemporary understanding of psychological and sociological phenomena."

It must grieve God when people slander Him by claiming that the Bible is outdated or isn't sophisticated enough for our educated society. Scripture needs no updating, editing, or refining. Whatever time or culture you live in, it is eternally relevant. It needs no help in that regard. It is pure, sinless, inerrant truth; it is enduring. It is God's revelation for every generation. It was written by the omniscient Spirit of God, who is infinitely more sophisticated than anyone who dares stand in judgment on Scripture's relevancy for our society, and infinitely wiser than all the best philosophers, analysts, and psychologists who pass like a childhood parade into irrelevancy.

SCRIPTURE IS TRUE, ALTOGETHER RIGHTEOUS

Verse 9 of Psalm 19 gives the final characteristic and effect of God's all-sufficient Word: "The judgments of the LORD are true; they are righteous altogether." "Judg-ments" in that context mean ordinances or divine verdicts from the bench of the Supreme Judge of the earth. The Bible is God's standard for judging the life and eternal destiny of every person.

Unbelievers can't know what is true because they are blind to God's Word. Being deceived by Satan, they search vainly for spiritual truth. But aside from God's Word they cannot discover ultimate truth about the things that really matter: origins, the purpose of life, morality, values, life, death, destiny, eternity, heaven, hell, true love, hope, security, and every other fundamental spiritual issue.

Recently I received a book on how to deal with depression, which was written by a contemporary psychiatrist. A section entitled "Reprogramming Your Conscious Mind" particularly caught my attention. The doctor's first suggestion was to shout, "Cancel!" every time you have a negative thought. She also recommended sleep programming—playing a tape recording all night that contains lots of positive feedback. During the day she said you should listen to positive music.

The doctor also thought it would be helpful to cultivate a meaningful spiritual philosophy. She said to find a belief system that works for you—any will do—but be sure to avoid people who talk about sin and guilt. Her final point was that you are to find the light in yourself. Unfortunately, that is the best human wisdom can do. [4]

Jesus illustrated the desperate, hopeless search for truth in human wisdom when He said to a group of unbelievers:

Why do you not understand what I am saying? It is because you cannot hear My word. You are of your father the devil, and you want to do the desires of your father. He was a murderer from the beginning, and does not stand in the truth, because there is no truth in him. Whenever he speaks a lie, he speaks from his own nature; for he is a liar, and the father of lies. But because I speak the truth, you do not believe Me . . . He who is of God hears the words of God; for this reason you do not hear them, because you are not of God. (John 8:43–45, 47)

By way of contrast, believers have the truth about everything that really matters. What an enormous privilege to possess the Word of truth!

Because Scripture is true it is "righteous altogether" (Ps. 19:9). The implication of that phrase is that its truthfulness produces a comprehensive righteousness in those who accept it. And because it is a complete and exhaustive source of truth and righteousness, we are forbidden to add to it, take from it, or distort it in any way (Deut. 4:2; Rev. 22:18–19; 2 Peter 3:15–16).

In Psalm 119 David gives further testimony to the righteous sufficiency of Scripture:

> Forever, O LORD,
> Thy word is settled in heaven.
> . . . I esteem right all Thy precepts concerning everything,
> I hate every false way.
> . . . Righteous art Thou, O LORD,
> And upright are Thy judgments.
> Thou hast commanded Thy testimonies in righteousness
> And exceeding faithfulness.
> . . . Thy righteousness is an everlasting righteousness,
> And Thy law is truth.
> . . . The sum of Thy word is truth,
> And every one of Thy righteous ordinances is everlasting.
> (vv. 89, 128, 137–38, 142, 160)

Contrary to what many are teaching today, there is no need for additional revelations, visions, or words of prophecy. In contrast to the theories of men, God's Word is true and absolutely comprehensive. Rather than seeking something more than God's glorious revelation, Christians need only to study and obey what they already have!

MORE THAN MUCH FINE GOLD

David concludes that God's Word is "more desirable than gold, yes, than much fine gold" (Ps. 19:10). Scripture is infinitely more precious than anything this world has to offer, perfectly sufficient for every need of life. Thus Scripture assesses its own immense value. As for its ability to satisfy our spiritual appetites, David writes that it is "sweeter also than honey and the drippings of the honeycomb." To David, meditating on God's Word was a source of great pleasure and enrichment. It meant more to him than the sweetest things in life.

Nothing this world has to offer is more precious than God's Word. I have a friend who collects rare Bibles. He owns a wonderful collection, with one Bible dating back to the fourth century. But my favorite is a Bible from sixteenth-century England, one of the earliest printed copies of God's Word. The top third of this Bible is covered with the blood of its original owner. My friend let me hold it in my hands, and tears came to my eyes as I leafed through it.

How did blood get on the pages of that Bible? When Bloody Mary ruled England, she terrorized Protestants, murdering as many as she could. Her soldiers would spill the person's blood, then take his Bible and dip it deep into the blood. A few of those Bibles have been preserved and are known as Martyrs' Bibles. Scientists have tested the paper and confirmed that the dark stains on every page of my friend's Bible are human blood.

I examined that Bible carefully, page by page. I could see where it was well worn from being studied. There are water stains, as if from tears, and places where a thumb had frayed favorite pages. This was someone's most valuable possession, and his or her blood is there to prove it.

In sad contrast, however, contemporary Christians tend to take their Bibles for granted, forgetting that many have given their lives just to own one copy. If the church today placed as high a value on God's Word as those martyrs did, perhaps there would not be so many people running off to experts in human theory and seeking counsel other than the perfect wisdom God gives us in His Word.

I am convinced that many who submit to various kinds of extrabiblical therapy do so precisely because they are looking for a way of solving their problems without surrendering to what they know God's Word requires of them.

Scripture hasn't failed them—they've failed Scripture. Many have never learned to let the Word of Christ richly dwell within them, as Paul instructs in Colossians 3:16. They have treated Scripture in a cursory way and never plumbed its depths. Their sinful neglect inevitably bears the fruit of doctrinal confusion and spiritual impotence. Because they never disciplined themselves to live according to biblical principles, they're now abandoning Scripture for worldly alternatives. They turn to psychoanalysis to solve their problems, to science to explain the origin of life, to philosophy to explain the meaning of life, and to sociology to explain why they sin. Churches, schools, and seminaries have thus made themselves vulnerable to the influence of such teachings.

In Psalm 19:11 David concludes his hymn on the sufficiency of Scripture: "Moreover, by [Thy judgments] Thy servant is warned; in keeping them there is great reward." The warnings of Scripture help to protect us against temptation, sin, error, foolishness, false teachers, and every other threat to our spiritual well-being. And to heed those warnings brings great reward. It is not a material prize; the Hebrew word for "reward" speaks of a spiritual blessing, not temporal riches. It is the settled joy and rest that come to those who live by God's Word.

There is no substitute for submission to Scripture. Your spiritual health depends on placing the utmost value on the Word of God and obeying it with an eager heart. If you think you can find answers to your spiritual problems through human counsel or worldly wisdom, you are forfeiting the most valuable and only reliable source of answers to the human dilemma. Don't relinquish the sweet, satisfying riches of God's Word for the bitter gall of this world's folly.

David ended this psalm by praying, "Let the words of my mouth and the meditation of my heart be acceptable in Thy sight, O LORD, my rock and my Redeemer" (v. 14). How can we be assured of having such acceptable thoughts and meditations? Joshua 1:8 gives us the answer and the results: "This book of the law shall not depart from your mouth, but you shall meditate on it day and night, so that you may be careful to do according to all that is written in it; for then you will make your way prosperous, and then you will have success."

2

HOLY, HOLY, HOLY[1]

Knowing that God is immutable, omnipotent, omnipresent, and omniscient is significant, but those attributes give limited insight into what God expects of us. What beyond His unchanging, all-powerful, infinitely knowing presence compels us to worship?

It is basically this: God is holy. Of all the attributes of God, holiness is the one that most uniquely describes Him and in reality is a summarization of all His other attributes. The word "holiness" refers to His separateness, His otherness, the fact that He is unlike any other being. It indicates His complete and infinite perfection. Holiness is the attribute of God that binds all the others together. Properly understood, it will revolutionize the quality of our worship.

When they exalted God, the angels didn't say, "Eternal, Eternal, Eternal"; they didn't say, "Faithful, Faithful, Faithful," "Wise, Wise, Wise," or "Mighty, Mighty, Mighty." They said, "Holy, Holy, Holy, is the Lord God, the Almighty" (Rev. 4:8). His holiness is the crown of all that He is.

Exodus 15:11 asks, "Who is like Thee among the gods, O LORD? Who is like Thee, majestic in holiness, awesome in praises, working wonders?" The answer, of course, is that no being is equal to God in holiness. In fact, holiness is so uniquely and exclusively an attribute of God that Psalm 111:9 says, "Holy and awesome is His name."

THE STANDARD OF ABSOLUTE HOLINESS

God doesn't conform to a holy standard; He *is* the standard. He never does anything wrong, He never errs, He never makes a misjudgment, He never causes something to happen that isn't right. There are no degrees to His holiness. He is holy, flawless, without error, without sin, fully righteous, utterly, absolutely, infinitely holy.

To be in God's presence, one must be holy. That was demonstrated when the angels sinned. God immediately cast them out and prepared a place for them separated from His presence. When men choose not to come to God, when they choose to reject Jesus Christ, their ultimate end is to be sent to the place prepared for the devil and his angels, out of the presence of God.

Miraculously, salvation imputes God's own holiness to the believer in Jesus Christ (see Phil. 3:8–9). Peter articulated that truth when he wrote: "It is written, 'You shall be holy, for I am holy'" (1 Peter 1:16).

God's holiness is best seen in His hatred of sin. God cannot tolerate sin; He is totally removed from it. Amos 5:21–23 records God's strong words to those attempting to worship Him while polluted with sin:

> I hate, I reject your festivals,
> Nor do I delight in your solemn assemblies.
> Even though you offer up to Me burnt offerings and your grain offerings,
> I will not accept them;
> And I will not even look at the peace offerings of your fatlings.
> Take away from Me the noise of your songs;
> I will not even listen to the sound of your harps.

That does not mean that God hates sacrifices and offerings and festivals and music. God desires all those things, because He instituted them. But when those instruments of worship are tainted with sin, God hates them.

God doesn't want you to sin, even if it would make your testimony more exciting or display His grace. He never wills sin. He will not keep you from sinning if you choose to, but God never tempts anyone to sin, and He cannot be tempted to sin (James 1:13). Sin is the object of His displeasure. God loves holiness. Psalm 11:7 says, "For the LORD is righteous; He loves righteousness."

THE PROOF OF GOD'S HOLINESS

God's holiness is visible in many ways. It is seen *in the creation of man,* to begin with. In Ecclesiastes 7:29, we read, "Behold, I have found only this, that God made men upright, but they have sought out many devices." In other words, when God made man, He made him to reflect His holiness. Sin was man's rebellion against that purpose.

Residual marks of God's holiness are still evident in man despite man's sin. Man has an innate sense of right and wrong. Although it is imperfect, that inborn understanding of good and evil manifests itself through man's conscience, his code of ethics, and his sense of justice. Romans 2:15 describes the accountability of the Gentiles to God: "They show the work of the Law written in their hearts, their conscience bearing witness, and their thoughts alternately accusing them or else defending them." Even the vilest, most rebellious man has at least a crude framework of righteousness inherent in his consciousness.

Second, God's holiness is seen *in the moral law.* One of the primary reasons God instituted the law under Moses was to demonstrate His holiness. When God laid down a legal standard of morality, He proved Himself to be a righteous, moral, holy being. In Romans 7:12 Paul says, "The Law is holy, and the commandment is holy and righteous and good." The moral aspects of the Mosaic Law are all reaffirmed in the teachings of the New Testament.

God's holiness is evident *in His sacrificial law,* although we might not normally think of it that way. When we see God commanding that animals be slain as sacrifices and their blood sprinkled all over, we see in a graphic way that death is the result of sin. Every time the Jews made a sacrifice, they illustrated the deadliness of sin, and that stated by contrast the holiness of God.

In a related sense, God's holiness is also seen *in judgment on sin.* When the Bible speaks, for example, as it does in 2 Thessalonians 1:7, of Jesus' coming in flaming fire and taking vengeance on those who do not know God and do not obey the gospel; and when it describes, as it does in Jude 15, the condemnation of the ungodly, we see how God hates sin. His judgment on sin is a reflection of His holiness; He must punish sin because He is holy.

The supreme demonstration of the holiness of God is seen *in the cross.* That is where God bore man's sin in the person of Christ and gave the greatest illustration of His holiness—His hatred of sin and power over it. God is so holy that He had to turn from His own Son because Christ bore man's sin. He paid the ultimate price necessary to satisfy His holiness—the death of His Son.

Hebrews 9:26 makes an amazing and mysterious statement: "He has been manifested to put away sin by the sacrifice of Himself." God in Christ paid the supreme price of dying Himself, bearing man's sin, because the price had to be paid even if it cost Him His own life. That's holiness.

WORSHIP THE LORD IN THE BEAUTY OF HOLINESS

A worshiping life must affirm the utter holiness of God; in fact, an acknowledgment and understanding of God's holiness is essential to true worship. In the words of Psalm 96:2–6, we are to:

> Sing to the LORD, bless His name;
> Proclaim good tidings of His salvation from day to day.
> Tell of His glory among the nations,
> His wonderful deeds among all the peoples.
> For great is the LORD, and greatly to be praised;
> He is to be feared above all gods.
> For all the gods of the peoples are idols,
> But the LORD made the heavens.
> Splendor and majesty are before Him,
> Strength and beauty are in His sanctuary.

That describes acts of worship. Verse 9 makes the key statement: "Worship the LORD in holy attire; tremble before Him, all the earth." "Holy attire" means the spiritual clothing of holiness. "Tremble before Him" implies fear. In fact, the King James version translates that verse, "O worship the LORD in the beauty of holiness: fear before him, all the earth."

Here we are introduced to the frequent biblical connection of the idea of God's holiness with fear on the part of the worshiper. It is a fear that grows out of an overwhelming sense of unworthiness in the presence of pure holiness. For example, in Genesis 18 Abraham confessed in the presence of God that he was dust and ashes. Similarly, Job said after his pilgrimage, "I have heard of Thee by the hearing of the ear; but now my eye sees Thee; therefore I retract, and I repent in dust and ashes" (Job 42:5–6). Ezra 9 records Ezra's sense of shame as he came before the Lord to worship. Habakkuk saw God revealed in the midst of his trial and circumstance, and his knees began to smash together.

ISAIAH'S ENCOUNTER WITH GOD

Isaiah 6 describes Isaiah's experience with God's holiness. Uzziah had been king in Judah for fifty-two years. Although he was superficially effective and had secured the country from its enemies, built a very formidable army, tightened up its defenses, created economic productivity, and brought great external security, inwardly the nation was corrupt, defiled, wretched, and superficially worshiping God.

As a result, in chapter 5, Isaiah pronounced half a dozen curses on Judah. The people had the illusion that things were going along well because they had a good leader. But in 740 B.C. their leader died of leprosy when God struck him down because of his pride.

When Uzziah died, the nation's sense of security was gone, and Isaiah sensed a tremendous need to enter into the presence of God. In Isaiah 6:1, Isaiah describes how he saw the Lord sitting on a throne, high and lifted up. And there he heard the seraphim cry back and forth to one another in antiphonal response, "Holy, Holy, Holy, is the LORD of Hosts, the whole earth is full of His glory" (v. 3). His holiness fills all.

As Isaiah in worship perceived the holiness of God, the posts of the place began to move at the voices of those angels who cried back and forth, and the house was filled with smoke. He tells us his response in verse 5: "Then I said, 'Woe is me, for I am ruined! Because I am a man of unclean lips, and I live among a people of unclean lips; for my eyes have seen the King, the LORD of hosts.'"

One of the seraphim flew and touched Isaiah's mouth with a live, hot coal as a symbol of cleansing. When he was thus purged and made clean, the Lord was ready to use him, and he was available (v. 8).

Some might think that Isaiah did not have a very good self-image. He was not thinking positively; he was not affirming his strengths. Surely Isaiah knew that he had the best mouth in the land! He was a prophet of God! He was the best man in the nation. And yet he cursed himself. Why?

The answer is very clear. We find it in the words "My eyes have seen the King, the LORD of Hosts" (v. 5). Isaiah had seen a vision of God in His holiness, and he was absolutely shattered to the very core of his being by a sense of his own sinfulness. His heart longed for purging.

WHATEVER HAPPENED TO THE FEAR OF GOD?

When we see God as holy, our instant and only reaction is to see ourselves as unholy. Between God's holiness and man's unholiness is a gulf. And until a man understands the holiness of God he can never know the depth of his own sin. We ought to be shaken to our roots when we see ourselves in comparison to Him. If we are not deeply pained about our sin, we do not understand God's holiness.

Without such a vision of God's holiness, true worship is not possible. Worship is not giddy. It does not rush into God's presence unprepared and insensitive to His majesty. It is not shallow, superficial, or flippant. Worship is life lived in the presence of an infinitely righteous and omnipresent God by one utterly aware of His holiness and consequently overwhelmed with his own unholiness.

You and I may not have a vision of God like Isaiah's, but nonetheless, the lesson is true that when we enter into the presence of God, we must see Him as holy. And our sense of sinfulness and fear is proportional to our experience of the presence of God. If you have never worshiped God with a broken and a contrite spirit, you've never fully worshiped God, because that is the only appropriate response to entering the presence of holy God.

My heartfelt concern is that there is too much shallowness today with regard to God's holiness. Our relationship to God has become too casual. In the modern mind, God has become almost human, so buddy-buddy that we don't understand His holy indignation against sin. If we burst into His presence with lives unattended to by repentance, confession, and cleansing by the Spirit, we are vulnerable to His holy reaction. It is only by His grace that we breathe each breath, is it not? He has every reason to take our lives, for the wages of our sin is death.

There is much supposed worship going on today that does not genuinely regard God as holy, and thus it falls woefully short. A lot of nice songs are being sung, nice feelings are being felt, nice thoughts are being thought, and nice emotions are being expressed, without a genuine acknowledgment of the holiness of God. That kind of worship bears no relationship to the worship we see in the Bible. It may be more psychological than theological, more fleshly than spiritual.

The response of a true worshiper to a vision of God is that like Isaiah he is overwhelmed with his own sinfulness and consequently consumed with a sense of holy terror. I am certain that if the people today who claim to have seen God really saw Him, they wouldn't be lining up to get on the latest Christian talk show; they'd be lying prostrate on the ground, grieving over their sin.

REVERENCE AND GODLY FEAR

A true worshiper comes into the presence of God in healthy fear. God punishes sin, even in those who are redeemed. And He says in Hebrews 12:6, "Whom the Lord loves, He disciplines, and He scourges every son whom He receives."

Hebrews 12:28 goes on to say, "Let us have grace, whereby we may serve God acceptably with reverence and godly fear" (KJV). The word for "serve" is *latreuo*, a word for worship. The writer is talking about acceptable worship, and he lists two key elements: "reverence and godly fear." Note the reason he gives for such worship: "For our God is a consuming fire" (v. 29).

"Reverence" carries a positive connotation. It describes a sense of awe as we perceive the majesty of God. "Godly fear," on the other hand, can be seen as a sense of intimidation as we see the power and holiness of God, who "is a consuming fire." That refers to His power to destroy, His holy reaction against sin.

True worship, then, demands the sense of God's holiness, the sense of my sinfulness, and the cry for purging. That's the essence of the proper attitude of worship. Let me illustrate that principle from the life of Christ.

THE RESPONSE TO JESUS

It seems to be difficult for Christians today to get away from the idea that Jesus was a passive, amiable, meek-and-mild being who walked through the world making people feel good. Actually, when our Lord was here on earth people were afraid of Him. It was overwhelming for people to come face to face with the living God incarnate. In fact, the normal reaction to Jesus from both believers and skeptics was fear. He traumatized people.

Jesus' very presence was intimidating. Many things contributed to that. His authority was apparent. "The multitudes were amazed at His teaching; for He was teaching them as one having authority, and not as their scribes" (Matt. 7:28–29). His words were unique. "Never did a man speak the way this man speaks" (John 7:46). His works were undeniably of God. The blind man said, "If this man were not from God, He could do nothing" (John 9:33). His wisdom was superhuman. "No one was able to answer Him a word, nor did anyone dare from that day on to ask Him a another question" (Matt. 22:46). His purity was undeniable. He said, "Which one of you convicts Me of sin?" (John 8:46). His truthfulness was unquestionable. He challenged those who tried Him, "If I have spoken wrongly, bear witness of the wrong" (John 18:23). His power was astounding. He fed the multitude, cast out demons, and spoke to a fig tree, causing it to die on the spot.

Even when He was a boy the teachers were shocked when He spoke. His knowledge was beyond anything the people of His day had ever known, and John 7:15 says, "The Jews therefore were marveling, saying, 'How has this man become learned, having never been educated?'" His independence made religious leaders shudder. The Pharisees marveled that He didn't wash before dinner. He defied their ceremonies. His composure and confidence were beyond anything human.

You see, Jesus' presence aroused a sense of fear in people. He intimidated them. One of the reasons the Pharisees wanted to get rid of Him was that they could not handle that intimidation.

Perhaps the most striking reactions to Jesus were from those who saw the blazing revelation of His deity. Whether they believed or not, the reaction was the same: they were terrified.

Even the disciples were fearful when they faced squarely the reality that He was God. In Mark 4:37–41, we read that while the disciples were crossing the lake in a boat with Jesus, a storm struck, and their boat began to sink. The disciples panicked and awoke Jesus, who was sleeping through it all. He calmed the storm and rebuked them for their unbelief, and verse 41 tells us that they were "exceedingly" terrified (KJV). It's far more frightening to face the holiness of God inside your boat than to have a storm outside your boat.

In the next chapter of Mark, Jesus encountered a man possessed by a legion of demons. When Jesus sent the demons into a herd of pigs that then went into the lake and drowned, the people of the town came out and pleaded with Him to leave their country (Mark 5:17). It was not because they owned the pigs, or they would have demanded compensation. Rather, they were terrified in His holy presence. They knew God was in action, and they were not willing to face their own sin before Jesus.

Later in Mark 5, we read that a crowd gathered around Jesus. In the crowd was a lady who had been sick for many years. She believed in her heart that Christ had so much power that she could just grab hold of His robe and be healed. She pushed her way through the crowd and reached out in her feeble way and clung to His garment, clutching it in her hand, and instantly she was healed.

Jesus said, "Who touched My garments?" Verse 33 says, "The woman fearing and trembling, aware of what had happened to her, came and fell down before Him, and told Him the whole truth." She knew she was in the presence of God.

The word for "trembling" is the word used in the Septuagint to describe the shaking of Mount Sinai when God gave the Law. She really shook! She was terrified. A sinner in the presence of the Holy God should be.

In Luke 5, Peter was fishing and couldn't catch anything. The Lord came along and told him where to let his nets down, and he did, and Peter's catch was so great that he couldn't haul it in. When he finally got help from another boat to bring in the catch, there were so many fish that both boats began to sink. It was a demonstration to Peter of Jesus' deity. Peter "fell down at Jesus' feet, saying, 'Depart from me, for I am a sinful man, O Lord!'" (v. 8). All he could see was his own sinfulness when confronted with the power and presence of holy God.

The true worshiper comes in that spirit. He is broken over his sinfulness. A true worshiping life is a life of contrition; it is a life that sees sin and confesses continually (see 1 John 1:9). It seeks to hide at first and then to be purged.

GOD'S GRACE DOES NOT CANCEL HIS HOLINESS

Perhaps we have lost the fear of God because we take His grace for granted. At the very beginning, God said to Adam and Eve, "The day that you eat from [the forbidden tree] you shall surely die" (Gen. 2:17). They ate from it, but they didn't die that day. God showed them grace.

Throughout the Bible we see that God is gracious. The Law called for death for adulterers, blasphemers, and even rebellious children. But many in the Old Testament violated God's laws without suffering the death penalty the Law prescribed. David committed adultery, but God didn't take his life. He was gracious.

And He continues to be gracious. We are alive only because God is merciful. But instead of our accepting the mercy of God with great thankfulness and keeping the perspective of fearing God, we begin to get used to it. Consequently, when God does punish sin, we think He's unjust.

People look at the Old Testament and question the goodness of God. Some have even suggested that we shouldn't teach the Bible to children because the God it speaks of is too violent. Why, they ask, would God command the Israelites to destroy all the people living in Canaan? What kind of God would snuff out the life of a man simply for touching the ark? What kind of God would cause a bear to destroy a group of children for making fun of a prophet's baldness? What kind of God would open the ground and swallow up people? What kind of God would drown the whole world?

We are so used to mercy and grace that we think God has no right to be angry with sin. Romans 3:18 sums up the world's attitude: "There is no fear of God before their eyes."

Do you know why God took the lives of certain people in the Bible? It was not because they were more sinful than anyone else; it was because somewhere along the line, in the long process of grace and mercy, God had to set some examples to make men fear. He turned Lot's wife into a pillar of salt, not because she did something worse than anyone else ever did, but because she was to be His example. First Corinthians 10 cites some Old Testament people who were destroyed, and verse 11 says, "Now these things happened to them as an example, and they were written for our instruction." The highway of history is paved with God's mercy and grace. But there are billboards all the way along, posted so that men may know that God at any moment has a right to take their lives.

God is gracious, but don't confuse His mercy with justice. God is not unjust when He acts in a holy manner against sin. Don't ever get to the place that you are so used to mercy and grace that you abuse it by going on in your sin. Or that you question God when He does what He has every right to do against a sinner. Don't abuse God's grace; He will judge you too. But know this: He is holy, and He is to be feared.

THE REAL QUESTION

The question is not why God so dramatically judges some sinners, but rather why He lets any of us live. God has every right to punish sin, and "the wages of sin is death" (Rom. 6:23). Lamentations 3:22 says, "It is of the LORD's mercies that we are not consumed, because His compassions fail not" (KJV).

God's mercy, however, is not His blessing on our sin. Most of us have been guilty of the same kind of sin of hypocrisy as Ananias and Sapphira. Or we have come to the Lord's Table in an unworthy manner like those in Corinth who died for their sin. Or we have acted in a worldly fashion like Lot's wife, who was turned to a pillar of salt. The real question is not why God judged them so quickly and harshly, but why He hasn't done the same with us.

One reason for God's mercy is that He is driving us to repentance. Romans 2:4 says "The kindness of God leads you to repentance." God, by His mercy and kindness to us, is often actually bringing us to the point where we see His love for us and our need of repentance.

The Chronicles of Narnia, a series of children's books by C. S. Lewis, are a fantasy based on the truths of Christianity. Aslan, the golden lion, represents Christ. And in his description of that fierce and loving lion, Lewis has given evidence of a remarkable understanding of Christ's character.

In one scene, some talking beavers are describing Aslan to Lucy, Susan, and Peter, who are newcomers to the realm of Narnia. In anticipation of meeting him, they ask questions that reveal their fears.

"Ooh! said Susan, "I'd thought he was a man. Is he—quite safe? I shall feel rather nervous about meeting a lion."

"That you will, dearie, and no mistake," said Mrs. Beaver, "if there's anyone who can appear before Aslan without their knees knocking, they're either braver than most or else just silly."

"Then he isn't safe?" said Lucy.

"Safe?" said Mr. Beaver. "Don't you hear what Mrs. Beaver tells you? Who said anything about safe? 'Course he isn't safe. But he's good. He's the King, I tell you."[2]

After the children met Aslan, Lucy observed that his paws were potentially very soft or very terrible. They could be as soft as velvet with his claws drawn in, or sharp as knives with his claws extended.

We in modern Christianity have somehow missed that truth. While we are thankful for the reality of His grace, and while we want to enjoy the experience of His love, we have somehow neglected the truth of His holiness. And it is eating at the heart of our worship.

God is a living, eternal, glorious, merciful, holy being. His worshipers must come in the contrition and humility and brokenness of sinners who see themselves against the backdrop of that holiness. And that should put such thanksgiving and joy in our hearts for the gift of His forgiveness that our worship is all it should be.

We are to live lives of confession, repentance, and turning from our sin so that our worship is that which fully pleases God. We dare not go rushing into His presence in unholiness. We cannot worship God acceptably except with reverence and godly fear, and in the beauty of holiness. We must return to the biblical teaching of God's utter and awesome holiness in order to be filled with the gratitude and humility that characterize true worship.

3

THE COST OF DISCIPLESHIP[1]

Jesus' call to discipleship was an invitation to salvation, not an offer of a "higher life," or a second step of faith following salvation. The contemporary teaching that separates discipleship from salvation springs from ideas that are foreign to Scripture.[2]

Every Christian is a disciple.[3] In fact, the Lord's Great Commission was to go into all the world and "make disciples . . . teaching them to observe all that I commanded you" (Matt. 28:19–20). That means the mission of the church, and the goal of evangelism, is to make disciples. Disciples are people who believe, those whose faith motivates them to obey all Jesus commanded. The word "disciple" is used consistently as a synonym for *believer* throughout the book of Acts (6:1, 2, 7; 11:26; 14:20, 22; 15:10). Any distinction between the two words is purely artificial. Though introduced by sincere and well-meaning men, it has given birth to a theology of easy-believism that disposes of the hard demands of Jesus.

When Jesus called disciples, He carefully instructed them about the cost of following Him. Halfhearted people who weren't willing to make the commitment did not respond. Thus He turned away anyone who was reluctant to pay the price—like the rich young ruler. He warned all who thought of becoming disciples to count the cost carefully. "Which one of you, when he wants to build a tower, does not first sit down and calculate the cost, to see if he has enough to complete it? Otherwise, when he has laid a foundation, and is not able to finish, all who observe it begin to ridicule him, saying, 'This man began to build and was not able to finish'" (Luke 14:28–30).

About those verses, John Stott has written penetratingly,

> The Christian landscape is strewn with the wreckage of derelict, half-built towers—the ruins of those who began to build and were unable to finish.

For thousands of people still ignore Christ's warning and undertake to follow him without first pausing to reflect on the cost of doing so. The result is the great scandal of Christendom today, so-called "nominal Christianity." In countries to which Christian civilization has spread, large numbers of people have covered themselves with a decent, but thin, veneer of Christianity. They have allowed themselves to become somewhat involved; enough to be respectable but not enough to be uncomfortable. Their religion is a great, soft cushion. It protects them from the hard unpleasantness of life, while changing its place and shape to suit their convenience. No wonder the cynics speak of hypocrites in the church and dismiss religion as escapism.[4]

A Christian is not one who simply buys "fire insurance," who "accepts Christ" just to escape hell. As we have seen repeatedly, true believers' faith expresses itself in submission and obedience. Christians follow Christ. They are committed unquestionably to Christ as Lord and Savior. They desire to please God. They are humble, meek learners (*mathetes* in the Greek text). When they fail, they seek forgiveness and move forward. That is their spirit and their direction.

The call to Christian discipleship explicitly demands just that kind of total dedication. It is full commitment, with nothing knowingly or deliberately held back. No one can come to Christ on any other terms. Those who think they can simply affirm a list of gospel facts and continue to live any way they please should examine themselves to see if they are really in the faith (2 Cor. 13:5).

In Matthew 10, Jesus challenged His disciples, saying:

> Everyone therefore who shall confess Me before men, I will also confess him before My Father who is in heaven. But whoever shall deny Me before men, I will also deny him before My Father who is in heaven . . . He who loves father or mother more than Me is not worthy of Me; and he who loves son or daughter more than Me is not worthy of Me. And he who does not take his cross and follow after Me is not worthy of Me. He who has found his life shall lose it, and he who has lost his life for My sake shall find it. (vv. 32–33, 37–39)

Our Lord gave no more definitive statement on discipleship than that. There He spells out in the clearest possible language the cost of discipleship. The words are addressed to the Twelve in particular (Matt. 10:5), but they are principles of discipleship applicable to us all. Verse 24 says, "A disciple is not above his

24

teacher." "A disciple" here means any disciple, and the words that follow, to the end of the chapter, apply to discipleship in general.

Those who see disciples as a separate class of more dedicated believers will point out that the Twelve—or at least eleven of them—were already believers in Christ and thus did not need instruction on what it means to come to Christ with saving faith. It is true that most of the disciples were undoubtedly already born again, but that does not negate the impact of these words for them. The fact is, these men were already called "disciples" too (10:1). This was not an invitation to a higher kind of relationship, but a reminder of what had already been established when they believed. Our Lord was continuing to teach them the meaning of faith and salvation and constantly reminding them of the commitment they had made when they chose to follow Him.

These words apply to you and me as well. Luke 14:25–35 contains similar words—in even stronger language—which Jesus spoke not just to the Twelve but to the multitudes that came to hear Him.

Matthew 10:2 refers to the Twelve as "apostles." That means "sent ones." Their basic training being complete, Jesus sent them out to preach. In this parting charge to them, however, He uses the word "disciple," not "apostle." His words apply to every disciple, serving as a signpost to every potential follower of Jesus.

CONFESSING CHRIST BEFORE OTHERS

Verses 32–33 are reminiscent of the awesome judgment scene in Matthew 7:21–23: "Everyone therefore who shall confess Me before men, I will also confess him before My father who is in heaven. But whoever shall deny Me before men, I will also deny him before My Father who is in heaven." Does that mean confession before others is a condition of becoming a true Christian? No, but it means that a characteristic of every genuine believer is that he or she *will* profess faith in Christ unreservedly. Paul wrote, "I am not ashamed of the gospel, for it is the power of God for salvation" (Rom. 1:16).

The heart of real discipleship is a commitment to be like Jesus Christ. That means both acting as He did and being willing to accept the same treatment. It means facing a world that is hostile to Him and doing it fearlessly. It means confessing before others that Jesus is Lord and being confident that He will also speak on our behalf before the Father.

"Confess" means to affirm, to acknowledge, to agree. It is a statement of identification, faith, confidence, and trust. One can confess Christ with the mouth, as Romans 10:9 says, and one can also confess Him through righteous behavior, as Titus 1:16 implies. We are to confess Christ "before men." This emphasizes the public character of the confession, and its meaning cannot be avoided. In Romans 10:10 we read, "With the heart man believes, resulting in righteousness, and with the mouth he confesses, resulting in salvation." If the heart truly believes, the mouth will be eager to confess. Confession is not merely a human work, it is prompted and energized by God, subsequent to the act of believing but inseparable from it. Again, confession is characteristic of true faith; it is not an additional condition of salvation.

First John 4:15 says, "Whoever confesses that Jesus is the Son of God, God abides in him, and he in God." What is the mark of a true Christian? He confesses Jesus as the Son of God.

This does not mean a disciple will always stand up for the Lord. Peter denied the Lord three times on the night He was betrayed. Then there was Timothy, perhaps the finest of Paul's disciples, pastor of the church at Ephesus. This dedicated young man with such marvelous pastoral gifts was a model disciple. But he may have experienced a temporary spiritual malfunction, or perhaps he was susceptible to fear. Paul had to write to him, "Do not be ashamed of the testimony of our Lord" (2 Tim. 1:8).

A moment of failure does not invalidate a disciple's credentials. We have all failed to confess Christ before others more often than we would like to admit. But if we are true disciples, we will not purposely and in a calculated way keep our faith hidden from everyone all the time. Even Joseph of Arimathea, whom the apostle John called a "secret disciple," had the boldness to go to Governor Pilate after the crucifixion and ask for the body of Jesus (John 19:38).

Christ says He will confess us before the Father in heaven (Matt. 10:32). What does that mean? Christ will say on the Day of Judgment, "This one belongs to Me." He will affirm His loyalty to those who have affirmed their loyalty to Him. The other side of it is also stated: "But whoever shall deny Me before men, I will also deny him before My Father who is in heaven" (v. 33). This does not speak primarily of open rejecters—people who would deny Christ flagrantly, have nothing to do with Him, despise Him, speak against Him, or blaspheme His name. The truth certainly applies to people like that, but our Lord is talking specifically about false disciples, people who claim to be Christians but are not.

When put to the test, they consistently deny the Lord, either by their silence, by their actions, or by their words. In fact, the idea here encompasses all those things. It speaks of someone whose entire life is a denial of Christ. He may claim to believe, but everything about his way of living exudes denial (cf. Titus 1:16).

Churches are filled with such people, masquerading as disciples, but denying the Lord in some very disturbing ways. Christ will deny them before God (v. 33).

Matthew 25:31–46 details what will happen in the judgment. Specifically, this describes in the separation of the sheep and goats at the end of the Tribulation, at the judgment of the nations (v. 32). But its principle applies to individuals in every phase of God's judgment. Here the Lord puts the sheep (those who have confessed Him) on His right hand, and the goats (those who have denied Him) on His left (v. 33), and He ushers the sheep into the kingdom. These are the righteous people who have confessed Him. How do we know? He says, "I was hungry, and you gave Me something to eat; I was thirsty, and you gave Me drink; I was a stranger, and you invited Me in; naked, and you clothed Me; I was sick, and you visited Me; I was in prison, and you came to Me" (vv. 35–36). Once again, we see that the pattern of their lives reveals the reality of their claim to know Christ. Those who fail to live in a way that is consistent with faith in Christ are sent to eternal punishment (v. 46).

GETTING THE PRIORITIES STRAIGHT

A second hallmark of a true disciple is loving Christ even more than his or her own family (Matt. 10:34–37). Verse 37 in particular is very strong: "He who loves father or mother more than Me is not worthy of Me; and he who loves son or daughter more than Me is not worthy of Me."

If you think that is forceful, look at the parallel passage in Luke 14:26–27: "If anyone comes to Me, and does not hate his own father and mother and wife and children and brothers and sisters, yes, and even his own life, he cannot be My disciple."

To be a disciple, must we literally hate our families? Obviously this does not call for hatred in any sense that would violate the clear commandments of God, such as "Honor your father and your mother" (Ex. 20:12), and "Husbands, love your wives" (Eph. 5:25). The key to this passage is the phrase "yes, and even his own life" (Luke 14:26). The Lord is saying we must be unquestioningly loyal to Him, even above our families—and especially above ourselves. Scripture teaches we are to deny self (Matt. 16:24), consider ourselves dead (Rom. 6:11), lay the old self aside (Eph. 4:22)—to treat the selfish aspect of our beings with the utmost contempt (cf. 1 Cor. 9:27). That is the same attitude we are to have toward our earthly possessions and even toward our families.

Why is this language so severe? Why does Christ use such offensive terms? Because He is as eager to drive the uncommitted away as He is to draw true disciples to Himself. He does not want halfhearted people to be deceived into thinking they are in the kingdom. Unless He is the number-one priority, He has not been given His rightful place.

TAKING UP THE CROSS

Those who are not willing lose their lives for Christ are not worthy of Him (Matt. 10:38). They cannot be His disciples (Luke 14:27). These statements cannot be made to accommodate the casual approach to conversion that is in vogue in our generation. Jesus is not asking people to add Him to the milieu of their lives. He wants disciples willing to forsake *everything*. This calls for full-scale self-denial—even willingness to die for His sake if necessary.

When Matthew 10:38 says, "He who does not take his cross and follow after Me is not worthy of Me," it does not mean bearing the "cross" of a difficult situation, a chronic disease, or a nagging spouse. I have heard devotional sermons spiritualizing the cross to mean everything from a cranky mother-in-law to a leaky roof to a 1957 Chevy! But that is not what the word "cross" meant to Jesus' first-century audience. It did not call to their minds the idea of long-term difficulties or troublesome burdens. It did not even evoke thoughts of Calvary—the Lord had not gone to the cross yet, and they did not understand that He would.

When Jesus said "take up your cross" to them, they thought of a cruel instrument of torture and death. They thought of dying in the most agonizing method known to man. They thought of poor, condemned criminals hanging on crosses by the roadside. Doubtless they had seen men executed in that fashion.

They understood He was calling them to die for Him. They knew He was asking them to make the ultimate sacrifice, to surrender to Him as Lord in every sense.

Jesus adds a final paradoxical thought on the meaning of discipleship: "He who has found his life shall lose it, and he who has lost his life for My sake shall find it" (Matt. 10:39). "He who has found his life" seems to refer to a person who has guarded his physical safety by denying Christ under pressure, or someone who clings to his life rather than taking up the cross. Because his first concern is securing his physical life, that person loses his eternal soul. Conversely, those who are willing to forfeit their lives for Christ's sake will receive eternal life.

The Bible does not teach salvation by martyrdom. The Lord was not advising the disciples to *try* to get themselves killed for Him. Again He was referring to a pattern, a direction. He was simply saying that genuine Christians do not shrink back, even in the face of death. To express it another way, when confronted with a decision between serving self and serving the Lord, the true disciple is the one who chooses to serve the Lord, even at great personal expense.

Again, this is not absolute in the sense that it disallows temporary failures like that of Peter. But even Peter *did* ultimately prove himself to be a true disciple, didn't he? The time came when he willingly gave His life for Jesus' sake.

Luke 9:23 records similar words of Jesus: "If anyone wishes to come after Me, let him deny himself, and take up his cross daily, and follow Me." Notice the addition of the one word: "daily." The life of a disciple invites persecution and therefore must be a life of daily self-denial. Paul wrote to the Corinthians, "I protest, brethren, by the boasting in you, which I have in Christ Jesus our Lord, I die daily" (1 Cor. 15:31).

The idea of daily self-denial does not jibe with the contemporary supposition that believing in Jesus is a momentary decision. A true believer is one who signs up for life. The bumper-sticker sentiment "Try Jesus" is a mentality foreign to real discipleship—faith is not an experiment, but a lifelong commitment. It means taking up the cross daily, giving all for Christ each day. It means no reservations, no uncertainty, no hesitation (Luke 9:59–62). It means nothing is knowingly held back, nothing purposely shielded from His lordship, nothing stubbornly kept from His control. It calls for painful severing of the tie with the world, a sealing of the escape hatches, a ridding oneself of any kind of security to fall back on in case of failure. Genuine believers *know* they are going ahead with Christ until death. Having put their hand to the plow, they will not look back (Luke 9:62).[5]

That's how it must be for all who would follow Jesus Christ. It is the stuff of true discipleship.

4

Just by Faith[1]

R. C. Sproul has written:

> The difference between Rome and the Reformation can be seen in these simple formulas:
>
> > Roman view
> > faith + works = justification
> > Protestant view
> > faith = justification + works
>
> Neither view eliminates works. The Protestant view eliminates human merit. It recognizes that though works are the evidence or fruit of true faith they add or contribute nothing to the meritorious basis of our redemption.
>
> The current debate over "Lordship/salvation" must be careful to protect two borders. On the one hand it is important to stress that true faith yields true fruit; on the other hand it is vital to stress that the only merit that saves us is the merit of Christ received by faith alone.[2]

In the 1500s a fastidious monk, who by his own testimony "hated God," was studying Paul's epistle to the Romans. He couldn't get past the first half of Romans 1:17: "[In the gospel] is the righteousness of God revealed from faith to faith" (KJV). He wrote:

> I greatly longed to understand Paul's Epistle to the Romans and nothing stood in the way but that one expression, "the [righteousness] of God,"

because I took it to mean that justice whereby God is just and deals justly in punishing the unjust. My situation was that, although an impeccable monk, I stood before God as a sinner troubled in conscience, and I had no confidence that my merit would assuage him. Therefore I did not love a just and angry God, but rather hated and murmured against him. Yet I clung to the dear Paul and had a great yearning to know what he meant.[3]

One simple biblical truth changed that monk's life—and ignited the Protestant Reformation. It was the realization that God's righteousness could become the sinner's righteousness—and that could happen through the means of faith alone. Martin Luther found the truth in the same verse he had stumbled over, Romans 1:17: "Therein is the righteousness of God revealed from faith to faith: as it is written, *The just shall live by faith*" (KJV, emphasis added). Luther had always seen "the righteousness of God" as an attribute of the sovereign Lord by which He judged sinners—not an attribute sinners could ever possess. He described the breakthrough that put an end to the dark ages:

> I saw the connection between the justice of God and the statement that "the just shall live by his faith." Then I grasped that the justice of God is that righteousness by which through grace and sheer mercy God justifies us through faith. Thereupon I felt myself to be reborn and to have gone through open doors into paradise. The whole of Scripture took on a new meaning, and whereas before the "justice of God" had filled me with hate, now it became to me inexpressibly sweet in greater love. This passage of Paul became to me a gate to heaven.[4]

Justification by faith was the great truth that dawned on Luther and dramatically altered the church. It is also the doctrine that brings equilibrium to the lordship position. Critics usually claim that lordship salvation is salvation by works. Justification by faith is the answer to that charge.

Because Christians are justified by faith alone, their standing before God is not in any way related to personal merit. Good works and practical holiness do not provide the grounds for acceptance with God. God receives as righteous those who believe not because of any good thing He sees in them—not even because of His own sanctifying work in their lives—but solely on the basis of *Christ's* righteousness, which is reckoned to their account. "To the one who does not work, but believes in Him who justifies the ungodly, his faith is reckoned as righteousness" (Rom. 4:5). That is justification.

DECLARED RIGHTEOUS: WHAT ACTUALLY CHANGES?

Theologically, justification is a forensic, or purely legal, term. It describes what God *declares* about the believer, not what He *does to change* the believer. In fact, justification effects no actual change whatsoever in the sinner's nature or character. Justification is a divine judicial edict. It changes our status only, but it carries ramifications that guarantee other changes will follow. Forensic decrees like this are fairly common in everyday life.

When I was married, for example, Patricia and I stood before the minister (my father) and recited our vows. Near the end of the ceremony, my father declared, "By the authority vested in me by the state of California, I now pronounce you man and wife." Instantly we were legally husband and wife. Whereas seconds before we had been an engaged couple, now we were married. Nothing inside us actually changed when those words were spoken. But our status changed before God, the law, and our family and friends. The implications of that simple declaration have been lifelong and life-changing (for which I am grateful). But when my father spoke those words, it was a legal declaration only.

Similarly, when a jury foreman reads the verdict, the defendant is no longer "the accused." Legally and officially he instantly becomes either guilty or innocent—depending on the verdict. Nothing in his actual nature changes, but if he is found not guilty he will walk out of court a free man in the eyes of the law, fully justified.

In its theological sense, justification is a divine verdict of "not guilty—fully righteous." It is the reversal of God's attitude toward the sinner. Whereas He formerly condemned, He now vindicates. Although the sinner once lived under God's wrath, as a believer he or she is now under God's blessing. Justification is more than simple pardon; pardon alone would still leave the sinner without merit before God. So when God justifies He imputes divine righteousness to the sinner (Rom. 4:22–25). Christ's own infinite merit thus becomes the ground on which the believer stands before God (Rom. 5:19; 1 Cor. 1:30; Phil. 3:9). And so justification elevates the believer to a realm of full acceptance and divine privilege equal to that of Jesus Christ.

Therefore because of justification, believers not only are perfectly free from any charge of guilt (Rom. 8:33), but they also have the full merit of Christ reckoned to their personal account (Rom. 5:17). At justification we are adopted as sons (Rom. 8:15); we become fellow heirs with Christ (Rom. 8:17); we are united with Christ so that we become one with Him (1 Cor. 6:17); and we are henceforth "in Christ" (Gal. 3:27) and He in us (Col. 1:27). Those are all foren-sic realities that flow out of justification.

HOW JUSTIFICATION AND SANCTIFICATION DIFFER

Justification is distinct from sanctification because in justification God does not *make* the sinner righteous; He *declares* that person righteous (Rom. 3:28; Gal. 2:16). Justification *imputes* Christ's righteousness to the sinner's account (Rom. 4:11); sanctification *imparts* righteousness to the sinner personally and practically (Rom. 6:1–7; 8:11–14). Justification takes place outside the sinner and changes his standing (Rom. 5:1–2); sanctification is internal and changes the believer's state (Rom. 6:19). Justification is an event, sanctification a process. The two must be distinguished but can never be separated. God does not justify whom He does not sanctify, and He does not sanctify whom He does not jus-tify. Both are essential elements of salvation.

Why differentiate between them at all? If justification and sanctification are so closely related that you can't have one without the other, why bother to define them differently?

That question is crucial to the lordship debate. It was also the central issue between Rome and the Reformers in the sixteenth century.

JUSTIFICATION IN ROMAN CATHOLIC DOCTRINE

Roman Catholicism blends its doctrines of sanctification and justification. Catholic theology views justification as an infusion of grace that *makes* the sin-ner righteous. In Catholic theology, then, the ground of justification is some-thing good within the sinner—not the imputed righteousness of Christ.

The Council of Trent, Rome's response to the Reformation, pronounced anathema on anyone who says "that the [sinner] is justified by faith alone—if this means that nothing else is required by way of cooperation in the acquisition of the grace of justification."[5] The Catholic council ruled that "justification is not only the remission of sins . . . but sanctification and renovation of the interior man through the voluntary reception of grace and gifts, whereby a man becomes just instead of unjust."[6] And so Catholic theology confuses the concepts of jus-tification and sanctification and substitutes the righteousness of the believer for the righteousness of Christ.

This difference between Rome and the Reformers is no example of theolog-ical hairsplitting. The corruption of the doctrine of justification results in several other grievous theological errors. If sanctification is included in justification, then justification is a process, not an event. That makes justification progressive, not complete. One's standing before God is then based on subjective experience, not secured by an objective declaration. Justification can therefore be experienced and then lost. Assurance of salvation in this life becomes practically impossible because security can't be guaranteed. And the ground of justification ultimately is the sinner's own continuing present virtue, not Christ's perfect righteousness and His atoning work.

Those issues were fiercely debated in the Reformation, and the lines were clearly drawn. Reformed theology to this day upholds the biblical doctrine of justification by faith against the Roman view of justification by sanctification.

JUSTIFICATION IN REFORMATION TEACHING

Advocates of no-lordship theology often suggest that lordship salvation has more in common with Roman Catholicism than with Reformation teaching. One outspoken advocate of the radical no-lordship view has repeatedly voiced alarm that lordship salvation is "not paving the road back to Wittenberg but, rather, paving the road back to Rome."[7]

The suggestion ignores both church history and the real issues in the contemporary lordship debate. No advocate of lordship theology I know of denies the doctrine of justification by faith. Rather, lordship theology represents a refusal to disengage justification and sanctification. On that we are in full accord with every significant Reformer.

Reformation teaching was clear on this issue. Calvin, for example, wrote,

> Christ . . . justifies no man without also sanctifying him. These blessings are conjoined by a perpetual and inseparable tie. Those whom he enlightens by his wisdom he redeems; whom he redeems he justifies; whom he justifies he sanctifies. But as the question relates only to justification and sanctification, to them let us confine ourselves. Though we distinguish between them they are both inseparably comprehended in Christ. Would ye then obtain justification in Christ? You must previously possess Christ. But you cannot possess him without being made a partaker of his sanctification: for Christ cannot be divided. Since the Lord, therefore, does not grant us the enjoyment of these blessings without bestowing himself, he bestows both at once, but never one without the other. Thus it appears how true it is that we are justified not without, and yet not by works, since in

the participation of Christ, by which we are justified, is contained not less sanctification than justification.[8]

Elsewhere, discussing James 2:21–22 ("Was not Abraham our father justified by works, when he offered up Isaac his son on the altar? You see that faith was working with his works, and as a result of the works, faith was perfected"), Calvin added,

> It appears certain that he is speaking of the manifestation, not of the imputation of righteousness, as if he had said, Those who are justified by true faith prove their justification by obedience and good works, not by a bare and imaginary semblance of faith. In one word, he is not discussing the mode of justification, but requiring that the justification of believers shall be operative. And as Paul contends that men are justified without the aid of works, so James will not allow any to be regarded as justified who are destitute of good works. Due attention to the scope will thus disentangle every doubt; for the error of our opponents lies chiefly in this, that they think James is defining the mode of justification, whereas his only object is to destroy the depraved security of those who vainly pretended faith as an excuse for their contempt of good works. Therefore, let them twist the words of James as they may, they will never extract out of them more than the two propositions: That an empty phantom of faith does not justify, and that the believer, not contented with such an imagination, manifests his justification by good works.[9]

Martin Luther championed justification by faith as passionately as any Reformer. Did he believe sanctification was optional? Not at all. When some of Luther's associates began to teach *antinomianism* (the idea that behavior is unrelated to faith, or that Christians are not bound by any moral law), he opposed them. He called their teaching "the crassest error," designed to "grind me under foot and throw the gospel into confusion." Such teaching, according to Luther, "kick[s] the bottom out of the barrel" of God's saving work.[10]

Someone reported to Luther that one of these men, Jacob Schenck, "had preached carnal license and had taught: 'Do what you please. Only believe and you will be saved.'"[11]

Luther replied, "This is a wicked disjunction. Turn the matter about: 'Dear fellow, believe in God, and then afterward, when you are reborn, are a new man, etc., do whatever comes to hand.' The fools don't know what faith is. They suppose it's just a lifeless idea . . . It's impossible to be reborn of God and yet sin, for these two things contradict each other."[12]

Although many more examples could be given, I'll just mention one other. The Formula of Concord, the definitive Lutheran statement of faith, written in 1576, dealt extensively with the relationship between justification and the believer's obedience. This document reveals that the questions at the heart of the contemporary lordship controversy were also on the minds of the Reformers. The Formula of Concord, like every other significant Protestant creed, refused to divorce justification from sanctification, though it underscored the distinction between the two.

According to this creed, "The renewing of man . . . is rightly distinguished from the justification of faith." The Formula stated explicitly that "antecedent contrition [repentance] and subsequent new obedience do not appertain to the article of justification before God."[13]

But it immediately added, "Yet we are not to imagine any such justifying faith as can exist and abide with a purpose of evil . . . But after that man is justified by faith, then that true and living faith works by love [Gal. 5:6], and *good works always follow justifying faith, and are most certainly found together with it.*"[14]

The Formula of Concord repudiated the teaching that *justify* means "[to] become in very deed righteous before God." But it also condemned the notion "that faith is such a confidence in the obedience of Christ as can abide and have a being even in that man who is void of true repentance, and in whom it is not followed by charity [love], but who contrary to conscience perseveres in sins."[15]

The well-known Reformation epigram is "Faith alone justifies, but not the faith that is alone." F. W. Robertson adds, "Lightning alone strikes, but not the lightning which is without thunder."[16] On these matters the principal Reformers all agreed. Only the antinomians taught that true faith might fail to produce good works.

JUSTIFICATION IN THE LORDSHIP DEBATE

Contemporary no-lordship doctrine is nothing but latter-day antinomianism. Although most no-lordship advocates object to that term,[17] it is a fair characterization of their doctrine.

Zane Hodges misses the point when he calls *antinomianism* "Reformed theology's favorite 'cuss word.'"[18] He writes,

> We could define "Antinomianism" in the way the *American Heritage Dictionary* (2nd College Edition, 1985) does as "holding that faith alone is necessary for salvation." If that were what was meant by the term, I would be quite comfortable with it. Unfortunately, because "Antinomianism" implies to many minds a disregard for moral issues, I must reject this designation. I urge my Reformed counterparts to drop this term because of its pejorative, and often unfair, connotations and overtones. But I will not hold my breath waiting for them to do so![19]

It is important to understand the term "antinomianism" in its theological sense. I do not use the word to be derogatory. To say someone is antinomian is not necessarily to say that person spurns holiness or condones ungodliness. Most antinomians vigorously appeal for Christians to walk in a manner worthy of their calling; but at the same time they minimize the relationship between obedience and faith. Antinomians typically believe Christians *should* yield to the lordship of Christ; they just do not believe surrender is a binding requirement in the gospel call to faith. Antinomians do not despise the law of God; they simply believe it is irrelevant to saving faith. And they suggest that obedience to the righteous principles of the law might not become a pattern in the Christian's life (Rom. 8:4; 10:4). In short, antinomianism is the belief that allows for justification without sanctification.

Antinomianism makes obedience elective. While most antinomians strongly *counsel* Christians to obey (and even urge them to obey), they do not believe obedience is a necessary consequence of true faith. Zane Hodges, for example, includes in his book *The Hungry Inherit* a chapter on obedience entitled "The Choice Is Yours" (pp. 117–126). And the leading theologian of the no-lordship movement, Charles Ryrie, has written, "The unsaved person has only one course of action—to serve sin and self, or to leave God out of his life—while the believer has an option. He may serve God, and as long as he is in a human body he may also choose to leave God out and live according to the old nature."[20] Clearly, no-lordship theology *does* make obedience optional. And that is what makes no-lordship theology antinomian.

This kind of antinomianism tends to see justification by faith as the whole of God's saving work. Antinomians minimize sanctification or even render it noncompulsory. Antinomian discussions of salvation typically omit any consideration of practical holiness. They emphasize justification by faith and Christian freedom to such an extreme that they become unbalanced, fearful of talking about personal righteousness, obedience, the law of God, or anything but the purely forensic aspects of salvation.

No-lordship theology is classic antinomianism. There is no way around that fact. And because it is important to understand the no-lordship view in the context of Reformation teaching, we cannot avoid the term "antinomianism," even though proponents of no-lordship teaching find it offensive. Their view is, after all, firmly in the tradition of historic antinomianism.[21]

One other point must be made about the no-lordship tendency to downplay sanctification. Most no-lordship advocates acknowledge the necessity for *some* degree of sanctification. Dr. Ryrie concedes that "every Christian will bear spiritual fruit. Somewhere, sometime, somehow. Otherwise the person is not a believer. Every born-again individual will be fruitful. Not to be fruitful is to be faithless, without faith, and therefore without salvation."[22]

Even Zane Hodges has lately affirmed that "some measure or degree of sanctification *will* indeed result from justification [and] that final sanctification *is* an inevitable result of justification."[23]

But those disclaimers must be understood in context. Ryrie, for example, is quick to add that some believers' "fruit" may be so meager and so fleeting as to be invisible to everyone around them.[24] Elsewhere Ryrie seems to suggest that *practical* sanctification is by no means guaranteed. He quotes Romans 8:29–30 ("Whom He foreknew, He also predestined to become conformed to the image of His Son, that He might be the first-born among many brethren; and whom He predestined, these He also called; and whom He called, these He also justified; and whom He justified, these He also glorified"). "But what of sanctification?" Ryrie asks.

> Nowhere does it appear in Paul's list in Romans 8:29–30. Only predestination, calling, justification, and glorification. Could it be that Paul didn't want to base our guarantee of ultimate glorification on our personal sanctification? Assuredly it does not rest on that, for the many sons who will be glorified will have exhibited varying degrees of personal holiness during their lifetimes. Yet all, from the carnal to the most mature, will be glorified.[25]

Ryrie outlines three facets of sanctification—*positional sanctification,* "an actual position that does not depend on the state of one's growth and maturity";

progressive sanctification, or practical holiness; and *ultimate sanctification,* perfect holiness that will be realized in heaven.[26] It is clear that Ryrie views the first and third aspects of sanctification as guaranteed. But he evidently believes *practical* sanctification can be forfeited or bypassed, for he makes room for "believers" who fall into utter carnality and permanent unbelief.[27]

Hodges holds a similar view. If anything, his tendency to depreciate the practical aspect of sanctification is more pronounced than Ryrie's. Hodges's most extensive book on the lordship debate, *Absolutely Free!,* omits any discussion of sanctification as a doctrine.[28] What Hodges does make clear from the beginning to the end of his book is that no measure of practical holiness is guaranteed in the life of a child of God.

Although no-lordship doctrine may give lip service to the necessity of sanctification, it seems certain that most no-lordship proponents do not really believe *practical* sanctification goes hand-in-hand with justification. That is, in fact, the fundamental point no-lordship advocates want to make. They have dismembered the biblical doctrine of salvation by severing justification from sanctification.[29] They are left with a crippled antinomianism that cannot guarantee any measure of holiness in the Christian experience. And therefore they have utterly missed the point of the biblical doctrine of justification by faith.

JUSTIFICATION IN THE NEW TESTAMENT

Justification is the heart and soul of New Testament *soteriology* (teaching about salvation). Realizing that is the case, a friend asked me why my book *The Gospel According to Jesus* had virtually no discussion of justification. The reason is that Jesus Himself had very little to say explicitly about justification by faith. That doctrine was first expounded in its fullness by the apostle Paul. In his epistle to the Romans, it is a major theme.

The first half of Romans divides naturally into three parts. Paul begins by showing that all men and women have sinned against God's perfect righteousness. This is his theme throughout the opening chapters of the book: "There is none righteous, not even one" (3:10). Beginning in 3:21 through the end of chapter 5, he explains in detail the doctrine of justification by faith. "Therefore having been justified by faith, we have peace with God through our Lord Jesus Christ" (5:1). And in chapters 6 through 8 he expounds the doctrine of sanctification. "That the requirement of the Law might be fulfilled in us, who do not walk according to the flesh, but according to the Spirit" (8:4).

So Paul talks about sin, saving faith, and sanctification. Or, as a friend of mine has said, Romans 1:1–3:20 speaks of *God's righteousness defied* by a sinful world. Romans 3:21–5:21 shows *God's righteousness supplied* for believing sinners. And chapters 6 through 8 focus on *God's righteousness applied* in the lives of the saints.

Justification by faith is the means through which God's righteousness is *supplied* on behalf of believing sinners. I wish there were space in this book for a full exposition of these crucial chapters (Rom. 3–5), which make up the core of biblical truth about justification. But that would require multiple chapters, so instead we will focus only on one section, Paul's main illustration of justification by faith—Abraham—found in Romans 4.

Here Paul writes,

> What then shall we say that Abraham, our forefather according to the flesh, has found? For if Abraham was justified by works, he has something to boast about; but not before God. For what does the Scripture say? "And Abraham believed God, and it was reckoned to him as righteousness." Now to the one who works, his wage is not reckoned as a favor, but as what is due. But to the one who does not work, but believes in Him who justifies the ungodly, his faith is reckoned as righteousness. (vv. 1–5)

Several crucial truths rise from this text.

TRUE SALVATION CANNOT BE EARNED BY WORKS

There are, after all, only two kinds of religion in all the world. Every false religion ever devised by mankind or by Satan is a *religion of human merit*. Pagan religion, humanism, animism, and even false Christianity all fall into this category. They focus on what people must *do* to attain righteousness or please the deity.

Biblical Christianity alone is the *religion of divine accomplishment*. Other religions say, "Do this." Christianity says, "It is done" (John 19:30). Other religions require that the devout person supply some kind of merit to atone for sin, appease deity, or otherwise attain the goal of acceptability. Scripture says Christ's merit is supplied on behalf of the believing Christian.

The Pharisees in Paul's day had turned Judaism into a religion of human achievements. Paul's own life before salvation was one long and futile effort to please God through personal merit. He had been steeped in the Pharisaic tradition, "a Pharisee, a son of Pharisees" (Acts 23:6), "a Hebrew of Hebrews; as to the Law, a Pharisee; as to zeal, a persecutor of the church; as to the righteousness which is in the Law, found blameless" (Phil. 3:5–6). Paul understood the religious culture of his day as well as anyone. He knew that the Pharisees revered Abraham as the father of their religion (John 8:39). So he singled him out to prove that justification before God is by faith in what God has accomplished.

By showing Abraham as the ultimate example of justification by faith, Paul was setting Christian doctrine against centuries of rabbinic tradition. And by appealing to the Old Testament Scriptures, Paul was showing that Judaism had moved away from the most basic truths affirmed by all believing Jews since Abraham himself. He was seeking to anchor the church so that it would not follow the drift of Israel.

Abraham's faith was the foundation of the Jewish nation and the basis for God's covenant with His chosen people. For the Pharisees' tradition to be at odds with Abraham was unthinkable. But, as Paul was about to prove, Abraham did not practice the Pharisees' religion of merit.

BOASTING IS EXCLUDED

If people could earn justification by works, they would indeed have something to boast about. The doctrine of justification by faith is therefore a humbling truth. We do not merit salvation. We cannot be good enough to please God. There is no room in God's redemptive plan for human pride. Even Abraham, the father of the faith, had no reason to glory in himself: "If Abraham was justified by works, he has something to boast about; but not before God. For what does the Scripture say? 'And Abraham believed God, and it was reckoned to him as righteousness'" (Rom. 4:2–3).

Paul was quoting Genesis 15:6: "[Abraham] believed in the LORD; and He reckoned it to him as righteousness." That single Old Testament verse is one of the clearest statements in all of Scripture about justification. The word "reckoned" shows the forensic nature of justification. In Romans 4, "reckoned" is translated from the Greek word *logizomai*, a term used for accounting and legal purposes. It speaks of something charged to an account.

This reckoning was a one-sided transaction. God designated righteousness to Abraham's spiritual account. Abraham *did* nothing to earn it. Even his faith was not meritorious. Faith is never said to be the *ground* for justification, only the channel through which justifying grace is received. Abraham believed God, and so God imputed righteousness to his account.

Again, the forensic nature of justification is clearly evident: "Now to the one who works, his wage is not reckoned as a favor, but as what is due. But to the one who does not work, but believes in Him who justifies the ungodly, his faith is reckoned as righteousness" (vv. 4–5). Those who attempt to earn justification by *doing* something will find a huge debt on their ledger. Those who receive God's gift by grace through faith have an infinitely sufficient asset applied to their account.

Faith, then, means the end of any attempt to earn God's favor through personal merit. God saves only those who do not trust in themselves—those who trust "Him who justifies the ungodly." And therefore, until a person confesses that he is ungodly, that person cannot be saved, because he still trusts in his own goodness. That is what Jesus meant when He said, "I have not come to call the righteous but sinners to repentance" (Luke 5:32). Those who are righteous in their own eyes have no part in God's redemptive work of grace. Consequently, those who are saved know they have nothing to boast about.

JUSTIFICATION BRINGS THE BLESSING OF FORGIVENESS

In verses 6 through 8 Paul quotes David as support for the idea of righteousness by imputation: "David also speaks of the blessing upon the man to whom God reckons righteousness apart from works: Blessed are those whose lawless deeds have been forgiven, and whose sins have been covered. Blessed is the man whose sin the Lord will not take into account.'" Paul is quoting from Psalm 32:1–2. The blessedness David refers to is salvation.

Notice that David speaks of both a positive and a negative accounting: righteousness is reckoned to the believer; sin is not taken into account. Justification has both positive and negative elements: the reckoning of righteousness to the individual, and the forgiveness of sins. This forgiveness would not be possible if our sin had not been paid for by the sacrifice of Christ's own blood. His death paid the price; and so "PAID" can be written on the believer's spiritual invoice.

As our sin was imputed to Christ (1 Peter 2:24), so His righteousness is imputed to the believer. No other payment or reimbursement is required.

ABRAHAM WAS NOT JUSTIFIED BY CIRCUMCISION

Paul anticipated the question that Jews would be asking themselves at this point in his argument: *If Abraham was justified by his faith alone, why did God demand circumcision of Abraham and all his descendants?*

Most Jews in New Testament times were thoroughly convinced that circumcision was the unique mark that set them apart as God's chosen people. They also believed it was the means by which they became acceptable to God. In fact, circumcision was considered such a mark of God's favor that many rabbis taught that no Jew could be sent to hell unless God first reversed his circumcision.

Genesis 17:10–14 records God's instructions that circumcision was to be a mark of God's covenant with Abraham and his descendants. On the basis of that passage the rabbis taught that circumcision itself was the means of getting right with God. But as Paul carefully points out, Abraham was not made righteous by his circumcision. When God commanded him to be circumcised he had *already* been declared righteous:

> Is this blessing then upon the circumcised, or upon the uncircumcised also? For we say, "Faith was reckoned to Abraham as righteousness." How then was it reckoned? While he was circumcised, or uncircumcised? Not while circumcised, but while uncircumcised; and he received the sign of circumcision, a seal of the righteousness of the faith which he had while uncircumcised, that he might be the father of all who believe without being circumcised, that righteousness might be reckoned to them, and the father of circumcision to those who not only are of the circumcision, but who also follow in the steps of the faith of our father Abraham which he had while uncircumcised. (Romans 4:9–12)

The chronology of Genesis proves that Abraham was declared righteous long before he observed God's command to be circumcised. At Abraham's circumcision he was ninety-nine years old, and Ishmael was thirteen (Gen. 17:24–25). But when Abraham was justified (15:6), Ishmael had not even been conceived (16:2–4). At Ishmael's birth Abraham was eighty-six (16:16). So Abraham was justified at least *fourteen years* before his circumcision. When Abraham was declared righteous he was actually no different from an uncircumcised Gentile.

Circumcision and other external rituals—including baptism, penance, holy orders, marriage, celibacy, extreme unction, fasting, prayer, or whatever—are no means to justification. Abraham was in God's covenant and under His grace long before he was circumcised, whereas Ishmael, although circumcised, was never in the covenant. Circumcision, a sign of man's need for spiritual cleansing, was only a mark of the covenant relationship between God and His people.

Paul had already stated in Romans 2:28–29: "For he is not a Jew who is one outwardly; neither is circumcision that which is outward in the flesh. But he is a Jew who is one inwardly; and circumcision is that which is of the heart, by the Spirit, not by the letter; and his praise is not from men, but from God." Only justification by faith makes someone a son of Abraham (4:12).

ABRAHAM WAS NOT JUSTIFIED BY THE LAW

> For the promise to Abraham or to his descendants that he would be heir
> of the world was not through the Law, but through the righteousness of
> faith. For if those who are of the Law are heirs, faith is made void and the
> promise is nullified; for the Law brings about wrath, but where there is
> no law, neither is there violation. (Romans 4:13–15)

Again the chronology of Scripture proves Paul's point beyond dispute.
Obviously, the Law was not revealed to Moses until more than half a millennium
after Abraham lived. Abraham clearly did not become righteous by means of
the law.

Justification has never been through ritual *or* law. God's law "is holy, and the
commandment is holy and righteous and good" (Rom. 7:12; cf. Gal. 3:21). But
the law has never been a means of salvation. "For as many as are of the works of
the Law," that is, seek to justify themselves on the basis of keeping the law, "are
under a curse; for it is written, 'Cursed is everyone who does not abide by all
things written in the book of the law, to perform them'" (Gal. 3:10). The law
demands perfection. But the only way to obtain perfect righteousness is by
imputation—that is, being justified by faith.

The purpose of the law was to reveal God's perfect standards of righteousness. At the same time, it sets a standard that is impossible for sinful humans to
live up to. That should show us our need for a Savior and drive us to God in
faith. Thus the law is a "tutor to lead us to Christ, that we may be justified by
faith" (Gal. 3:24).

God has never recognized any righteousness but the righteousness of faith.
The law cannot save because the law only brings wrath. The more someone
seeks justification through the law, the more that person proves his or her sinfulness, and the more judgment and wrath is debited to that person's account
(Rom. 4:4).

Then comes the climax.

ABRAHAM WAS JUSTIFIED BY GOD'S GRACE

> For this reason it is by faith, that it might be in accordance with grace, in
> order that the promise may be certain to all the descendants, not only to
> those who are of the Law, but also to those who are of the faith of Abraham,
> who is the father of us all, (as it is written, "A father of many nations have

I made you") in the sight of Him whom he believed, even God, who gives life to the dead and calls into being that which does not exist. (4:16–17)

The gist of this entire passage is stated in verse 16: "*It is by faith, that it might be in accordance with grace.*" The dynamic of justification is God's grace. Abraham's faith was not in itself righteousness. Faith is only *reckoned* for righteousness. Justification is wholly a work of God's grace.

Again, we see here the purely forensic nature of justification: God "calls into being that which does not exist." The King James Version says He "calleth those things which be not as though they were." That is a fascinating statement about God.

If you or I were to declare "things that [are] not as though they were," we would be lying. God can do it because He is God, and His decrees carry the full weight of divine sovereignty. God spoke, and the worlds were created. "What is seen was not made out of things which are visible" (Heb. 11:3). He spoke things that were not, and behold! They were. He can call people, places, and events into existence solely by His divinely sovereign decrees. And He can declare believing sinners righteous even though they are not. That is justification.

But justification never occurs alone in God's plan. It is always accompanied by sanctification. God does not declare sinners righteous legally without making them righteous practically. Justification is not just a legal fiction. When God declares someone righteous, He will inevitably bring it to pass. "Whom He justified, these He also glorified" (Rom. 8:30). When justification occurs, the process of sanctification begins. Grace always encompasses both.

The apostle Paul clearly taught both truths. He did not end with a discussion of justification and forget the matter of sanctification. The salvation he described in his epistle to the Roman church was not a single-faceted, merely forensic reckoning. But the forensic element—justification—was without doubt the footing on which Paul based the whole of Christian experience.

5

DOES GOD PROMISE
HEALTH AND WEALTH?[1]

O ne of the most unusual legacies of World War II has been the cargo cults of the South Pacific. Many aboriginal island peoples ranging from North Australia to Indonesia were first exposed to modern civilization through the Allied armed forces during the war. The American military in particular often used the remote islands that dot that part of the globe as sites for temporary landing strips and supply depots.

> White men came bearing cargo; then they left as quickly as they had come. The tribal peoples had no time to learn the ways of civilization. But for a brief time they saw high technology up close. Cargo planes would swoop from the sky, land, leave their payload, then take off. Island natives saw cigarette lighters produce fire instantly and believed it to be miraculous. They saw large machinery push aside whole forests to build airstrips. They saw for the first time jeeps, modern weaponry, refrigerators, radios, power tools, and many varieties of food. They were fascinated by all that and many concluded the white men must be gods. When the war was over and the armies were gone, tribesmen built shrines to the cargo gods. Their tabernacles were perfect replicas of cargo planes, control towers, and airplane hangars—all made of bamboo and woven material. These structures all looked exactly like the real thing, but they were nonfunctional except for their use as temples to the cargo gods.

On some of the more remote islands, the cargo cults still thrive today. Some have personified all Americans in one deity they call Tom Navy. They pray for holy cargo from every airplane that flies over. They venerate religious relics—such as Zippo lighters, cameras, eyeglasses, ballpoint pens, nuts and bolts, and so on. As civilization has begun to penetrate some of these cultures, their fascination for cargo has not diminished. Missionaries who have been sent to areas where cargo cults have flourished receive a warm reception at first; the cargo cultists view their arrival as a sort of second coming. But the cultists are looking for cargo, not the gospel, and missionaries have found it very difficult to penetrate the materialism that is the very essence of the islanders' religion.

In recent years the charismatic movement has spawned its own variety of cargo cult. The Word Faith movement, known otherwise as the Faith movement—or Word, Faith-Formula, Word of Faith, Hyper-Faith, Positive Confession, Name It and Claim It, or Health, Wealth, and Prosperity teaching—this subdivision of the charismatic movement is every bit as superstitious and materialistic as the cargo cults in the South Pacific. The leaders of the Word Faith movement, including Kenneth Hagin, Kenneth and Gloria Copeland, Robert Tilton, Fred Price, and Charles Capps, promise each believer financial prosperity and perfect health. Anything less, they argue, is not God's will.

FALSE AND TRUE RELIGION

Virtually every false religion ever spawned by man worships a god whose function is to deliver some sort of cargo. That is, human religions invent gods for utilitarian reasons; the deities exist to serve men, rather than the other way around. Word Faith theology has turned Christianity into a system no different from the lowest human religions—a form of voodoo where God can be coerced, cajoled, manipulated, controlled, and exploited for the Christian's own ends.

I received a mailing sent out by one rather extreme Word Faith teacher named David Epley. A brochure was included with "a bar of prayer-blessed soap." "We are going to WASH away all BAD LUCK, SICKNESS, MISFOR-TUNES and EVIL! Yes, even that evil person you want out of your life! Jesus helped a man wash blindness from his eyes. I want to help you concerning Hexs [sic], Vexs [sic], Home Problems, Love, Happiness and Joy!" the brochure said. Inside were testimonies from people who had been blessed by that ministry: "Door opens to NEW JOB!"; "An $80,000 dollar dream comes true!"; "Couldn't use my hand for 12 years!" Also inside was a "personal" letter from the pastor, closing with a full page of instructions on how to use the soap for healing or a "money miracle": "Now, after you wash the poverty from your hands . . . take out the largest bill or check you have . . . that $100, $50, or $20 bill . . . Hold it in your clean hands and say, 'In Jesus' Name I dedicate this gift to God's work . . . and expect a miracle return of money.'" Of course, your "largest bill or check" must be sent to Epley's organization.

The last paragraph in the letter said,

> Through this Gift of Discernment I see someone sending a $25.00 offering and God is showing me a large check coming to them in the next short while. *I mean LARGE* . . . it looks like over a $1000 dollars. I know this sounds strange but you know me well enough to know I have to obey God when He speaks.

> I'll be here waiting for your answer.

That sounds more like black magic than faith. It is certainly a more outrageous example than most. Still, it reflects a *style* that is typical of nearly all Word Faith ministries. If it were merely hucksterism, that would be bad enough. But Word Faith teachers have corrupted the heart of New Testament Christianity, moving the believer's focus off sound doctrine, worship, service, sacrifice, and ministry, shifting it instead to promised physical, financial, and material "blessings." Those blessings are the cargo that God is expected to deliver to those who know and follow the Word Faith formulas.

Word Faith writings carry titles like "How to Write Your Own Ticket with God,"[2] "Godliness Is Profitable,"[3] *The Laws of Prosperity,*[4] "God's Creative Power Will Work for You,"[5] *Releasing the Ability of God Through Prayer,*[6] *God's Formula for Success and Prosperity,*[7] *God's Master Key to Prosperity,*[8] and *Living in Divine Prosperity.*[9]

In Word Faith religion, the believer uses God, whereas the truth of biblical Christianity is just the opposite: God uses the believer. Word Faith theology sees the Holy Spirit as a power to be put to use for whatever the believer wills. The Bible teaches, however, that the Holy Spirit is a *person* who enables the believer to do *God's* will.[10] Many Word Faith teachers claim that Jesus was born again so that we might become little gods. Scripture, however, teaches that Jesus is God, and it is *we* who must be born again.

I have little tolerance for the deceptions, corruptions of Scripture, and false claims of the Word Faith movement. The movement closely resembles some of the destructive greed sects that ravaged the early church. Paul and the other apostles were not accommodating to or conciliatory with the false teachers who propagated such ideas. Rather, they identified them as dangerous false teachers and urged Christians to avoid them. Paul warned Timothy, for example, about men of depraved mind and deprived of the truth, *who suppose that godliness is a means of gain* . . . But those who want to get rich fall into temptation and a snare and many foolish and harmful desires which plunge men into ruin and destruction. For the love of money is a root of all sorts of evil, and some by longing for it have wandered away from the faith, and pierced themselves with many a pang. But flee from these things, you man of God; and pursue righteousness, godliness, faith, love, perseverance and gentleness. (1 Timothy 6:5, 9–11, emphasis added)

Jude wrote of the greed-mongers,

Woe to them! For they have gone the way of Cain, and *for pay* they have rushed headlong into the error of Balaam, and perished in the rebellion of Korah. These men are those who are hidden reefs in your love feasts when they feast with you without fear, caring for themselves; clouds without water, carried along by winds; autumn trees without fruit, doubly dead, uprooted; wild waves of the sea, casting up their own shame like foam; wandering stars, for whom the black darkness has been reserved forever . . . These are grumblers, finding fault, following after their own lusts; they speak arrogantly, flattering people for the sake of gaining an advantage. (Jude 11–13, 16, emphasis added)

Peter wrote,

But false prophets also arose among the people, just as there will also be false teachers among you, who will secretly introduce destructive heresies, even denying the Master who bought them, bringing swift destruction upon themselves. And many will follow their sensuality, and because of them the way of the truth will be maligned; and *in their greed they will exploit you with false words*; their judgment from long ago is not idle, and their destruction is not asleep . . . For speaking out arrogant words of vanity *they entice by fleshly desires, by sensuality*, those who barely escape from the ones who live in error, promising them freedom while they themselves are slaves of corruption; for by what a man is overcome, by this he is enslaved. (2 Peter 2:1–3, 18–19, emphasis added)

Paul said covetousness is idolatry (Eph. 5:5) and forbade the Ephesians to be partakers with anyone who brought a message of immorality or covetousness (vv. 6–7).

How closely do modern Word Faith teachers resemble the greedy false teachers the apostles decried? Is it fair to write the movement off as sub-Christian or heretical?

I hesitate to label the Word Faith movement a cult only because its boundaries are as yet somewhat hazy. Many sincere believers hover around the periphery of Word Faith teaching, and some in the movement who adhere to the core of Word Faith teaching reject some of the most extreme teachings of the group. Nevertheless, all the elements that are common to the cults exist within the movement: a distorted christology, an exalted view of man, a theology based on human works, a belief that new revelation from within the group is unlocking "secrets" that have been hidden from the church for years, extrabiblical human writings that are deemed inspired and authoritative,[11] and an exclusivity that compels adherents to shun any criticism of the movement or teaching that is contrary to the system. Without some exacting corrections in the movement's doctrinal foundations, the movement is well on its way to being established as a false cult in every sense of the term. It is, I am convinced, the closest thing on earth to the greed cults of the New Testament era, which the apostles bluntly labeled heresy.

I realize that is a grave verdict, but abundant evidence bears it out. At almost every crucial point, the Word Faith movement has tainted, twisted, garbled, misunderstood, corrupted, or obliterated the crucial doctrines of our faith.

THE WRONG GOD

The god of the Word Faith movement is not the God of the Bible. Word Faith teaching, in effect, sets the individual believer above God and relegates God to the role of a genie, or Santa Claus, or a valet who is at the Christian's beck and call. Word Faith believers are their own supreme authority. As we will note, disciples in this movement are explicitly taught and encouraged to act like little gods.

Word Faith teaching has no concept of God's sovereignty. Scripture says, "The LORD has established His throne in the heavens; and His sovereignty rules over all" (Ps. 103:19). God is "the blessed and *only* Sovereign, the King of kings and Lord of lords" (1 Tim. 6:15, emphasis added). Yet in the volumes of Word Faith material I have read, I have not found one reference to the sovereignty of God. The reason is clear: Word Faith teachers don't believe God is sovereign. Jesus, according to Word Faith theology, has no authority on earth, having delegated it all to the church.[12]

Furthermore, Word Faith theology teaches that God is bound by spiritual laws that govern health and prosperity. If we say the right words, or believe without wavering, God is forced to respond however we determine. Robert Tilton claims that God is already committed to His part of a covenant relationship with us. We can make whatever commitment or promise to Him we want, "then we can tell God on the authority of His word what we would like Him to do. That's right! You can actually tell God what you would like His part in the covenant to be!"[13]

In the Word Faith system God is not Lord of all; He can't work until we release Him to do so. He is dependent on human instruments, human faith, and above all human words to get His work done. "It is in your power to release the ability of God," Charles Capps has written.[14] On the other hand, according to Capps, "Fear activates the devil."[15] If you succumb to fear—even doubting a little—"You've moved God out of it . . . *You have stopped God's ability immediately.* Maybe it was just about to come into manifestation, but now you have established satan's word in the earth—that it's not getting any better, it's getting worse. *YOU have established his word.*"[16]

According to Capps, God has turned over His sovereignty—including His creative authority—to people. Capps has written:

> In August of 1973, the Word of the Lord came unto me saying, "If men would believe me, long prayers are not necessary. Just speaking the Word will bring you what you desire. My creative power is given to man in Word form. I have ceased for a time from my work and have given man the book of MY CREATIVE POWER. That power is STILL IN MY WORD.
>
> "For it to be effective, man must speak it in faith. Jesus spoke it when He was on earth and as it worked then so it shall work now. *But it must be spoken by the body.* Man must rise up and have dominion over the power of evil by my Words. It is my greatest desire that my people create a better life by the spoken Word. For my Word has not lost its power just because it has been spoken once. It is still equally as powerful today as when I said, 'Let there be light.'
>
> "But for my Word to be effective, *men must speak it,* and that creative power will come forth performing that which is spoken in faith."[17]

Why pray at all if our words have so much creative force? Indeed, some Word Faith teachers come dangerously close to explicitly denying the need to seek any help from God through prayer. Norvel Hayes says it is better to talk to your checkbook, your disease, or whatever predicament you're in than to turn to God in prayer:

> You aren't supposed to talk to Jesus about it. You're supposed to talk directly to the mountain in Jesus' name—whatever the mountain is in your life.

> . . . Stop talking to Jesus about it. Stop talking to anybody else about it. Speak to the mountain itself in Jesus' name!

> Don't say, "Oh, God, help me. Remove this sickness from me." Say, "Flu, I am not going to let you come into my body. Go from me in the name of Jesus! Nose, I tell you to stop running. Cough, I tell you to leave in Jesus' name." Say, "Cancer, you can't kill me. I will never die of cancer in Jesus' name."

> Do you have a financial mountain in your life? Start talking to your money. Tell your checkbook to line up with God's Word. Talk to your business. Command customers to come into your business and spend their money there. Talk to the mountain![18]

Hayes also teaches that believers can exercise dominion over their guardian angels. "Since Angels are ministering spirits sent to minister to and for us Christians," he reasons, we can learn "how to put them into action on our behalf."[19] "We believers ought to be keeping those angelic creatures busy!" Hayes writes. "We ought to have them working for us all the time."[20]

And so Word Faith theology denies God's sovereignty, removes the need to pray to God for any relief from burdens or needs, and gives the Christian himself both dominion and creative power.

Indeed, by far the most controversial teaching of the Word Faith movement is the notion that God created mankind to be a race of "little gods." Kenneth Copeland has explicitly stated what many Word Faith teachers more subtly imply:

> He imparted in you when you were born again—Peter said it just as plain, he said, "We are partakers of the divine nature." That nature is life eternal in absolute perfection. And that was imparted, injected into your

spirit man, and you have that imparted into you by God just the same as you imparted into your child the nature of humanity. That child wasn't born a whale! [It was] born a human. Isn't that true?

Well, now, you don't *have* a human, do you? You *are* one. You don't *have* a god in you. You *are* one.[21]

Copeland teaches that Adam was "created in the god class," that is, he was a reproduction of God. "He was not *subordinate* to God, even . . . [Adam] was walking as a god . . . What he said, went. What he did, counted. [And when he] bowed his knee to Satan and put Satan up above him, then there wasn't anything God could do about it, because a *god* had placed [Satan] there."[22] Adam, remember, was "created in the god class, but when he committed high treason, he fell below the god class."[23]

On the cross, according to Copeland, Jesus won the right for believers to be born again back into the "god class." In doing so, Copeland believes that Jesus

won healing, He won deliverance, He won financial prosperity, mental prosperity, physical prosperity, family prosperity . . . He said He'd meet my needs according to His riches in glory by Christ Jesus, and I'm walking around and saying, "Yes! My needs are met according to His riches in glory by Christ Jesus! Glory to God! . . . I'm covenanting to the need meeter. I'm covenanting to the I AM!" Hallelujah.

And I say this with all respect, so that it don't upset you too bad. But I say it anyway: When I read in the Bible where He says, "I Am," I just smile and say, "Yes, I Am, too."[24]

That is so blasphemous it ought to make every true child of God cringe. Yet it is typical of Word Faith teaching. In the face of criticism for some of his statements about the deity of the believer, Copeland appeared with Paul and Jan Crouch on the Trinity Broadcasting Network's nationwide program *Praise the Lord* to defend and explain his teaching. The following conversation ensued:

PC: [God] doesn't even draw a distinction between Himself and us.
KC: Never, Never! You never can do that in a covenant relationship.
PC: Do you know what else that has settled, then, tonight? This hue and cry and controversy that has been spawned by the devil to try

and bring dissension within the body of Christ that we are gods. I
am a little God!

KC: Yes! Yes!

JC: Absolutely! (giggling) He gave us His name.

KC: The *reason* we are—

PC: I have His name. I'm one with Him. I'm in covenant relations—I
am a little god! Critics, be gone!

KC: You are anything that He is.

PC: Yes.[25]

Paul Crouch, head and on-air host of Trinity Broadcasting Network, and therefore one of the most powerful and influential people in religious broadcasting
today, has reaffirmed repeatedly his commitment to the "little gods" doctrine
of the Word Faith:

That new creation that comes into new birth is created in His image . . .
It is joined, then, with Jesus Christ. Is that correct? And so in that sense—
I saw this many years ago—whatever that union is that unites Father,
Son, and Holy Spirit, He says, "Father, I want them to be one with Me
even as You and I are one in Us." So apparently, what He does, He opens
up that union of the very godhead, and brings us into it![26]

Other Word Faith teachers have reiterated the heresy. Charles Capps writes, "I
have heard people say, 'Those who confess God's Word and say the promises of
God over and over are just trying to act like God!' Yes! That's exactly what we're
trying to do: *Act as God would in a similar situation* . . . What did He do? *He spoke
the thing desired.*"[27] Earl Paulk wrote, "Until we comprehend that we are little gods
and we begin to act like little gods, we cannot manifest the kingdom of God."[28]
Robert Tilton also calls the believer "a God kind of creature . . . designed to be as
a god in this world . . . designed or created by God to be the god of this world."[29]
And Morris Cerullo had this televised conversation with Dwight Thompson:

MC: See, when God created us in His image, He didn't put any strings
on us, did He? He didn't make us puppets.

DT: No, not at all.

MC: He didn't say—He didn't say, Morris, raise your hand. Raise
your—You know, and then here we are, we have no absolute—no
control over us, so—

DT: No. No. No.

MC: He made Dwight Thompson, He made Morris Cerullo a *small, miniature god*. Of course! The Bible says we are created in the image of God. His likeness. Where is that godlikeness? He gave us power . . . He gave us authority, He gave us dominion. He didn't tell us to act like a man! He told us to act like a *god*![30]

Benny Hinn adds, "The new creation is created after God in righteousness and true holiness. The new man is after God, like God, godlike, complete in Christ Jesus. The new creation is just like God. May I say it like this: 'You are a little god on earth running around'?"[31] Hinn responded to criticism of such teaching this way:

Now are you ready for some *real* revelation knowledge? OK. Now watch this: He laid aside His divine form . . . so one day I would be clothed on earth with the divine form.

Kenneth Hagin has a teaching. A lot of people have problems with it. Yet it is absolute truth. Kenneth Copeland has a teaching. Many Christians have put holes in it, but it's divine truth. Hagin and Copeland say: You are god. Ye are gods.

"Oh! I can't be god." Hold it. Let's bring balance to this teaching. The balance is being taught by Hagin. It's those that repeat him that mess it up. The balance is being taught by Copeland, who is my dear friend, but it's those that repeat what he say that are messing it up.

You see there brother? When Jesus was on earth, the Bible says that first He disrobed Himself of the divine form. He, the limitless God, became a man, that we men, may become as He is.[32]

Hagin, whom most major Word Faith teachers acknowledge as a major influence in shaping their theology, has said, "If we ever wake up and realize who we are, we'll start doing the work that we're supposed to do. Because the church hasn't realized yet that they are Christ. That's who they are. They are Christ."[33]

Thus have the Word Faith teachers deposed God and put the believer in His place. From that basic error nearly all their other fallacies flow. Why do they teach that health and prosperity are every Christian's divine right? Because in their system, Christians are gods, deserving of those things. Why do they teach that a believer's words have creative and determinative force? Because in their system, the believer is sovereign, not God.

They have bought Satan's original lie: "The serpent said to the woman, 'You surely shall not die! For God knows that in the day you eat from it your eyes will be opened, and you *will be like God,* knowing good and evil'" (Gen. 3:4–5, emphasis added). The idea that man can be like God is and always has been a satanic lie. In fact, it was the very lie that brought the devil himself down (cf. Isa. 14:14).

Two proof texts are often used by the Word Faith teachers as support for their teaching. In Psalm 82:6, God says to the rulers of earth, "You are gods, and all of you are sons of the Most High." A simple reading of the psalm, however, reveals that those words were spoken to unrighteous rulers on the verge of their judgment. God was deriding them for their haughtiness. It was *they* who thought they were gods. Read verses 6 and 7 together: "You are gods . . . nevertheless you will die like men." There was a clear note of irony in God's condemnation of them. Far from affirming their godhood, He was condemning them for thinking too highly of themselves!

Word Faith teachers will immediately turn to their other favorite proof text, where Jesus Himself quoted Psalm 82 in defense of His deity: "The Jews answered Him, 'For a good work we do not stone You, but for blasphemy; and because You, being a man, make Yourself out to be God.' Jesus answered them, 'Has it not been written in your Law, "I said, you are gods"?'" (John 10:33–34). But don't fail to notice Jesus' purpose for choosing that verse. It would have been a familiar one to the scribes and Pharisees, who understood its meaning as a condemnation of evil rulers. Jesus was echoing the irony of the original psalm. Walter Martin wrote,

> Jesus mocks the people as if to say, "You all think you're gods yourselves. What's one more god among you?" Irony is used to provoke us, not to inform us. It is not a basis for building a theology.

> It is also pertinent to an understanding of John 10 that we remember that Satan is called "the ruler of this world" by no less an authority than the Lord Jesus Christ (John 14:30, NASB). And Paul reinforces this by calling him "the god of this age" (2 Corinthians 4:4). We can make a "god" out of anything—money, power, status, position, sex, patriotism, family, or, as in Lucifer's case, an angel. We can be our own "god." But to *call* some-

thing deity or to worship it or treat it as divine is quite another thing than its being by nature and in essence deity.[34]

God said to the rebellious Israelites, "You turn things around! Shall the potter be considered as equal with the clay?" (Isa. 29:16) According to the Word Faith movement, the answer is yes. But according to Scripture, there is only one God, and beside Him there is no other (Deut. 4:35, 39; 32:39; 2 Sam. 7:22; Isa. 43:10; 44:6; 45:5–6, 21–22; 1 Cor. 8:4).

THE WRONG JESUS

It should come as no surprise that the Jesus of the Word Faith movement is not the Jesus of the New Testament. Word Faith teachers say Jesus gave up His deity and even took on Satan's nature, in order to die for our sins. Kenneth Copeland, defending his infamous "prophecy" that seemed to call doubt on the deity of Christ, wrote, "Why didn't Jesus openly proclaim Himself as God during His 33 years on earth? For one single reason. He hadn't come to earth as God, He'd come as man."[35]

The Word Faith Jesus often sounds like nothing more than a divinely empowered man:

> [Most Christians] mistakenly believe that Jesus was able to work wonders, to perform miracles, and to live above sin because He had divine power that we don't have. Thus, they've never really aspired to live like He lived.
>
> They don't realize that when Jesus came to earth, He voluntarily gave up that advantage, living His life here not as God, but as a man. He had no innate supernatural powers. He had no ability to perform miracles until after He was anointed by the Holy Spirit as recorded in Luke 3:22. He ministered as a man anointed by the Holy Spirit.[36]

Evidently it matters little to Copeland's system whether Jesus was God or man:

> The Spirit of God spoke to me, and He said, "Son, realize this."
>
> (Now follow me in this. Don't let your tradition trip you up.)
>
> He said, "Think this way: A twice-born man whipped Satan in his own domain."

And I threw my Bible and I sat up like that. I said, "What?"

He said, "A born-again man defeated Satan. The first-born of many brethren defeated him." He said, "You are the very image and the very copy of that one."

I said, "*Good*-ness gracious sakes alive!" I began to see what had gone on in there. And I said, "Well, now You don't mean—You couldn't *dare* mean that I could've done the same thing."

He said, "Oh yeah! If you'd known that—had the knowledge of the Word of God that he did, you could've done the same thing. Because you're a reborn man, too." He said, "The same power that I used to raise him from the dead, I used to raise you from your death in trespasses and sins." He said, "I had to have that copy and that pattern to establish judgment on Satan so that I could recreate a child and a family and a whole new race of mankind." And he said, "You are in his likeness."[37]

That utterance is glaringly blasphemous.[38] It is astonishing to me that anyone with the barest knowledge of biblical truth could accept it as true revelation. But judging from the response to Copeland's ministry, hundreds of thousands do.

The atonement of Christ—His sacrificial death on the cross—was the primary work our Lord came to earth to accomplish. The atonement is a major emphasis of the New Testament and is central to all that we believe and teach as Christians. Yet the Word Faith movement's teachings about the work of Christ are aberrant to the point of blasphemy.

Copeland says,

Jesus was the first man to ever be borned from sin to righteousness. He was the pattern of a new race of men to come. Glory to God! And you know what he did? The very first thing that this reborn man did—See, you have to realize that he died. You have to realize that he went into the pit of hell as a mortal man made sin. But he didn't stay there, thank God. He was reborn in the pit of hell.

The righteousness of God was made to be sin. He accepted the sin nature of Satan in his own spirit, and at the moment that he did so, he cried, "My God! My God! Why hast Thou forsaken me?"

You don't know what happened at the cross. Why do you think Moses, upon the instruction of God, raised a serpent up on that pole instead of a lamb? That used to *bug* me. I said, "Why in the world have you got to put that snake up there—the sign of Satan. Why didn't you put a lamb on that pole?"

The Lord said, "Because it *was* the sign of Satan that was hanging on the cross." He said, "I accepted in my own spirit spiritual death, and the light was turned off."[39]

Later in that same message Copeland adds:

The spirit of Jesus accepting that sin, and making it to be sin, he separated from his God, and in that moment, he's a mortal man. Capable of failure. Capable of death. Not only that, he's fixing to be ushered into the jaws of hell. And if Satan is capable of overpowering him there, he'll win the universe, and mankind is doomed. Don't get the idea that Jesus was incapable of failure, because if he had been, it would have been illegal.[40]

Illegal? Copeland has embraced a heresy known as the ransom theory of the atonement. It is the view that Christ's death was a ransom paid to Satan to settle the legal claim the devil had on the human race because of Adam's sin. That view contradicts the clear biblical teaching that Christ's death was a sacrifice offered to God, not to Satan (Eph. 5:2).

Moreover, Copeland and the Word Faith teachers move outside of orthodoxy with their teaching that Christ actually died spiritually. We sometimes refer to Christ's separation from the Father on the cross (cf. Matt. 27:46) as spiritual death. It is error to teach, however, that Christ's spirit ceased to exist ("the light was turned off"), or that the Trinity was somehow broken up ("he separated from his God, and in that moment, he's a mortal man"). Nor was Jesus dragged into hell by Satan and tormented for three days and three nights, as Fred Price wrote in a newsletter:

Do you think that the punishment for our sin was to die on a cross? If that were the case, the two thieves could have paid your price. No, the punishment was to go into hell itself and to serve time in hell separated from God . . . Satan and all the demons of hell thought that they had him bound, and they threw a net over Jesus, and they dragged Him down to the very pit of hell itself to serve our sentence.[41]

Could a *zillion* thieves on the cross have paid the price of our sin? Of course not. Jesus' deity and His sinlessness qualified Him alone to be our Great High Priest (Heb. 4:14–15) and perfect sacrifice ("You were not redeemed with perishable things like silver or gold from your futile way of life inherited from your forefathers, but with precious blood, as of a lamb unblemished and spotless, the blood of Christ. For He was foreknown before the foundation of the world, but has appeared in these last times for the sake of you"—1 Peter 1:18–20). Depreciating the death of Christ is serious error indeed.

Nevertheless, Copeland boldly preaches an aberrant view similar to Price's:

> Jesus had to go through that same spiritual death in order to pay the price—Now it wasn't the physical death on the cross that paid the price for sins, because if it had've been, any prophet of God that had died for the last couple of thousand years before that could've paid that price. It wasn't the physical death. Anybody could do that.[42]

Once again, Kenneth Hagin's influence is behind all these teachings. Hagin says,

> Jesus tasted death—*spiritual* death—for every man. See, sin is more than a physical act, it's a spiritual act. And so, He became what we were, that we might become what He is. Praise God. And so therefore, His spirit was separated from God.

> Why did He need to be begotten, or born? Because He became like we were: separated from God. Because He tasted spiritual death for every man. And His spirit and inner man went to hell. In my place. Can't you see that? Physical death wouldn't remove your sins. "He's tasted death for every man"—He's talking about tasting spiritual death.

> Jesus is the first person that was ever born again. Why did His spirit need to be born again? Because it was estranged from God.[43]

And so the Word Faith movement has concocted a theology that makes sinners gods and requires the sinless Son of God to be born again. Such teaching is totally unbiblical. It demeans our Lord and His work. Jesus does not merely *have* eternal life, nor did He *buy* it for us by paying off the devil. He *is* eternal life. As He said in John 14:6, "I am the way, and the truth, and the life" (cf. John 1:4; 5:26; 11:25). Although Jesus took upon Himself human nature in the Incarnation, and although He bore our sins on the cross, He never ceased to be God.

Furthermore, the Atonement did not take place in hell. It was completed on the cross when Jesus cried, "It is finished!" (John 19:30). First Peter 2:24 says that Christ "bore our sins in His body *on the cross*," not in hell. Colossians 2:13–14 says He canceled the debt of our sin, "and He has taken it out of the way, having nailed it to the cross." Ephesians 1:7 says, "We have redemption through His blood ["blood" here refers to His physical death—the actual shedding of His blood on the cross], the forgiveness of our trespasses" (cf. Matt. 26:28; Acts 20:28; Rom. 3:25; 5:9; Eph. 2:13; Col. 1:20; Heb. 9:22; 13:12; 1 Peter 1:19; 1 John 1:7; Rev. 1:5; 5:9). Jesus promised the repentant thief on the cross, "Today you shall be with Me in Paradise" (Luke 23:43). Clearly, He was not preparing to serve a sentence in hell. Instead, He served *notice* to hell that the powers of evil were defeated (cf. 1 Peter 3:19). The Bible knows nothing of the kind of atonement that the Word Faith movement describes. That's because the Jesus of the Bible is not the Jesus Word Faith teachers are talking about.

THE WRONG FAITH

Word Faith teaching sees faith as an immutable, impersonal "law" that, like gravity or the laws of thermodynamics, rules the universe: a principle that works regardless of who is exercising it—or for what. Pat Robertson, asked if the laws of the kingdom work even for non-Christians, wrote, "Yes. These are not just Christian and Jewish principles, anymore than the law of gravity is Christian and Jewish . . . The laws of God work for anybody who will follow them. The principles of the Kingdom apply to all of creation."[44] Applied to the "law" of faith, that reasoning means anyone—Christian or otherwise—who claims a blessing without doubting, can have whatever he claims.

Faith, according to Word Faith doctrine, is not submissive trust in God; faith is a formula by which to manipulate the spiritual laws they believe govern the universe. "Words governed by spiritual law become spiritual forces working for you. Idle words work against you. The spirit world is controlled by the word of God. The natural world is to be controlled by man speaking God's words."[45]

As the name "Word Faith" implies, this movement teaches that faith is a matter of what we *say* more than whom we trust or what truths we embrace and affirm in our hearts. A favorite term in the Word Faith movement is "Positive Confession." It refers to the Word Faith teaching that words have creative power. What you *say*, Word Faith teachers claim, determines everything that happens to you. Your "confessions," that is, the things you say—especially the favors you demand of God—must all be stated positively and without wavering. Then God is required to answer.

Kenneth Hagin writes, "You can have what you say. *You can write your own ticket with God.* And the first step in writing your own ticket with God is: *Say it.*"[46] He adds later, "If you talk about your trials, your difficulties, your lack of faith, your lack of money—your faith will shrivel and dry up. But, bless God, if you talk about the Word of God, your lovely Heavenly Father and what He can do—your faith will grow by leaps and bounds."[47]

Those ideas have bred festering superstition within the movement. Word Faith disciples believe, in effect, that all their words are magical incantations, determining their fate. Charles Capps warns against the dangers of speaking a negative confession, albeit unintentionally:

> We have programmed our vocabulary with the devil's language. We have brought sickness and disease into our vocabulary, and even death. The main word so many people use to express themselves is death—the word, *"death."*
>
> *"I'm just dying to do that." They will say, "I'm going to die if I don't. That just tickled me to death."*
>
> Now that, my friend, is *perverse speech.* That is contrary to God's Word. *Death is of the devil . . .* We need not *buddy-up* with death. All men are going to die soon enough, so don't start *buddying up* with it now.[48]

Positive confession would seem to rule out confession of sin. Indeed, Word Faith books on prayer and spiritual growth are utterly lacking in any teaching on confessing one's sin. They have undermined the crucial teaching of 1 John 1:9, which indicates believers should be constantly confessing their sin.

In fact, positive-confession teaching actually *encourages* believers to ignore and deny the reality of their sins and limitations. It has produced multitudes who perpetually wear emotionless smiles out of fear that a negative confession will bring them bad fortune.[49] Hagin admits he feels that way himself:

> I wouldn't tell anybody if I had a doubt-thought, or a fear-thought. I wouldn't accept it. I wouldn't tell somebody if the thought came to me— and you know the devil can put all kinds of thoughts in your mind.

We are a product of WORDS. Did you ever stop to think that the Bible teaches that there is health and healing in your tongue? Did you notice that he said here, [Prov. 12:18] *"the tongue of the wise is health"?*

I never talk sickness. I don't believe in sickness. I talk health . . . I believe in healing. I believe in health. I never talk sickness. I never talk disease. I talk healing.

I never talk failure. I don't believe in failure. I believe in success. I never talk defeat. I don't believe in defeat. I believe in winning, hallelujah to Jesus![50]

That perspective is rife with obvious problems. Bruce Barron tells of one Word Faith church where

the pastor rose sheepishly to instruct his congregation on a ticklish concern. Some of the church members, he had heard, were spreading contagious diseases among the church's little ones by bringing their sick babies to the nursery. Against the nursery volunteers' protests, these parents were positively confessing that their children were well. Since the parents had claimed their healing, there was nothing to worry about. They may have been dismissing those persistent whines and coughs as lying symptoms, but those lying symptoms proved to be contagious, and only an announcement from the pulpit could succeed in putting an end to the problem.[51]

In addition, the Word Faith denial of diseases and problems as "lying symptoms" robs believers of an opportunity to minister with compassion and understanding to suffering people. How can you help someone whose symptoms you believe are lies of Satan—or worse, the result of sinful unbelief in the sick person's life? Consequently, many Word Faith devotees tend to be unfeeling, even to the point of being coarse and abrasive toward people they assume don't have enough faith to claim a healing.

Barron tells of a pastor and his wife, unable to bear children, who "were told by a member of their church that they needed to 'confess' a pregnancy and display their faith by purchasing a baby stroller and walking down the street with it!"[52] A few years ago I received a heartrending letter from a dear woman who, deceived by "positive confession" theology, believed God wanted her to write everyone she knew with a baby announcement for the child she was hoping to conceive. Tragically, that poor woman was physically incapable of bearing children. Months later she had to write to everyone again to explain that the expected "faith baby" had not arrived. She was quick to add that she was still claiming a pregnancy by faith, however. She was obviously fearful that someone might take her second letter as a "negative confession."

Hagin seems callous even about the death of his own sister from lingering cancer:

> My sister got down to 79 pounds. The Lord kept telling me that she was going to die. I kept asking the Lord why I couldn't change the outcome. He told me she had had five years in which she could have studied the Word and built up her faith (she was saved), but she hadn't done it. He told me she was going to die, and she did. This is a sad example, but it's so true.[53]

Word Faith theology makes the healer a hero when miraculous cures are claimed, but it always blames the seeker for a lack of faith when a healing doesn't happen. Hagin describes an incident when he was attempting to heal an arthritic woman. Her disease had crippled her so badly that she was unable to walk. Hagin became frustrated at her unwillingness to let go of her wheelchair.

> I pointed my finger at her and said, "Sister, you don't have an ounce of faith, do you?" (She was saved and baptized with the Holy Spirit, but I meant she didn't have faith for her healing.)
>
> Without thinking, she blurted out, "No, Brother Hagin, I don't! I don't believe I'll ever be healed. I'll go to my grave from this chair." She said it, and she did it.
>
> We weren't to blame.[54]

Remember, positive confession teaches people that their words are determinative. God is no longer the object of faith; Word Faith devotees learn to put their faith in their own words—or as Hagin bluntly puts it, "faith in [their] own faith."[55] Try to follow his logic as he attempts to substantiate that concept:

> Did you ever stop to think about having faith in your own faith? Evidently God had faith in His faith, because He spoke the words of faith

and they came to pass. Evidently Jesus had faith in His faith, because He spoke to the fig tree, and what He said came to pass.

In other words, *having faith in your* words *is having faith in your* faith.

That's what you've got to learn to do to get things from God: *Have faith in your faith.*

It would help you to get faith down in your spirit to say out loud, "Faith in my faith." Keep saying it until it registers on your heart. I know it sounds strange when you first say it; your mind almost rebels against it. But we are not talking about your head; we're talking about faith in your heart. As Jesus said, *". . . and shall not doubt in his heart. . . ."*[56]

Notice that once again, Hagin manages to depreciate the Father and Son (Does God have faith? Can we accurately speak of the *faith* of an omniscient, sovereign God?) and deify himself as a worthy object of trust. Moreover, he turns faith into a magical formula and our words into some kind of abracadabra by which one may "get things from God."[57] There is no biblical basis for any of those ideas. The only appropriate objects for our faith are God and His infallible Word, certainly not our own words.

Nevertheless, Word Faith believers view their positive confessions as an incantation by which they can conjure up *anything* they desire. "Believe it in your heart; say it with your mouth. That is the principle of faith. *You can have what you say,*" Kenneth Hagin claims.[58] Quoting John 14:14 ("If you ask Me anything in My name, I will do it"), ignoring the plain implications of the phrase "in My name," they take that verse to be an unqualified promise they can use in extorting from God whatever kind of cargo they fancy.

Such teachings have led many Word Faith proponents into the grossest kind of materialism. John Avanzini, one of the lesser-known Word Faith teachers, spent an evening on Trinity Broadcasting Network arguing that Jesus was actually rich.[59] He pointed to Judas's role as treasurer and said, "You've got to handle lots of money to need a treasurer."[60] As a guest on Kenneth Copeland's broadcast, Avanzini said he believes Scripture teaches that Jesus had a big house and wore designer clothes.[61] All of that is touted as justification for the Word Faith teachers' own lavish lifestyles and materialistic philosophies.

Robert Tilton goes a step further: "Being poor is a sin, when God promises prosperity."[62] "My God's rich! And He's trying to show you how to draw out of your heavenly account that Jesus bought and paid for and purchased for you at

Calvary."[63] Tilton says, "New house? New car? That's chicken feed. That's nothing compared to what God wants to do for you."[64]

How is this cargo to be obtained? Tilton suggests that his followers make a "vow of faith" in the form of a gift to his ministry:

> I like a thousand-dollar vow, because I like—don't like—half-hearted people, lukewarm, just, "Well, I'll do a little . . . " I like a thousand-dollar vow of faith . . . I'm not talking to you that's got it. You that's got it don't pay a bit of attention to me. I'm talking to you that don't have it, and I'm showing you how you can get it! Yes, the Lord's work gets a portion of it. But you get the biggest portion. You get the biggest blessing. I'm trying to talk you out of that dump you're in! I'm trying to talk you into a decent car! . . . I'm trying to help you! Quit cursing me! Quit cursing me! God, what will pull this blessing from you? I am a blessing. I have been blessed supernaturally by God. I bring a blessing to you this day, and I know it, and my responsibility is to take it to you.[65]

Tilton encourages his listeners to pray the prayer of faith, "not one of those, 'Lord, if it be Thy will—' I *know* what the will of God is when it concerns healing, and prosperity, and divine direction . . . I don't have to pray a prayer of doubt and unbelief."[66] In other words, Robert Tilton wants you to make a thousand-dollar vow of faith to his ministry, especially if you *can't* afford to give away that much money. He doesn't want you to pray for God's will on the matter. After all, you can demand what you want and God must give it to you. Set your vow at a thousand, and demand that God provide the money. That's deceitful, blasphemous folly, but literally millions are sucked into such traps.

Richard Roberts, echoing his father's "Seed-Faith" concept, "urged viewers to 'sow a seed on your MasterCard, your Visa or your American Express, and then when you do, expect God to open the windows of heaven and pour you out a blessing.'"[67] Oral Roberts once mailed out plastic bags full of "holy water" from the River of Life Fountain at Oral Roberts University. To demonstrate how to use the stuff, he poured a bag of it over his own wallet on his television program.[68]

If it's that simple to get the cargo, why do so many Word Faith believers "claim" material blessings they never receive?[69] Fred Price explains:

> If you've got one-dollar faith and you ask for a ten-thousand-dollar item, it ain't going to work. It won't work. Jesus said, "according to your [faith],"

not according to *God's will for you*, in His own good time, if it's according to His will, if He can work it into His busy schedule. He said, "According to *your* faith, be it unto you."

Now, I may want a Rolls Royce, and don't have but bicycle faith. Guess what I'm going to get? A bicycle.[70]

Thus God's ability to bless us supposedly hangs on our faith.

Note that both Price and Tilton recoil from praying, "If it be Thy will." That is a common characteristic of Word Faith teachers. As we noted, they love to quote John 14:14: "If you ask Me anything in My name, I will do it." But 1 John 5:14 is noticeably missing from their database: "This is the confidence which we have before Him, that, if we ask anything *according to His will*, He hears us" (emphasis added). Hagin goes so far as to claim that no such truth is taught in the New Testament:

Because we didn't understand what Jesus said, and because we've been religiously brainwashed instead of New Testament-taught, we watered down the promises of God and tacked on something that Jesus didn't say, and added on something else to it: "Well, He will all right if it's His will, but it might not be His will," people have said. And yet, you don't find that kind of talk in the New Testament.[71]

Hagin has also written, "It is unscriptural to pray, 'If it is the will of God.' When you put an 'if' in your prayer, you are praying in doubt."[72]

Yet 1 John 5:14 clearly includes an "if." Furthermore, Romans 8:27 tells us that even the Holy Spirit "intercedes for the saints *according to the will of God*" (emphasis added).

And what will the Word Faith movement do with James 4:13–16? Does not their most fundamental teaching utterly contradict this passage?

Come now, you who say, "Today or tomorrow, we shall go to such and such a city, and spend a year there and engage in business and make a profit." Yet you do not know what your life will be like tomorrow. You are just a vapor that appears for a little while and then vanishes away. Instead, you ought to say, "If the Lord wills, we shall live and also do this or that." But as it is, you boast in your arrogance; all such boasting is evil.

What of the Word Faith movement's emphasis on material wealth and prosperity? Is that what real faith is all about? Hardly.

Far from stressing the importance of wealth, the Bible warns against pursuing it. Believers—especially leaders in the church (1 Tim. 3:3)—are to be free from the love of money (Heb. 13:5). Love of money leads to all kinds of evil (1 Tim. 6:10). Jesus warned, "Beware, and be on your guard against every form of greed; for not even when one has an abundance does his life consist of his possessions" (Luke 12:15). In sharp contrast to the Word Faith gospel's emphasis on gaining money and possessions in this life, Jesus said, "Do not lay up for yourselves treasures upon earth, where moth and rust destroy, and where thieves break in and steal" (Matt. 6:19). The irreconcilable contradiction between the Word Faith gospel and the gospel of our Lord Jesus Christ is best summed up in the words of Jesus in Matthew 6:24: "You cannot serve God and mammon [riches]."

CHRISTIAN SENSE OR CHRISTIAN SCIENCE?

The concept that the universe (including God) is governed by impersonal spiritual laws is not biblical.[73] It is a denial of God's sovereignty and providence. It is nothing less than deism. Furthermore, the notion that we can use words mystically to control reality is far removed from the biblical pattern of faith, especially as revealed in Hebrews 11.[74] Both ideas have more in common with the cult of Christian Science than with biblical truth.

Most Word Faith teachers vehemently deny that their teachings have anything to do with Christian Science or the other metaphysical cults. Charles Capps has written,

> You see, sometimes when I start teaching on this folks will say it sounds like *Christian Science.* One lady punched her husband in a service in Texas and said (my wife overheard them), *"That sounds like Christian Science."*
>
> *It's not Christian Science.* I like what Brother Kenneth Hagin says, *"IT'S CHRISTIAN SENSE"!*[75]

Later he adds, "No, It's not Christian Science. I don't deny the existence of disease. I deny the right of that disease to exist in this body, because I'm the Body of Christ."[76]

Still, the distinction is a fine one. It is a simple matter of fact that many of the doctrines central to Word Faith teaching are similar to those of Christian Science. There is a reason for that. A direct line of relationship ties the modern Word Faith movement to the metaphysical cults that flourished earlier in this century.

That connection has been carefully and conclusively documented in an excellent critique of the Word Faith movement, *A Different Gospel* by D. R. McConnell.[77] McConnell chronicles the development of the Word Faith movement, showing that nearly every major figure in the movement was mentored by Kenneth Hagin or one of his close disciples. Every doctrinal distinctive of the movement is traceable to Hagin.

Moreover, McConnell demonstrates convincingly that Word Faith teachings are not original with Hagin; Hagin gleaned them from the writings of a faith evangelist named E. W. Kenyon.[78] Hagin borrowed not only the *ideas* from Kenyon; McConnell includes several pages of column-by-column text that proves beyond question that Hagin has repeatedly plagiarized long sections of his writings *word-for-word* from Kenyon's material.[79]

Why is that significant? Because McConnell also reveals that Kenyon's roots were in the metaphysical cults. He was a faith healer not in the pentecostal tradition, but in the tradition of Mary Baker Eddy and Christian Science. He attended a college that specialized in training lecturers for the metaphysical science cults. And he imported and adapted into his system most of the essential ideas these cults propagated.[80] Hagin absorbed them from there.[81]

In short, McConnell's book is a devastating exposé of the Word Faith movement. It demonstrates irrefutably that Word Faith teachers owe their ancestry to groups like Christian Science, Swedenborgianism, Theosophy, Science of Mind, and New Thought—not to classical pentecostalism. It reveals that at their very core, Word Faith teachings are corrupt. Their undeniable derivation is cultish, not Christian.

The sad truth is that the gospel proclaimed by the Word Faith movement is not the gospel of the New Testament. Word Faith doctrine is a mongrel system, a blend of mysticism, dualism, and neo-gnosticism that borrows generously from the teachings of the metaphysical cults. Its perverse teachings are causing untold harm to the church in general and charismatics in particular. Word Faith is, in the words of the apostle Peter, a "destructive heresy" (2 Peter 2:1). No wonder it is as riddled with greed and materialism—and as spiritually bankrupt—as the crudest cargo cult.

The Word Faith movement may be the most dangerous false system that has grown out of the charismatic movement so far. Because so many charismatics are unsure of the finality of Scripture, and because they feel they cannot discount tales of people who claim to have had visitations from Christ, they are particularly susceptible to the movement's lies—and often at a loss to answer them.

Despite what Word Faith teachers say, however, our God is not merely a source of cargo. We are His servants, not He ours. He has called us to lives of loving service and worship, not godlike supremacy. He blesses us, but not always materially. In no way can we "write our own ticket" and expect Him to follow our script—nor should any real believer ever desire such a scenario. The life of the Christian is a life spent in pursuit of God's will—not a strategy to get Him to go along with ours. No one who rejects that fundamental truth can genuinely live unto God's glory. And no one who has known the emancipation from sin and selfishness wrought by God's grace should ever be willing to exchange that freedom for the cheapened cargo of the Word Faith doctrines.

6

WHAT ARE THE FUNDAMENTALS
OF CHRISTIANITY?[1]

A woman once wrote me to say she thought Christianity was fine but, personally, she was "into Zen." She liked to listen to Christian radio while she was driving because the music "smoothed out her karma." Occasionally, however, she would tune in one of the Bible-teaching ministries. In her opinion, all the preachers she heard were too narrow-minded toward other religions, so she was writing several radio ministers to encourage them to be more broad-minded.

"God doesn't care *what* you believe, as long as you're sincere," she wrote, echoing an opinion I have heard many times. "All religions lead ultimately to the same reality. It doesn't matter which road you take to get there, as long as you follow your chosen road faithfully. Don't be critical of the alternative roads other people choose."

To those who accept the Bible as God's Word, the folly of that thinking should be immediately evident. What does the Bible say about following your chosen road faithfully? "There is a way that seemeth right unto a man, but the end thereof are the ways of death" (Prov. 16:25; 14:12 KJV). Jesus said, "The gate is wide, and the way is broad that leads to destruction, and many are those who enter by it" (Matt. 7:13). He urged people to change directions, to enter the small gate that leads to the narrow way that few find.

Actually it is *Satan* who doesn't care what you believe—or how sincerely you believe it—as long as what you believe is error. To portray God as tolerant of all forms of worship is to deny the God of Scripture. After all, this was His first commandment: "I am the LORD your God . . . You shall have no other gods before Me" (Ex. 20:2–3).

If we believe the Bible, we cannot concede that other religions might be true as well. If we believe that Christ is Lord of all, and if we truly love Him, we cannot countenance the doctrines of those who deny Him (1 Cor. 16:22). Christianity, if true at all, is exclusively true. Inherent in the claims of Christ is the assertion that He alone offers truth, and all religious systems that deviate from His truth are false. Jesus said, "I am the way, and the truth, and the life; no one comes to the Father, but through Me" (John 14:6). Peter proclaimed, "There is salvation in no one else; for there is no other name under heaven that has been given among men, by which we must be saved" (Acts 4:12). If this is true, every other religion is a lie (cf. Rom. 3:4).

So the content of our faith *is* crucial. Sincerity is not sufficient.

Of course, such a view contradicts the relativistic values of modern culture. Pluralism and diversity have been enshrined as higher virtues than truth itself. We're not supposed to say our beliefs are right and all others are wrong. That is regarded as backward, outmoded, discourteous. In other words, we're not really supposed to *believe* our religious beliefs; we're only allowed to hold them as personal preferences.

Evangelicalism is beginning to absorb that latitudinarianism. Not that most evangelicals would accept Islam, Hinduism, or other overtly non-Christian religions. But many seem to think it doesn't really matter what you believe, as long as you label it Christianity. With the exception of a few cults that blatantly renounce the Trinity, almost everything taught in the name of Christ is accepted by evangelicals—from Roman Catholicism (which denies that sinners are justified solely by faith) to the extreme charismatic Word Faith movement (which both corrupts the doctrine of Christ and makes temporal health and wealth the focus of salvation).

In the name of unity, such matters of doctrine are expressly *not* supposed to be contested. We are being encouraged to insist on nothing more than a simple affirmation of faith in Jesus. Beyond that, the specific *content* of faith is supposed to be a matter of individual preference.

THE RISE AND FALL OF FUNDAMENTALISM

These are not new issues; the church has waged an ongoing struggle over these very matters at least since the turn of the century. This very same appeal for broad-mindedness has always been at the heart of the agenda of theological liberalism; indeed, it is precisely what the term "liberal" originally meant. What is new about today's appeals for tolerance is that they come from within the evangelical camp.

Liberalism first began to dominate the major Protestant denominations nearly a hundred years ago. Schools formerly committed to biblical truth began to attack the very doctrines they had been founded to uphold. Even Princeton Seminary, long a bastion of Reformed orthodoxy, ultimately succumbed to the spirit of the age. For a time it seemed that evangelicalism would be completely overwhelmed and overthrown by liberalism.

Liberals characterized evangelicalism as outmoded, unenlightened, and hopelessly intolerant. They argued that Christianity should be broad enough to embrace all kinds of beliefs. In their opinion the narrowness and intolerance of historic evangelicalism did not appropriately represent Christ; tolerance and liberality were more fitting for modern Christianity. That argument evidently fell on receptive ears. Sound doctrine began to give way to compromise, liberalism, and even rank unbelief within the church.

Then a remarkable movement began. Evangelicals from both sides of the Atlantic united in writing and publishing a series of articles titled *The Fundamentals*.[2] Originally published in twelve volumes, those articles laid the basis for a movement that became known as fundamentalism. With men like J. Gresham Machen, James Orr, and R. A. Torrey leading the way, fundamentalism employed sound doctrine to combat liberalism, higher criticism, evolutionary theory, and modernism.

The doctrinal basis for fundamentalism was broad enough to involve evangelical Anglicans, Presbyterians, Methodists, Baptists, Mennonites, Independents, and others—including theologians from both Reformed and Dispensationalist backgrounds. The issues they identified as "fundamentals" were doctrines they collectively viewed as essential, primary, nonnegotiable truths. These were, of course, the very articles of faith that distinguished evangelicalism from liberalism. The fundamentalists believed they were also the doctrines that separated the true church from false Christianity. What were the fundamental articles they identified?

The most basic were the authority, inspiration, and infallibility of Scripture. Against the higher critics, fundamentalists argued that the Bible is the literal Word of God, that it is historically and factually accurate, and that it is the complete and only binding rule of faith for believers. These precepts, of course, determine a host of other issues. If we agree that Scripture is the authoritative and inerrant Word of God, we have no legitimate reason to dispute its historical assertions, such as the creation account, the virgin birth of Christ, His bodily resurrection, and the miracles. If we believe Scripture is the *only* authority in matters of faith and practice, we cannot set religious speculation or church tradition alongside it.

All those issues were enumerated as fundamentals, along with the deity of Christ, the doctrine of the Trinity, Christ's substitutionary atonement on the cross, the Resurrection, justification by faith alone, salvation by grace through faith, the necessity of sanctification, and the rejection of every cult that distorts or contradicts any of the other fundamental doctrines.

In short, the early fundamentalists used *sound doctrine* to define true Christianity—against the liberals, who insisted that the only issues that really mattered were practical, not theoretical. A well-worn liberal slogan was "Christianity is a life, not a doctrine." The fundamentalists correctly argued that true Christianity is a doctrine that affects all of life.

So in contrast to those who were willing to enlarge the designation "Christian" to embrace the broadest possible spectrum of beliefs, the fundamentalists sought to identify the core of objective truth that was absolute and nonnegotiable. That body of sound doctrine, they claimed, is the very foundation of all genuine Christianity. Every brand of religion that rejected the fundamentals was regarded as pseudo-Christian or non-Christian.

Fundamentalists were not able to recover most of the mainline denominations from encroaching liberalism. But they did manage to establish new schools, new denominations, and new churches faithful to historic biblical truth. Those institutions have enjoyed a century of vigorous growth and spiritual influence, while mainline denominational churches have suffered severe decline.

Sadly, however, the fundamentalist movement began to unravel almost as soon as it had experienced its initial successes. One wing of fundamentalism, desperate for academic respectability, could not resist the pluralism of the modern age. Schools that had been founded to counter theological liberalism were overexposed to liberal theology and began to compromise on the issue of biblical inerrancy, capitulating at the very point where early fundamentalism had taken its strongest stand. Incredibly, some fundamentalist schools and churches abandoned their commitment to biblical inerrancy within *one generation* of their founding![3] Most of these institutions and the people associated with them quickly repudiated the designation "fundamentalist."

Another wing of fundamentalism moved the opposite direction. They were keenly aware that an obsession with academic respectability had led their brethren to abandon the fundamentals. For that reason they distrusted scholarship or spurned it altogether. This right wing of the fundamentalist movement was relentlessly fragmented by militant separatism. Legalism led to an extreme emphasis on external issues. Petty concerns often replaced serious doctrine as the matter for discussion and debate. This branch of the movement quickly reached the point where some of its adherents spent more time arguing about men's hair length and women's clothing than they spent defending the real fundamentals of the faith.

All the squabbling and extreme legalism eventually sullied the term "fundamentalism." Intellectually and temperamentally, these fundamentalists utterly abandoned the high ground that the fathers of the movement had held so tenaciously. As a consequence the movement succumbed to a subtle depreciation of doctrine. The published material from this side of fundamentalism is notable for its lack of any significant works with real doctrinal or biblical depth. The term "fundamentalist" became exclusively linked with this militant group.

In recent years, the term "fundamentalist" has been hijacked by the secular media, who apply it to every conceivable kind of religious fanatic.

SACKING THE FUNDAMENTALS

The polemical, theological spirit of early fundamentalism is all but dead. Modern evangelicals are too willing to downplay doctrine. Unlike our fundamentalist forebears, many today are perfectly agreeable to the suggestion that true Christianity ought to be broad enough to accommodate widely differing— even contradictory—belief systems. Many evangelicals are seeking to forge spiritual alliances with Catholicism, Eastern Orthodoxy, charismatic extremists, and even liberals—without regard to the fundamental doctrinal differences.

Historically, evangelicals and fundamentalists have almost universally rejected the ecumenical movement. The primary force in ecumenism has been the World Council of Churches, an organization that never really cared for biblical Christianity. Consequently, ecumenism has had little or no influence among evangelicals.

Even during the ecumenical movement's most prosperous era, evangelical churches experienced dramatic growth while ecumenical churches were quickly dying. Consequently, the ecumenical movement peaked in the 1960s and began quickly to wane. As recently as ten years ago the World Council of Churches appeared to be a monument to a lost cause.

But now the picture is changing. Incredibly, today's most powerful ecumenical forces are all under the banner of a foundering evangelicalism: the charismatic movement, Catholic-evangelical accords, cooperative mass evangelism, and a host of voices in the Christian media.

An aggressive effort is being made to divest "the fundamentals" of key evangelical distinctives. Influential voices within evangelicalism are urging us to pare back the essentials to the barest possible statement of faith. These voices can be heard across the spectrum of evangelicalism. Appeals for broader tolerance and more inclusivism have come from charismatics, dispensationalists, Calvinists and Arminians, Reformed and Lutheran leaders—so-called evangelicals of almost every stripe.

Paul Crouch, for example, president of the Trinity Broadcasting Network, writes, "As I have said so often, one theologian's heresy is another theologian's orthodoxy."[4] Crouch nevertheless acknowledges that Jude 3 commands us to contend earnestly for the faith once delivered to the saints. "So what is 'the faith'?" he asks rhetorically, then writes,

> The answer is simple; read it in the Apostle's [*sic*] Creed or any number of other confessions such as the Heidelberg Confession: Jesus Christ, born of a virgin, crucified, risen again, ascended to heaven, by whose blood our sins are forgiven, who will return in power and glory to judge the living and the dead. Beyond these absolute essentials of "FAITH," there is infinite room for honest men and women to disagree and debate the limitless issues of "doctrinal purity."

In other words, Crouch suggests that all who profess faith in those few essentials he lists should be permitted to teach whatever else they feel is right, and no one should publicly subject those teachings to any further theological scrutiny. It is all right for us to disagree, he concedes, but Christians should "NEVER judge a brother or sister by name" in any sort of critical doctrinal appraisal. To do so, he believes, is unbecoming to the cause of Christ. He labels the practice "heretic hunting."[5]

The Apostles' Creed is one of the earliest and simplest statements of faith in the history of creeds. We will examine it more closely later in this chapter, but for now we simply note that the creed was probably not written by the apostles. But it does summarize some of the major points of apostolic doctrine. It is not an exhaustive statement of faith, nor was it ever intended to be. It was a brief, rudimentary confession designed to distinguish Christianity from Judaism or pagan religions. It does not even address the issue of Jesus' deity.

Crouch's reference to "the Heidelberg Confession" is difficult to decipher. Perhaps he refers to the Heidelberg *Catechism* (1563). The principal author of this catechism was Ursinus, a student of Philipp Melanchthon. The document is far more detailed in its teachings than the Apostles' Creed. In fact, this catechism was written to address a controversy that arose when a fight broke out over the communion cup during a church service. The dispute had to do with whether the real presence of Christ was present in the communion elements.[6] Of course, this was one of the issues that was hotly debated in the Reformation. Ursinus rejected the Catholic view that the elements literally *become* the body and blood of Christ (transubstantiation). He also rejected Luther's view that the elements *contain* the real presence of Christ (consubstantiation). He embraced instead the view of Zwingli and most of the Reformers; namely, that the communion elements are *only symbolic*. The Heidelberg Catechism therefore includes several questions about the Lord's Supper designed to clarify these issues: such as "Do, then, the bread and wine become the real body and blood of Christ?" and "What difference is there between the Lord's Supper and the Popish Mass?" Far from being an elementary list of basic beliefs, the Heidelberg Catechism was a rather intensive theology lesson, a polemic designed to draw a clear line between Lutheranism and Reformed theology. It is actually a far more meticulous form of theological hairsplitting than has been practiced by the critics Paul Crouch wishes to silence.

The Heidelberg Catechism *does* contain a lengthy commentary on the Apostles' Creed. But even that section of the catechism is designed to take the meager statements of the Apostles' Creed and explain them in terms of the Reformed faith. The catechism explicitly interprets the creed in a way that refutes Roman Catholic doctrine.

The truth is that virtually all the historic creeds of the church serve a purpose that is diametrically opposed to the benign broad-mindedness Crouch is appealing for. The creeds were written to confront error. They present truth dogmatically, in specific and well-delineated terms. All of them are polemic, controversial, argumentative. They aim at separation, not unity. The Nicene Creed (381) defended the doctrine of the Trinity. The Athanasian Creed (c. 425) spells out the doctrine of Christ's two natures. Then there are Roman Catholic creeds, Greek and Russian creeds, and Protestant creeds. Virtually every creed after the Apostles' Creed addressed matters of doctrinal controversy.

So despite Paul Crouch's assertion that "any number of other confessions" might be adduced to make his point, it is very unlikely that he could point to *any* creed ever adopted by a church council or denominational body that fits his parameters. He is almost certainly attempting to define "the faith" in terms of the Apostles' Creed only. In fact, his list of essentials is actually an abbreviated paraphrase of the Apostles' Creed.

Paul Crouch is not alone in suggesting that the test of orthodoxy ought to be nothing more than the Apostles' Creed. That view is evidently shared by increasing numbers of evangelical leaders.

Perhaps the most popular and persuasive defender of this view is Charles Colson, former counsel to the Nixon White House and founder of Prison Fellowship. Colson is an influential and highly respected leader within evangelicalism, known for his well-honed writing and speaking ministries. I have deeply appreciated much of what he has written over the years. Often his insights are extremely perceptive. I find myself on the same side of the fence with him on most important issues. It is evident that he has a warm heart for the things of the Lord.

That is why it is so hard to understand the way Colson defines Christian orthodoxy. His frequent appeals for Christian unity are surely noble efforts, but he fails to identify which doctrines are truly essential to real Christianity. Colson is by no means the only evangelical leader to make this error. But because he is one of the most outspoken and aggressive proponents of the new ecumenism, we need to examine some of the ideas he has proposed.

Appeals for broader Christian unity have been a running theme in Colson's writings over the years, but the subject is especially prominent in his 1992 book, *The Body*.[7] Again, there is much in this book with which we can wholeheartedly agree. For example, Colson writes,

> We must begin with a renewed commitment to the truth . . . We must stand boldly in the tradition of those who have gone before us, many of whom have shed blood in their defense of the historic, orthodox confession of our faith. In theology, as in other areas of life, fads come and go, but truth is validated as it survives the assaults that come its way. Tested through the centuries, the tenets of Christian orthodoxy have been passed on and entrusted to us. And here we must stand—without equivocation—even when the world hangs labels on us that represent everything considered ugly and backward.[8]

Colson acknowledges that the kind of ecumenism that means "reducing all elements of faith to the lowest common denominator" is not true unity.[9] It is obvious that Colson desires to avoid the trap of doctrinal minimalism that led the World Council of Churches into destructive radical politics. He says he is *not* in favor of that brand of ecumenism. True unity, he correctly observes, is achieved by finding a "common ground of orthodoxy on which [Christians] can stand together."[10]

Colson mounts a brilliant attack against moral relativism. He laments the fact that "relativism is firmly established as the reigning orthodoxy of American life."[11] And he notes a Gallup poll that revealed 69 percent of Americans question the existence of any moral absolutes, comparing the rise of such existentialism in society to a "moral lobotomy." "As a result, the only stable virtue left in this relativistic world is unbridled tolerance," he writes. "There are no absolutes except the absolute that there can be no absolute."[12]

Colson also declares that he is a fundamentalist. He defends the term "fundamentalism," recounting briefly how *The Fundamentals* came into being after the turn of the century. He rehearses, much as I have in this chapter, how the fundamentalist movement took a stand against early liberalism.[13] Fundamentalism, he writes, "means adherence to the fundamental facts—in this case, the fundamental facts of Christianity. It is a term that was once a badge of honor, and we should reclaim it."[14] To all of that I heartily say Amen.

But then Colson lists his idea of the fundamentals: the infallibility of Scripture, the deity of Christ, the virgin birth and miracles of Christ, Christ's substitutionary death, and Christ's physical resurrection and eventual return. (Note, by the way, that his list includes two items missing from the Apostles' Creed and Paul Crouch's list: the infallibility of Scripture and the deity of Christ.)

Those five doctrines, Colson says, are "the backbone of orthodox Christianity." He writes, "If a fundamentalist is a person who affirms these truths, then there are fundamentalists in every denomination—Catholic, Presbyterian, Baptist, Brethren, Methodist, Episcopal . . . Everyone who believes in the orthodox truths about Jesus Christ—in short, every Christian—is a fundamentalist."[15]

Colson's thesis in *The Body* is that all who adhere to those basic doctrines ought to view one another as members of the same body, refuse to allow any other doctrinal differences to divide them, and put up a united front against what Colson believes are the church's two great enemies—secularism and Islam.[16] The church universal desperately needs to get back to "mere Christianity," he suggests. "Articulated in the classic confessions and creeds, ['mere Christianity'] embraces such fundamentals as the Virgin Birth, the deity of Christ, the Atonement, the Resurrection, the Authority of Scripture, and the Second Coming."[17]

Is Colson's list of fundamental doctrines really comprehensive enough? Although he seems to be affirming *The Fundamentals*, his appeal for solidarity with Rome is seriously out of sync with the design of those tracts.[18] Moreover, his five- or six-point creed lacks any reference to the way of salvation. He excludes justification by faith. He says nothing about the *sufficiency* of Scripture as our sole rule of faith. What in his brief list of doctrines would exclude Mormonism? Do these few doctrines really provide an adequate creed to exclude false Christianity?

IS THE APOSTLES' CREED A FULL ENOUGH STATEMENT OF FAITH?

Note that Colson, like Paul Crouch, suggests that "the classic confessions and creeds" all support his bare-bones platform of fundamentals. Yet as we noted earlier, virtually all the historic creeds served purposes that were controversial, not conciliatory. Not one of the major creeds was written to try to bring together widely differing religious bodies. On the contrary, those who drafted the creeds had exactly the opposite design in mind. The Roman Catholic Council of Trent wrote a creed that assails the work of the Reformers. All the Reformed creeds are outspokenly anti-Catholic. Which of those creeds would Colson select as an acceptable standard for the whole church? He must either reject them all or abandon his crusade to blend the Catholic-evangelical-Orthodox traditions. Ecumenical efforts cannot be supported by an appeal to the church's creedal heritage.

Colson also implies that the true nonnegotiables of Christianity were all settled by the Apostles' Creed.[19] He suggests that all evangelical Christians should be willing to embrace as brothers and sisters in Christ everyone who can give assent to this ancient creed.

What is the Apostles' Creed? Is it a full enough statement of faith? Does it contain sufficient safeguards against false doctrine to serve as a test of fellowship?

The Apostles' Creed cannot be traced to any specific author or date. The earliest known text comes to us from the middle of the fourth century, but it is assumed to have existed before then. This is the most common form of the creed as it is recited today:

I believe in GOD THE FATHER Almighty; Maker of heaven and earth.

And in JESUS CHRIST His only Son our Lord; who was conceived by the Holy Ghost, born of the Virgin Mary; suffered under Pontius Pilate, was crucified, dead, and buried; he descended into hell; the third day he rose from the dead; he ascended into heaven; and sitteth at the right hand of God the Father Almighty; from thence he shall come to judge the quick and the dead.

I believe in the HOLY GHOST; the holy catholic church; the communion of saints; the forgiveness of sins; the resurrection of the body; and the life everlasting. Amen.

Roman Catholic tradition says the apostles themselves wrote the creed, each contributing one article of faith. But the historical evidence does not support that.[20] The phrase "he descended into hell," for example, was not part of the creed until the late fourth century; it is borrowed from another creed of that era. The word "catholic," the phrase "the communion of saints," and the final phrase ("life everlasting") are all later additions to the creed.[21] The full creed as it is known today did not come into general use until the seventh or eighth century.[22]

IS THIS A FULL STATEMENT OF ALL THE ESSENTIALS?

The creed is by no means a complete statement of all the doctrines essential to genuine Christianity. For example, since there is no statement about the deity of Christ, a Jehovah's Witness could give full assent to the creed as it stands. In fact, the ancient forerunners of Jehovah's Witnesses, the followers of a heretic named Arius, defended themselves by appealing to the creed. William Cunningham wrote, "Nay, it is well known that Arians, who deny the divinity of the Son and the Holy Ghost, have no hesitation in expressing their concurrence in the creed."[23]

In 1681, a godly Dutch Reformed theologian named Herman Witsius published in Latin a series of dissertations on the Apostles' Creed. The two-volume English translation of this work has recently been republished. Witsius wrote,

> If you consider only the truths expressly mentioned in the Creed, *all the necessary articles of our Religion are not contained in this summary*. For it contains *nothing about the Word of God*, which is the immediate object, the rule, and the source of our faith . . . [It contains] *nothing respecting our sin and misery*, the knowledge of which is inculcated in Scripture as particularly necessary [Jer. 3:13]:—*Nothing relative to justification by faith without the works of the law*, the knowledge of which article, however, the Apostle valued so highly, that in comparison of it he accounted all other things but loss and dung [Phil. 3:8–9]—so highly, that he declares that whosoever desire to be justified by the law, have no part in Christ, and are fallen from grace [Gal. 5:4]:—*Nothing even regarding the worship and service of God*, and the leading of a holy life; which cannot be rightly performed, unless they are both known, and believed to be necessary.[24]

Moreover, Witsius points out, there are issues in the creed that are clearly *not* essential. Is salvation prerequisite on knowing that it was Pontius Pilate who condemned Christ to death? Must a person understand in what sense Christ "descended into hell" in order for that person to be saved? Must every truly regenerate person be able to define "the holy catholic church," or "the communion of saints"? William Cunningham wrote in 1882, "If men appeal to the Creed as a proof of their orthodoxy, they are of course bound to explain its meaning, and to show that they hold its statements in a reasonable sense."[25]

WHOSE INTERPRETATION OF THE CREED IS VALID?

The truth is, many of the statements in the Apostles' Creed are open to widely varying, or even contradictory, interpretations. There is no general agreement on how those statements should be interpreted. "Therefore although heretics may say that they receive the [Creed], yet they do not because they reject its true and genuine sense."[26] It is not merely the *words* of the creed that must be affirmed, but their true meaning. Unfortunately, there is little agreement between the major Christian traditions about what the words mean.

Christ's descent into hell, for example, is interpreted by some to mean that He actually went into the infernal flames—although Scripture teaches nothing like that. Others, appealing to the Latin terminology, believe the creed simply means that He descended into *hades*, the realm of the dead. In other words, the phrase "he descended into hell" simply means that he actually died. The Roman Catholic Church teaches that Christ descended into hades, gathered up the souls of all the righteous who had died before Him, and carried them to heaven. Still other interpreters suggest that the phrase means only that Christ experienced all the torments of hell in His sufferings on the cross.

Which of those interpretations conveys the actual truth that the creed intends to teach?

Or what about "the holy catholic church"? Those who follow the pope dogmatically interpret that as a reference to the *Roman* Catholic Church. Protestants interpret "catholic" in accord with its literal meaning, "universal." Thus according to most Protestants the phrase refers to the whole worldwide body of true believers regardless of their denomination.

"The communion of saints" has been interpreted by various commentators as a reference to the fraternity of saints already in heaven, actual communion between earthly and heavenly saints, or simply fellowship among believers here on earth.[27]

William Cunningham cited an essay written by a Lutheran writer named

Ittigius, who "exhibited in parallel columns the Lutheran, the Calvinistic, and the Popish interpretations of all the different articles in the Creed . . . Another writer afterward added a fourth column, containing the Arminian or Pelagian interpretation of all the articles."[28] According to Cunningham, it could not be proved that any one of these systems was inconsistent with the intent of the creed—though they clearly contradict each other. The words of the creed are simply not specific enough to determine which of these views it intends to affirm.

But the differences between these various interpretations make the difference between true Christianity and false Christianity. As Cunningham wrote,

> The Apostles' Creed, as it is called . . . is not fitted to be of much use, as a summary of the leading doctrines of Christianity. A document which may honestly be assented to by Papists and Arians, by the adherents of the great apostasy and by the opposers of the divinity of our Saviour, can be of no real utility as a directory, or as an element or bond of union among the churches of Christ.[29]

All of this comes back to the problem raised by Charles Colson in his book *The Body*. Having argued so convincingly against moral relativism, how can he defend a position that is essentially spiritual and doctrinal relativism? If, as Colson points out, "ideas do have consequences,"[30] how can he declare these doctrinal differences inconsequential—especially since they involve matters as significant as the way of salvation and the source of spiritual authority? Having lamented the "moral lobotomy" secular society has been subjected to, does he now plead for the visible church to undergo a spiritual lobotomy?[31]

Again, I deeply appreciate much that Charles Colson has to say, but it seems this matter produces a considerable amount of confusion—and it is contributing to the rise of reckless faith in the evangelical church. *The Body* has been widely hailed as a landmark statement of true unity. At least in part because of the widespread influence Colson has had, the movement to embrace Roman Catholicism and Eastern Orthodoxy is fast gaining momentum. It is essential that evangelicals think these matters through more carefully.

HOW SERIOUS ARE DIFFERENCES OVER THE CENTRAL DOCTRINES OF CHRISTIANITY?

All who call themselves Christian should agree that there is a body of doctrine that is nonnegotiable. The articles of faith that make up this constitutional body of truth are the very essence of "the faith which was once for all delivered to the saints" (Jude 3). These are the real fundamentals of the faith. They are doctrines so indispensable to true Christianity that we ought to break fellowship with professing Christians who deny them (2 Cor. 6:14–17).

Nothing is more clear from Scripture than the teaching that such a boundary exists between true and false doctrine. Paul wrote, "Even though we, or an angel from heaven, should preach to you a gospel contrary to that which we have preached to you, let him be accursed. As we have said before, so I say again now, if any man is preaching to you a gospel contrary to that which you received, let him be accursed" (Gal. 1:8–9). In a similar vein, the apostle John wrote, "Beloved, do not believe every spirit, but test the spirits to see whether they are from God; because many false prophets have gone out into the world" (1 John 4:1). And, "Anyone who goes too far and does not abide in the teaching of Christ, does not have God . . . If anyone comes to you and does not bring this teaching, do not receive him into your house, and do not give him a greeting; for the one who gives him a greeting participates in his evil deeds" (2 John 9–11).

Those are just a few of the passages in the New Testament that command us to draw a clear line of distinction between sound doctrine and pseudo-Christianity. These verses *command* us to keep spiritually separate from those who corrupt the essential truths of the gospel. Not only that, they attach the guilt of the false teacher's evil deeds to the one who fails to distinguish clearly between truth and error. We who love Christ should be very conscientious about interpreting and applying those commandments with the utmost care.

Without question, the biblical call to separation is sometimes abused by people who improperly apply it. Some Christians read such commands as if they were a prescription for abusive, spiteful, or venomous behavior toward others. That is not at all the attitude these verses call for. Nor are these passages guidelines for dealing with mere differences of opinion among true believers. They instruct us how to deal with false teachers who have gone astray with regard to the fundamental doctrines of Christianity.

Note the sternness of the language. The apostle, writing under divine inspiration, pronounces a severe curse on those who preach a corrupt gospel. In doing so he condemns both the false teachers and the bogus religious systems they devise. He thus places false Christianity in a category with the most heinous sins imaginable.

Surely, therefore, we ought to be extremely cautious about whom we receive into fellowship. Above all, we cannot possibly justify any sort of spiritual union with anyone whose teaching corrupts the New Testament gospel.

No one who really believes the Bible should dispute those things. But it is precisely at this point that the real difficulty begins. What *are* the doctrines that are truly fundamental, and how do we decide what they are? Can we take them from a creed that was given to us by tradition, not by inspiration? Shouldn't we turn instead to God's Word for instruction about what is really essential to our faith?

The answer is automatic for those who truly love the Word of God.

HOW DO WE DECIDE WHICH DOCTRINES ARE TRULY FUNDAMENTAL?

Does the Bible itself identify specific doctrines as fundamental? Indeed it does. We have already noted that the strongest words of condemnation in all the New Testament are aimed at false teachers who corrupt the gospel. Therefore the gospel message itself must be acknowledged as a primary point of fundamental doctrine.

It would seem obvious, then, that two religious groups with contradictory evangelistic messages could not unite together for evangelism. Yet that is precisely what many today are appealing for. Charles Colson appeals for ecumenical unity for precisely this reason: "For it means we can cooperate for common witness."[32]

But what message will determine the content of our testimony? The biblical message of instantaneous justification through faith alone—or a system of rituals and sacraments that are supposed to convey grace to the participants with no guarantee of ultimate salvation? What authority will we point people to? The Scriptures alone—or a papal hierarchy and church tradition? Those two gospels are flatly contradictory and mutually exclusive.

All these considerations determine what message we proclaim and whether that message is the authentic gospel of true Christianity. Therefore we are dealing with matters that go to the very heart of the doctrines Scripture identifies as fundamental.

Can we get more specific? Let's turn to Scripture itself and attempt to lay out some biblical principles for determining which articles of faith are truly essential to authentic Christianity.[33]

All Fundamental Articles of Faith Must Be Drawn from the Scriptures

First, if a doctrine is truly fundamental, it must have its origin in Scripture, not tradition, papal decrees, or some other source of authority. Paul reminded

Timothy that the Scriptures are "able to make thee wise unto salvation" (2 Tim. 3:15 KJV). In other words, if a doctrine is essential for salvation, we can learn it from the Bible. The written Word of God therefore must contain all doctrine that is truly fundamental. It is able to make us "adequate, equipped for every good work" (2 Tim. 3:17). If there were necessary doctrines not revealed in Scripture, those promises would ring empty.

The psalmist wrote, "The law of the LORD is perfect, restoring the soul" (Ps. 19:7). That means Scripture is *sufficient*. Apart from the truths revealed to us in Scripture there is no essential spiritual truth, no fundamental doctrine, nothing essential to soul restoration. We do not need to look beyond the written Word of God for any essential doctrines. There is nothing necessary beyond what is recorded in God's Word.

This, of course, is the Reformation principle of *sola Scriptura*—Scripture alone. It contrasts starkly with the practice of the Roman Catholic Church, which commonly threatens eternal damnation for anyone who questions the decrees of the pope or the dogma of church councils. For example, Canon 1 of the seventh session of the Council of Trent pronounces anathema on anyone who says that there are more or less than the seven sacraments established by the council. That means if any Catholic questions the sacraments of confirmation, penance, or extreme unction—mentioned nowhere in Scripture—that person is subject to excommunication and in the church's eyes is worthy of eternal damnation. The canons and decrees of the Council of Trent are larded with similar anathemas—in effect making all the council's dictums fundamental doctrines. In Turretin's words, they "are impudent enough often to declare as fundamental their own hay and stubble and whatever the Romish church teaches."[34]

But according to the Bible itself, no supposed spiritual authority outside "the sacred writings" of Scripture can give us wisdom that leads to salvation. No papal decrees, no oral tradition, no latter-day prophecy can contain truth apart from Scripture that is genuinely fundamental.

THE FUNDAMENTALS ARE CLEAR IN SCRIPTURE

Second, if an article of faith is to be regarded as fundamental, it must be clearly set forth in Scripture. No "secret knowledge" or hidden truth formula could ever qualify as a fundamental article of faith. No key is necessary to unlock the teaching of the Bible.

The truth of God is not aimed at learned intellectuals; it is simple enough for a child. "Thou didst hide these things from the wise and intelligent and didst reveal them to babes" (Matt. 11:25). The Word of God is not a puzzle. It does not speak in riddles. It is not cryptic or mysterious. It is plain and obvious to those who have spiritual ears to hear. "The testimony of the LORD is sure, making wise the simple" (Ps. 19:7).

The point is not that every fundamental article of faith must be supported with an explicit proof text. The doctrine of the Trinity, for example, is certainly essential to true Christianity—and it is very clear in Scripture—but you will find no comprehensive statement of the Trinity from any single passage of Scripture. Witsius wrote,

> Among articles clearly contained in the Scriptures . . . we must include not only those which they teach in express words, but also those which, to all who apply their minds to the subject, are obviously deducible from them by necessary consequence. Our Lord and his Apostles very frequently confirmed even fundamental articles of faith by consequences deduced from Scripture [cf. Luke 20:37–38] . . . The knowledge of a fundamental article consists not in understanding this or the other passage of the Bible; but in an acquaintance with the truth, which in one passage, perhaps, is more obscurely traced, but is exhibited in other places in a clear, nay, in the clearest possible light.[35]

Nor does this mean that a doctrine must be noncontroversial in order to be considered a fundamental article. Some would argue that the only test of whether something is essential to true Christianity is whether it is affirmed by all the major Christian traditions. Perhaps this is the very idea behind Charles Colson's appeals for ecumenical unity. But as Witsius points out, according to that rule, hardly anything of any substance would remain to distinguish the Christian gospel from the "salvation" offered by pagan morality or Islamic theology. "There is much truth in the remark of *Clement of Alexandria;* 'No Scripture, I apprehend, is so favourably treated, as to be contradicted by no one.'"[36]

EVERYTHING ESSENTIAL TO SAVING FAITH IS FUNDAMENTAL

Third, a doctrine *must* be regarded as fundamental if eternal life depends on it. Scripture is full of statements that identify the terms of salvation and the marks of genuine faith. "Without faith it is impossible to please Him, for he who comes to God must believe that He is, and that He is a rewarder of those who seek Him" (Heb. 11:6). That verse makes faith itself essential to a right relationship with God. It also expressly identifies both the existence and the veracity of God as fundamental articles of the Christian faith.

Elsewhere we are told that eternal life is obtained through the knowledge of the true God and Jesus Christ (John 17:3; 14:6; Acts 4:12). Since Jesus Himself *is* the true God incarnate (1 John 5:20; John 8:58; 10:30), the fact of His deity (and by implication the whole doctrine of the Trinity) is a fundamental article of faith (cf. 1 John 2:23). Our Lord Himself confirmed this when He said all must honor Him as they honor the Father (John 5:23).

The truths of Jesus' divine sonship and messiahship are also fundamental articles of faith (John 20:31).

Of course, the bodily resurrection of Christ is a fundamental doctrine, because 1 Corinthians 15:14 tells us, "If Christ has not been raised, then our preaching is vain, your faith also is vain."

Romans 10:9 confirms that the Resurrection is a fundamental doctrine and adds another: the lordship of Christ. "If you confess with your mouth Jesus as Lord, and believe in your heart that God raised Him from the dead, you shall be saved."

And according to Romans 4:4–5 justification by faith is a fundamental doctrine as well: "Now to the one who works, his wage is not reckoned as a favor, but as what is due. But to the one who does not work, *but believes in Him who justifies the ungodly,* his faith is reckoned as righteousness" (emphasis added). In other words, those who seek acceptance before God on the ground of their own righteousness will find they fall short (Rom. 3:27–28; Gal. 2:16–3:29). Only those who trust God to impute Christ's perfect righteousness to them are accounted truly righteous. This is precisely the difference between Roman Catholic doctrine and the gospel set forth in Scripture. It is at the heart of all doctrine that is truly fundamental.

In fact, an error in understanding justification is the very thing that was responsible for the apostasy of the Jewish nation: "For not knowing about God's righteousness, and seeking to establish their own, they did not subject themselves to the righteousness of God" (Rom. 10:3). Is that not the precise failure of Roman Catholicism? But "Christ is the end of the law for righteousness to everyone who believes" (v. 4).

EVERY DOCTRINE WE ARE FORBIDDEN TO DENY IS FUNDAMENTAL

Certain teachings of Scripture carry threats of damnation to those who deny them. Other ideas are expressly stated to be affirmed only by unbelievers. Such doctrines, obviously, involve fundamental articles of genuine Christianity.

The apostle John began his first epistle with a series of statements that establish key points of the doctrine of sin (*hamartiology*) as fundamental articles of faith. "If we say that we have fellowship with Him and yet walk in the darkness, we lie and do not practice the truth" (1 John 1:6). That condemns wanton antinomianism and makes some degree of doctrinal and moral enlightenment essential to true Christianity. A second statement rules out the humanistic notion that people are basically good: "If we say that we have no sin, we are deceiving ourselves, and the truth is not in us" (v. 8). And a third suggests that no true Christian would deny his or her own sinfulness: "If we say that we have not sinned, we make Him a liar, and His word is not in us" (v. 10).

First Corinthians 16:22 makes love for Christ a fundamental issue: "If anyone does not love the Lord, let him be accursed." And a similar verse, 1 Corinthians 12:3, says that no one speaking by the Spirit of God can call Jesus accursed.

The truth of Jesus' incarnation is also clearly designated a fundamental doctrine: "Every spirit that confesses that Jesus Christ has come in the flesh is from God; and every spirit that does not confess Jesus is not from God; and this is the spirit of the antichrist" (1 John 4:2–3). "For many deceivers have gone out into the world, those who do not acknowledge Jesus Christ as coming in the flesh. This is the deceiver and the antichrist" (2 John 7). Those verses by implication also condemn those who deny the virgin birth of our Lord, for if He was not virgin-born, He would be merely human, not eternal God come in the flesh.

And since those who twist and distort the Word of God are threatened with destruction (2 Peter 3:16), it is evident that both a lofty view of Scripture and a sound method of Bible interpretation (*hermeneutics*) are fundamental tenets of true Christianity.

THE FUNDAMENTAL DOCTRINES ARE ALL SUMMED UP IN THE PERSON AND WORK OF CHRIST

Paul wrote, "No man can lay a foundation other than the one which is laid, which is Jesus Christ" (1 Cor. 3:11). Christ Himself embodied or established every doctrine that is essential to genuine Christianity. Those who reject any of the cardinal doctrines of the faith worship a christ who is not the Christ of Scripture.

How are the fundamentals of the faith personified in Christ?

With regard to *the inspiration and authority of Scripture*, He is the incarnate Word. He upheld the written Word's authority (Matt. 5:18). Christ Himself established *sola Scriptura* as a fundamental doctrine when He upbraided the Pharisees for nullifying Scripture with their own traditions:

Rightly did Isaiah prophesy of you hypocrites, as it is written,
"This people honors Me with their lips,
But their heart is far away from Me.
But in vain do they worship Me,
Teaching as doctrines the precepts of men."
Neglecting the commandment of God, you hold to the tradition of
men . . . You nicely set aside the commandment of God in order
to keep your tradition. (Mark 7:6–9)

Our Lord had much to say about the authority and infallibility of the Word of God.

In the doctrine of *justification by faith*, it is Christ's own perfect righteousness, imputed to the believer, that makes the pivotal difference between true biblical justification and the corrupted doctrine of Roman Catholicism and the cults. That is what Paul meant when he wrote, "Christ is the end of the law for righteousness to everyone who believes" (Rom. 10:4). It is also why Paul wrote that Christ is become to us righteousness (1 Cor. 1:30), and it is why Jeremiah called Him "The LORD our righteousness," *Jehovah Tsidkenu* (Jer. 23:6). The Lord Himself, Jesus Christ, *is* our righteousness (Jer. 33:16). That is the very essence of justification by faith alone, *sola fide*.

Of course all the fundamental doctrines related to the Incarnation—the virgin birth of Christ, His deity, His humanity, and His sinlessness—are part and parcel of who He is. Deny any of those doctrines and you have attacked Christ Himself.

The essential doctrines related to His work—His atoning death, His resurrection, and the reality of His miracles—are the very basis of the gospel (cf. 1 Cor. 15:1–4; Heb. 2:3–4). Reject them and you nullify the heart of the Christian message.

The fundamentals of the faith are so closely identified with Christ that the apostle John used the expression "the teaching of Christ" as a kind of shorthand for the set of doctrines he regarded as fundamental. To him, these doctrines represented the difference between true Christianity and false religion.

That is why he wrote, "Anyone who goes too far and does not abide in the teaching of Christ, does not have God; the one who abides in the teaching, he has both the Father and the Son" (2 John 9). Far from encouraging union with those who denied the fundamental truths of the faith, John forbade any form of spiritual fellowship with or encouragement of such false religion (vv. 10–11).

RECOVERING THE SPIRIT OF
EARLY FUNDAMENTALISM

It is not my purpose here to attempt to give an exhaustive list of fundamental doctrines. To do so would be beyond the scope of this book and certainly beyond my own abilities as a theologian. Witsius wrote,

> To point out the articles necessary to salvation, and precisely determine their number, is a task, if not utterly impossible, at least extremely difficult. There are, doubtless, more articles fundamental, than those to which the Scriptures have appended an express threatening of destruction . . .
>
> Nor is it absolutely necessary that we should possess an exact list of the number of fundamental articles. It is incumbent on each of us to labour with the utmost of diligence to obtain an enlargement of saving knowledge, lest, perhaps we should be found ignorant of truths that are necessary . . . [But] to ascertain precisely the number of necessary articles, is not requisite to our spiritual comfort . . .
>
> It is of no great importance, besides, to the church at large, to know quite correctly the precise number of fundamental articles.[37]

In a similar vein, Turretin wrote,

> The question concerning the number of fundamental articles . . . besides being rash (since Scripture says nothing definitely about it) is also useless and unnecessary because there is no need of our knowing particularly the number of such articles, if we can prove that [our adversaries] err fundamentally in one or more . . . Nor does it follow from this that the perfection of Scripture in necessary things is detracted from . . . For the Scriptures [still] contain most fully all things necessary to salvation, although their actual number is not accurately set forth.[38]

Certainly any list of fundamentals would have to begin with these doctrines Scripture explicitly identifies as nonnegotiable: the absolute authority of Scripture over tradition (*sola Scriptura*), justification by faith alone (*sola fide*), the deity of Christ, and the Trinity. Since the Apostles' Creed omits *all* those doctrines, it clearly cannot be regarded as a doctrinal basis for building ecumenical bridges.

At the same time, we must acknowledge that some people are tempted to wield fundamental doctrines like a judge's gavel and consign multitudes to eternal doom. It is not our prerogative to exercise such judgment. As Witsius sagely observed, "It does not become us to ascend into the tribunal of God, and to pronounce concerning our neighbour, for how small a defect of knowledge, or for how inconsiderable an error, he must be excluded from heaven. It is much safer to leave that to God."[39]

Wise advice. We dare not set ourselves up as judges of other people's eternal fate.

Nevertheless, we must recognize that those who have turned away from sound doctrine in matters essential to salvation are condemning themselves. "He that believeth not is condemned already" (John 3:18 KJV). Our passion as true fundamentalists ought to be to proclaim the fundamentals with clarity and precision, in order to turn people away from the darkness of error. We must confront head-on the blindness and unbelief that will be the reason multitudes will one day hear the Lord say, "I never knew you; depart from Me" (Matt. 7:23). Again it must be stressed that those who act as if crucial doctrines were of no consequence only heap the false teacher's guilt on themselves (2 John 11).

We have no right to pronounce a sentence of eternal doom against anyone (John 5:22). But by the same token, we have no business receiving just anyone into the communion and fellowship of the church. We should no more forge spiritual bonds with people whose religion is fundamentally in error than we would seek fellowship with those guilty of heinous sin. To do so is tantamount to the arrogance shown by the Corinthians, who refused to dismiss from their fellowship a man living in the grossest kind of sin (1 Cor. 5:1–3).

We must also remember that serious error can be extremely subtle. False teachers don't wear a sign proclaiming who they are. They disguise themselves as apostles of Christ (2 Cor. 11:13). "And no wonder, for even Satan disguises himself as an angel of light. Therefore it is not surprising if his servants also disguise themselves as servants of righteousness" (vv. 14–15). And it should not be surprising to hear false teachers and heretics recite the Apostles' Creed. Again, hear Witsius:

> Our faith consists not in words, but in sense; not in the surface, but in the substance; not in the leaves of a profession, but in the root of reason. All the heretics of the present day, that claim the name of Christians, are

willing enough to subscribe to the words of the [Apostles'] Creed; each however affixing to them whatever sense he pleases, though diametrically opposed to sound doctrine.[40]

Witsius concludes his chapter by pointing out that people who plead for all creeds to be as brief and general as possible—as well as people who reject all doctrinal expressions not confined to the precise words of Scripture—usually do so because they "are secretly entertaining some mischievous design."[41]

Nothing is more desperately needed in the church right now than a new movement to reemphasize the fundamental articles of the faith. Without such a movement to restore true biblical discernment, the true church is in serious trouble. If the current hunger for ecumenical compromise gains a foothold within evangelicalism, it will result in an unmitigated spiritual disaster. Reckless faith will virtually have free reign in the church. And far from strengthening the church's witness to an unbelieving world, it will spell the end of any clarion voice of truth.

7

THE POWER OF GOD UNTO SALVATION[1]

Where the gospel is fully and powerfully preached, with the Holy Ghost sent down from heaven, our churches do not only hold their own, but win converts; but when that which constitutes their strength is gone—we mean when the gospel is concealed, and the life of prayer is slighted—the whole thing becomes a mere form and fiction. For this thing our heart is sore grieved.

CHARLES HADDON SPURGEON[2]

A recent book in the "user-friendly" genre includes a section titled, "Different Times Require Different Messages." That title caught my eye, so I began reading. This author—who pastors a large, user-friendly church—says modern times have ravaged people's self-esteem so badly that people today actually need to hear a different message from what was appropriate a hundred years ago. He writes,

> In times past the human spirit was far more sturdy than it is now. Modernity has taken a high toll of the human spirit, as has the high cost of the American dream. The stress of modern life has had a greatly negative impact on the self-esteem of modern man.
>
> Consequently, there is a high level of fragility in the modern human ego. [Baby] boomers particularly have been fragmented and shattered by the fast pace of modern-day development. That's why our baby boomers today are in a very fragile state.
>
> Have you ever taken the time to read messages by some of the great nineteenth-century preachers . . . ? If you have, you will probably have noted that [men of that era] addressed quite a different crowd than we do today and they addressed them in a very different manner. And because

of those differences, I disagree with those who say that such messages are appropriate for our time.

You see, people in our culture are truly broken and deeply wounded. They need desperately to be healed and put back together. But the process of healing, I believe, is different for every era and every generation, including this one.

Yes, different times do require different messages.[3]

That author is unusually frank in stating his perspective. He candidly admits he believes preaching should accommodate the spirit of the age. (His book also carries unqualified endorsements from several of the top names in the user-friendly, church-marketing, and church-growth movements.) How does this pastor think we should determine what is the appropriate message for our time? He gives this list of suggestions for preachers:

1. Visit those how-to sections in your local bookstores.

2. Regularly have a small group submit a list of their greatest challenges at home and on the job.

3. Similarly, acquire inventories of needs from several secular people in your community.

4. Periodically, examine issues of *Time, Newsweek* and *USA Today,* as these publications tend to be on the cutting edge of the felt needs and fears that people are facing.

5. Apply practical aims to every study, message or program in your church.

6. Practice composing practical, catchy titles for your messages (sermons) from various biblical texts.

7. Limit your preaching to roughly 20 minutes, because boomers don't have too much time to spare. And don't forget to keep your messages light and informal, liberally sprinkling them with humor and personal anecdotes.[4]

That list is a recipe for weak and insipid preaching. It is also diametrically opposed to biblical ministry.

In a superb critique of the church-marketing movement, Douglas D. Webster compares biblical preaching to user-friendly methods:

Biblical preaching was God-centered, sin-exposing, self-convicting and life-challenging—the direct opposite of today's light, informal sermons that Christianize self-help and entertain better than they convict.

There are so many illustrations in today's market-sensitive sermons that the hearer forgets the biblical truth that is being illustrated; so many personal anecdotes that the hearer knows the pastor better than she knows Christ; so many human-interest stories that listening to the sermon is easier than reading the Sunday paper; so practical that there is hardly anything to practice.

No wonder nominal Christians leave church feeling upbeat. Their self-esteem is safely intact. Their minds and hearts have been sparked and soothed with sound-bite theology, Christian maxims and a few practical pointers dealing with self-esteem, kids or work. But the question remains: has the Word of God been effectively and faithfully proclaimed, penetrating comfort zones and the veneer of self-satisfaction with the truth of Jesus Christ?[5]

The simple reality is that one *cannot* follow a market-driven strategy and remain faithful to Scripture. Preachers who concern themselves with user-friendliness cannot fearlessly proclaim the whole counsel of God. Those who aspire to preach a timely message will find themselves at odds with the timeless truth of the Bible. Ministers who take their cues from *USA Today* rather than from God's Word will quickly discover the message that seemed so relevant last week is now yesterday's news. Preaching that conceals the unchanging gospel behind the fleeting issues of our time cloaks the very force that makes good preaching truly powerful. After all, it is not our anecdotes, applications, how-tos, jokes, catchy titles, clever outlines, or other contrivances—but the *gospel* that is "the power of God unto salvation" (Rom. 1:16 KJV).

I AM SET APART FOR THE GOSPEL

Paul's epistle to the Romans is a thorough exposition of the gospel in almost point-by point fashion. In the first verse of the epistle, Paul describes himself as one "set apart for the *gospel*." The gospel was the foundation of Paul's ministry, and in Romans he gives a clear and thorough presentation of it. He writes about God's wrath and human sin (chapters 1–3), justification and imputed righteousness (3–5), sanctification and practical righteousness (6–8), election and Israel's rejection of Christ (9–11), and then makes practical applications of various gospel truths in chapter 12 through the end of the epistle. The gospel is his theme throughout, and one of Paul's reasons for writing Romans seems to be to demonstrate the centrality of the gospel to all Christian life and ministry.

When we speak of "the gospel" we tend to think of an evangelistic message—and surely the gospel is that. But it is not only a four- or five-point outline of salvation truths. The *gospel*—in the sense Paul and the apostles employed the word—includes all the truth about Christ (cf. Rom. 1:1–6). It does not stop at the point of conversion and justification by faith but embraces every other aspect of salvation, from sanctification to ultimate glorification. The gospel's significance therefore does not end the moment the new birth occurs; it applies to the entire Christian experience. And when Paul and the other New Testament writers spoke of "preaching the gospel," they were not talking about preaching only to unbelievers (cf. v. 15).

All ministry in the early church revolved around the gospel. No one would have suggested a debate about secular politics, a weight-loss program, a comedy act, a stage show, or a seminar on time management for businessmen as means to boost church attendance. The church and all its ministries were single-mindedly committed to the one task of strengthening believers for the furthering the gospel in the world.

Paul's personal commitment to the gospel as the heart of all ministry is seen clearly in the opening chapter of Romans, where Paul expresses his desire to come to Rome and minister to the saints there. He desperately wanted to get to Rome. Not to renew old personal relationships, though he had many good friends who were part of the church there. Not so he could minister in one of his own churches, for Paul did not plant the church at Rome. Not to escape persecution elsewhere, for he was certain to become a target in a city that was militantly opposed to Christianity. But Paul's passion was to preach the gospel, and he couldn't wait to do it in Rome, the center of the civilized world.

I SERVE GOD BY PREACHING THE GOSPEL

Paul writes,

> I thank my God through Jesus Christ for you all, because your faith is being proclaimed throughout the whole world. For God, whom I serve in my spirit in the preaching of the gospel of His Son, is my witness as to

how unceasingly I make mention of you, always in my prayers making request, if perhaps now at last by the will of God I may succeed in coming to you. (Romans 1:8–10)

There's a wealth of spiritual truth about biblical ministry in those brief verses, and I have commented on them in depth elsewhere.[6] Here I want to begin by focusing on one brief phrase in verse 9: "I serve [God] in my spirit in the preaching of the gospel of His Son."

For Paul, preaching the gospel was an act of spiritual worship. The Greek word translated "serve" is *latreuō*, the same word translated "worship" in Philippians 3:3: "We are the true circumcision, who worship in the Spirit of God and glory in Christ Jesus and put no confidence in the flesh." Paul "served" (worshiped) God in his spirit by preaching the gospel. In other words, Paul viewed his ministry like that of a priest before God rendering high and holy duty: "If I preach the gospel, I have nothing to boast of, for I am under compulsion; for woe is me if I do not preach the gospel" (1 Cor. 9:16). Yet it was not only a duty; it was an immense privilege as well. "I am eager to preach the gospel to you" (Rom. 1:15).

Paul's eagerness to serve God emanated from his spirit from the moment of his salvation. His first question as a Christian was, "What shall I do, Lord?" (Acts 22:10). His heart and energies were fixed on preaching, and he did it with his whole soul.

Notice that Paul's concern was for the *spiritual* welfare of those to whom he ministered: "I long to see you in order that I may impart some spiritual gift to you" (v. 11). He was not wanting to visit Rome as a tourist. He was not interested in merely entertaining the Roman believers or seeing how many unbelievers he could draw to their meetings. He wasn't thinking of his own rewards or reputation or remuneration. He wanted to give of himself for their spiritual benefit.

What "spiritual gift" did Paul want to impart to the Romans? He was not, of course, speaking about spiritual gifts such as those listed in 1 Corinthians 12 and Romans 12. Those gifts are imparted by the Holy Spirit to every believer (1 Cor. 12:7–11), not handed out from person to person. Paul was speaking of a gift of spiritual value, something that would help them "be established." What he had in mind involved preaching to them (cf. Rom. 1:15). He wanted to encourage them with the full riches of gospel truth and be encouraged in return by their faith that truth: "That is, that I may be encouraged together with you while among you, each of us by the other's faith, both yours and mine" (v. 12).

So Paul's burden for the church at Rome was bound up in his desire to serve them through the preaching and ministry of the gospel. Ultimately Paul did make it to Rome, but at a very dear price. He was brought there in chains, bound to Roman guards. Had he known when he wrote this epistle what it would finally cost him to get to Rome, Paul's desire to preach the gospel in Rome would not have been diminished in the least. After all, he went to Jerusalem even though he knew he would be imprisoned there (cf. Acts 21:10–15). When the brethren tried desperately to talk him out of going to Jerusalem, he replied, "What are you doing, weeping and breaking my heart? For I am ready not only to be bound, but even to die at Jerusalem for the name of the Lord Jesus" (Acts 21:13). Paul would have willingly gone to Rome under the same circumstances—and ultimately he did. He wrote to the Philippians from Rome, "All the saints greet you, especially those of Caesar's household" (Phil. 4:22). Paul was under house arrest when he wrote that, waiting for the verdict of the imperial court. Even under those trying circumstances Paul was faithfully preaching the gospel. Evidently he had even been used to lead people from Caesar's own household to a saving knowledge of Christ.

Obviously, proclaiming the gospel was a compulsion for Paul. That's why he spoke of himself as "set apart for the gospel" (Rom. 1:1). He knew of no other kind of ministry.

I AM DEBTOR TO ALL THE LOST

Paul wrote, "I am under obligation both to Greeks and to barbarians, both to the wise and to the foolish" (Rom. 1:14). The King James Version renders that verse, "*I am debtor* both to the Greeks, and to the Barbarians; both to the wise, and to the unwise" (emphasis added). Paul did not preach the gospel for personal reasons or because the calling seemed attractive. He considered himself under obligation.

At the time of Paul's conversion, he was the church's most determined opponent. He hated Christ and all Christians. When Stephen, the first martyr, was killed, Paul was there, "in hearty agreement with putting him to death" (Acts 8:1). After his salvation, Paul's zeal for Christ was even greater than his zeal to persecute Christians had been before. This verse gives us an insight as to why. Paul's perspective was that since God had chosen and called an enemy like him, "foremost of all sinners" (1 Tim. 1:15), Paul was then obligated to other sinners to preach the gospel to them. He knew he had been sovereignly appointed to this role, and he was obliged to carry it out.

All of us who have believed the gospel are under the same kind of obligation. First, as we noted earlier, Christ Himself commands us to preach the gospel (Mark 16:15). And second, we who know the way of eternal life are obligated to unbelievers in the same sense we would be responsible to warn someone whose house is on fire, or morally constrained to give water to someone dying of thirst.

Paul was equally obligated to Jews and Gentiles, educated people and barbarians. He didn't target the young, upwardly mobile, cultured people and ignore the slaves and dregs of society. He preached the gospel to them all, because he was obligated to them all. "There is no respect of persons with God" (Rom. 2:11); so Paul was no respecter of persons.

"Target marketing" is a key concept in the user-friendly church movement. George Barna has written,

> To successfully market your product, you have to identify its prospective market. The key to market identification—sometimes referred to as "target marketing"—is to be as specific as possible in selecting the audience to whom you will market the product. By matching the appeal of your product to the interests and needs of specific population segments, you can concentrate on getting your product to your best prospects without wasting resources on people who have no need or interest in your product . . . By knowing the product's market, the product itself can be developed to address the special needs of that segment, and the entire marketing effort can be designed with maximum efficiency.[7]

In other words, decide whom you're going to minister to, fashion the "product" to suit that audience, and don't "waste resources" on people outside that targeted group.

Why do you suppose nearly all the user-friendly churches identify their "target market" as young suburban professionals and other moneyed groups? Why are so few of these churches ministering to poor and inner-city congregations or mixtures of all classes and types of people? The answer may be obvious. One leading pastor in the movement says, "A pastor can define his appropriate target audience by determining with whom he would like to spend a vacation or an afternoon of recreation."[8] It would be hard to imagine a ministry philosophy more at odds with the Word of God than that. Doesn't Scripture say, "My brethren, do not hold your faith in our glorious Lord Jesus Christ with an attitude of personal favoritism" (James 2:1). And "did not God choose the poor of this world to be rich in faith and heirs of the kingdom which He promised to those who love Him?" (v. 5). "But if you show partiality, you are committing sin and are convicted by the law as transgressors" (v. 9).

Those who narrow their ministry to a select "target audience" certainly are not ministering in the spirit of Paul, who considered himself debtor to all and ministered to all alike.

I AM EAGER TO PREACH THE GOSPEL

But by saying he was "under obligation" to preach the gospel, Paul was in no way implying that he was a grudging witness for Christ. He makes this clear to the Romans: "For my part, I am eager to preach the gospel to you also who are in Rome" (Rom. 1:15). He was not only willing but also eager, even *determined* to preach the gospel.

The King James Version translates verse 15, "So, as much as in me is, I am ready to preach the gospel." That captures even more of Paul's eagerness. With every fiber of his being, he desired to preach the gospel at Rome. Paul would not have been able to understand preachers who, given the privilege of preaching the gospel, choose instead to entertain people, tell anecdotes, or give speeches on self-esteem. He was ready to suffer persecution, be beaten, go to prison, or even be killed for the privilege of preaching the gospel.

C. H. Spurgeon said,

> The apostle was ready to go anywhere with the gospel, but he was not ready to preach another gospel; no one could make him ready to do that. He was not ready to hide the gospel, he was not ready to tone it down, he was not ready to abridge it or to extend it. He said, "I am not ashamed of the gospel of Christ: for it is the power of God unto salvation to everyone that believeth; to the Jew first, and also to the Greek." As to the matter of preaching the gospel, Paul was always ready for that; he kept not back any one of its truths, nor any part of its teaching. Even if it should bring upon him ridicule and contempt, though it should be to the Jews a stumbling block, and to the Greeks foolishness, Paul would say, "As much as in me is, I am ready to preach the gospel" to them all. He did not always feel fit for the work; he did not always find the same openings, or the same freedom in speech; but he was always ready to preach wherever the Lord gave him the opportunity.[9]

At the end of his life, Paul was able to say, "I have fought the good fight, I have finished the course, I have kept the faith" (2 Tim. 4:7). That's because he never allowed himself to be deterred from his calling. He never gave in to the temptation to seek popularity. He never compromised with the enemies of the gospel. He never allowed his ministry to be conformed to the world. He never tickled the ears of the crowds.

Externally, it may have seemed to the world that Paul was a failure. He was arrested, imprisoned for years, and finally killed by the Roman officials. Yet even in those dark hours Paul kept preaching. When he couldn't preach to crowds, he preached to the soldiers assigned to guard him. When he couldn't minister in the churches, he ministered in the prisons. He was always ready to preach—but never to compromise.

I AM NOT ASHAMED OF THE GOSPEL

Paul's next statement could be called the thesis statement of the epistle: "I am not ashamed of the gospel, for it is the power of God for salvation to everyone who believes" (Rom. 1:16). That is one of the most potent, penetrating statements in all the New Testament. Paul equates the gospel itself with God's almighty power! No wonder he says he is not ashamed of the gospel.

The rest of the epistle is an exposition of this one statement, unfolding in brilliant detail the truth of the gospel and showing why it is so powerful. No wonder Romans takes such a prominent place among the Pauline epistles. Paul was so committed to the gospel that occasionally he referred to it as "my gospel" (Rom. 2:16; 16:25; 2 Tim. 2:8). Far from being ashamed of it, he spoke of it as if it were his own prized possession!

But as Paul well knew, the cost of standing up for the gospel could be great. Consequently, too many Christians *did* behave as if they were ashamed of the gospel.

Mockery was a key weapon used by the earliest enemies of Christianity. The Romans especially tended to look upon Christianity as a crude and uncultured religion. Rumors circulated among Roman society that Christians were cannibals, because they partook of the Lord's Supper. Christians were accused of sedition, murder, and other treacherous crimes. Some enemies of the gospel claimed the Christians were having orgies. Pagans even attacked believers as atheists because they rejected all the mythological gods. The price for following Christ could be extremely high.

The gospel itself is disagreeable, unattractive, repulsive, and alarming to the world. It exposes sin, condemns pride, convicts the unbelieving heart, and shows human righteousness—even the best, most appealing aspects of human nature—

to be worthless, defiled, filthy rags (cf. Isa. 64:6). It affirms that the real problems in life are not because of anyone but ourselves. We are fallen sinners, with deceitful hearts, evil motives, pervasive pride. We cannot blame anyone else for our failure and misery. That is not a popular view, particularly in today's psychological climate. It comes as bad news to those who love sin, and many who hear it for the first time react with disdain against the messenger.

It is not easy to take a bold stand for the gospel and not be ashamed. Most of us must confess that we have a lot in common with the weakness of Peter, who on the night of Jesus' crucifixion denied the Lord three times, cowering in fear before a servant girl and others who recognized him as a follower of Christ (Luke 22:56–62).

There is no record of any incident like that in Paul's life, however. From the moment of his conversion, Paul was a man with a mission, and he never wavered from his one purpose: to preach the gospel. He knew the gospel's remarkable power to transform lives, and he longed to be the herald to proclaim it. How could he ever be ashamed of the gospel? Having received the gospel directly from the risen Jesus Himself (Acts 20:24; 1 Cor. 11:23; 15:3), Paul was eager to proclaim it to everyone, without fear or shame.

The Gospel Is the Power of God

It is hard to imagine that anyone who truly understands the power of the gospel can possibly be ashamed to proclaim it. "It is the power of God" (1:16). *Dunamis* is the Greek word translated "power." We derive the word "dynamite" from the same Greek word, and *dynamite* is not too strong a word to express what Paul is saying here.

Inherent in the gospel message is the power of an omnipotent God. That power alone is sufficient to save the vilest sinner and transform the hardest heart—apart from any human arguments, illustrations, or ingenuity.

The prophet Jeremiah wrote, "Can the Ethiopian change his skin or the leopard his spots? Then you also can do good who are accustomed to do evil" (Jer. 13:23). The truth is, people are utterly powerless to overcome their own sin. Sin is part of our nature, like a leopard's spots. We cannot change ourselves. Self-help techniques and recovery programs might temporarily help people feel better about themselves, but they have no power to remove sin or change the human heart.

That only the gospel can do. "It is the power of God unto salvation." In other words, the objective truth of the gospel is inherently powerful for transforming lives when divinely applied. Peter spoke of the Word of God as the seed that generates new life and a new birth: "You have been born again not of seed which is perishable but imperishable, that is, through the living and abiding word of God" (1 Peter 1:23). Both apostles were saying essentially the same thing: God's Word—the message of the gospel—is the vehicle through which God's transforming power invades a life and brings about the new birth.

Paul wrote: "The word of the cross is to those who are perishing foolishness, but *to us who are being saved it is the power of God"* (1 Cor. 1:18, emphasis added). And, "We preach Christ crucified, to Jews a stumbling block, and to Gentiles foolishness, but to those who are the called, both Jews and Greeks, Christ *the power of God and the wisdom of God"* (vv. 23–24). The gospel is the *only* message God uses for salvation. There is a place for persuasion, graphic illustration, and relevant application. Certainly every worthy preacher or evangelist will seek ways to stimulate people's interest—but only to capture a hearing for the gospel. If the plain truth of the gospel doesn't penetrate the heart, no amount of cajoling or salesmanship on the part of the evangelist is going to bring a person to salvation.

Note that the gospel "is the power of God for salvation *to everyone who believes"* (v. 16, emphasis added). Some people remain unaffected by the gospel. As powerful as the message is, it has no positive effect on those who turn away, disbelieving. Paul, of course, experienced much rejection and mocking from those who rejected the gospel. Nevertheless he refused to change his methods or adapt the message to their tastes. He did not assume unbelievers' rejection was due to any lack of power in the gospel. He knew too well the unrivaled power of the gospel to transform "everyone who believes."

In referring to the gospel as "the power of God for salvation," Paul was also affirming that the gospel reveals the *only way* of salvation. Jesus said, "I am the way, and the truth, and the life; no one comes to the Father, but through Me." (John 14:6). Acts 4:12 says, "There is salvation in no one else; for there is no other name under heaven that has been given among men, by which we must be saved." Biblical preaching means preaching Jesus Christ (2 Cor. 4:5)—His person and work. Perhaps the most serious indictment of contemporary market-conscious preaching is the absence of Christ. His name or some fact about Him may be thrown in at the end, but He is rarely central in the trendy preaching of today.

THE GOSPEL REVEALS GOD'S RIGHTEOUSNESS

The term "the gospel" is much abused these days. Elsewhere I have addressed in detail some of the contemporary fallacies regarding the gospel.[10] Here it is sufficient to note that many evangelicals have redefined the gospel in man-centered terms. Instead of declaring Christ crucified and focusing on God's righteousness, they talk about human needs. But the gospel is first of all a message about God's righteousness: "For in it the righteousness of God is revealed from faith to faith; as it is written, 'But the righteous man shall live by faith'" (Rom. 1:17).

The word "righteousness" and its derivatives appear at least thirty-five times in Romans. Divine righteousness is the starting point and the theme of the gospel message. God's righteousness, defied by sinning humanity, was perfectly fulfilled by Christ incarnate, is imputed to the sinner who repents and believes in the Lord Jesus, and will be manifested in practical ways in the life of the Christian. That is a summary of the gospel as Paul unfolds it in Romans.

"The righteousness of God" carries two connotations. In one sense it speaks of God's holy hatred of sin. In the early 1500s, Martin Luther sat in the tower of the Black Cloister, Wittenberg, reading this verse. "That expression 'righteousness of God' was like a thunderbolt in my heart," Luther said years later. "I hated Paul with all my heart when I read that the righteousness of God is revealed in the gospel."[11] Luther saw God's righteousness as an unassailable obstacle to eternal life. Luther was deeply aware of his own sinfulness, and he knew because of it he was unacceptable to a righteous God. Therefore as he read this verse he was seized with despair.

But there is a second connotation of righteousness in verse 17: "As it is written, 'But the righteous man shall live by faith.'" This speaks of Christ's perfect righteousness, which is imputed to the account of the believing sinner (Rom. 4:24). When Luther finally understood this sense of the word "righteousness," he knew the true meaning of the gospel, and that discovery resulted in the Protestant Reformation.

The doctrine is known as *justification.* It means that God freely reckons all of Christ's perfect righteousness to the assets side of the believer's ledger, and He cancels out all the sin on the debit side. When God looks at the believing one, He sees that person as if he or she were as fully righteous as Christ Himself. That's how God "justifies the ungodly" (Rom. 4:5). Because Christ made full atonement for sin by His death and resurrection, God can justify sinners without compromising His own righteousness—"That He might be just and the justifier of the one who has faith in Jesus" (Rom. 3:26). This is the very heart of the gospel. It is why the message is *good news.*

THE GOSPEL REVEALS GOD'S WRATH

But the gospel is not *all* good news. In fact, it is not good news at all for those who turn away from Christ. Note that the starting point for Paul's gospel is God's wrath against sin: "For the wrath of God is revealed from heaven against all ungodliness and unrighteousness of men" (Rom. 1:18). Paul then spends more than two full chapters systematically proving that all humanity is sinful and under the wrath of God.

God's wrath is almost entirely missing from modern presentations of the gospel. It is not fashionable to speak of God's wrath against sin or to tell people they should fear God. The typical presentation today starts exactly opposite where Paul started. He wrote of "the wrath of God . . . against all ungodliness and unrighteousness of men." But modern evangelism begins with "God loves you and wants to make you happy."

Read the literature of the user-friendly movement and you'll notice a preoccupation with conveying every message in a positive tone. One leading pastor in the movement writes,

> Though unchurched [baby] boomers may privately acknowledge they are flawed—and maybe even sinful—they are hardly going to sit in a public place and listen to themselves being described as worms, wretches, fallen creatures and other totally depraved types . . .

> As a pastor to boomers, I'm convinced that they need to hear even negative messages presented in positive terms. It's the grid through which we filter things. So if we can't be positive—even when talking about negative topics—boomers will probably not listen.

> We need to be very careful, therefore, about the tone we take in our services . . . I've made a deliberate practice of making sure that the messages I direct to my age-group always strike a positive note.[12]

Comments like that in recent church-growth writings almost always come with disclaimers assuring readers that what the author has in mind is not compromise—and this one is no exception. He goes on to say, "Now, I'm not backing down on the biblical premise that we are all fallen sinners and desperately need to be saved. Admittedly, we are depraved; yet the gospel also presents the premise that because we were created in God's image, God considered us of high enough value to send His Son to redeem us." He goes on to say again that those who want to minister effectively in this generation must remember to keep their tone "optimistic."[13]

Let me say first of all that I minister to a rather large group from the baby-boom generation, and I disagree with that writer's unwarranted generalization that they automatically tune out negative truth. Furthermore, it is one thing to say "that we are all fallen sinners and desperately need to be saved," and quite another to say, as Paul does, that "the wrath of God is revealed from heaven against all ungodliness and unrighteousness of men." Both statements are true, of course. The gospel is not complete without both sides, however. It is Paul's starting point—the wrath of God, not a statement about human need—that is frequently left out by preachers today.

There is simply no way to synthesize the truth about God's wrath with a positive-only presentation of the gospel. There is no way to declare the truth about God's wrath to an unbelieving sinner in an "optimistic" tone. As a result, the gospel preached in these churches is often truncated—and the point that is most deliberately censored is the very place Paul began his gospel presentation— the reality of divine wrath!

Those who feel they must be forever optimistic are forced to ignore crucial sections of Scripture, including most of Romans 1, Luke 16, all the Hebrews warning passages, much of the core of Old Testament truth, and about half of Jesus' teaching. And so the philosophy shapes the message.

Don't get the impression I am in favor of preaching that is dour, always negative, oppressive, and grim. Of course I am not. But as we have noted repeatedly, there must be a biblical balance of negative *and* positive, or we're not ministering according to the will of God. And the strategy currently in fashion is to try to style the gospel so that it is entirely positive. That can't be the biblical message. It is certainly not the gospel that is the power of God unto salvation.

For Paul, the threat of God's eternal wrath was the *first* point to be taken up. He was determined that people understand the awful reality of God's holy wrath and the desperate heinousness of human depravity. It was not an upbeat way to introduce the subject. But that is how Paul, under the inspiration of the Holy Spirit, dealt with it.

God's wrath is crucial to who He is. All His attributes are balanced in divine perfection. If He had no righteous anger, He would not be God. Apart from His wrath, the concept of His love is rendered meaningless: "Thou hast loved righteousness, and hated wickedness" (Ps. 45:7). Furthermore, God hates sin just as perfectly and as thoroughly as He loves fallen sinners. One side without the other is utterly hollow.

Often the twin emphases of wrath and mercy are side by side. "He who believes in the Son has eternal life; but he who does not obey the Son shall not see life, but the wrath of God abides on him" (John 3:36). That verse appears in the same chapter as the more familiar words of John 3:16. Without an under-standing of the severity of God's wrath against sin, even the phrase "should not perish" in John 3:16 loses its significance.

God's wrath is not a secondary theme in Scripture. It is emphasized throughout both the Old and New Testaments. Psalm 7:11–12 says, "God is a righteous judge, and a God who has indignation every day. If a man does not repent, He will sharpen His sword; He has bent His bow and made it ready." The phrase "The anger of the LORD burned against Israel" and similar expres-sions are found repeatedly in the Old Testament (e.g. Judges 2:14, 20; 3:8; 10:7; 2 Sam. 6:7; 24:1; 2 Kings 13:3; Ps. 106:40). The New Testament is replete with warnings about God's wrath (e.g. Rom. 2:5; 3:5; 9:22; Eph. 5:6; Col. 3:6; Rev. 14:10). The writer to the Hebrews says simply, "Our God is a consuming fire" (Heb. 12:29; cf. Deut. 4:24; 9:3).

Those truths are not *supposed* to make us feel comfortable or self-confident. They are supposed to fill us with severe anxiety and fear. After all, "The fear of the LORD is the beginning of wisdom" (Prov. 9:10). Only when the gospel pro-vokes a holy dread of God can it be appreciated for the truly good news it is. "In the fear of the LORD there is strong confidence" (Prov. 14:26); "The fear of the LORD is a fountain of life" (v. 27); "The fear of the LORD is the instruction for wisdom" (15:33); and "The fear of the LORD leads to life, so that one may sleep satisfied, untouched by evil" (19:23).

A DIFFERENT MESSAGE FOR A DIFFERENT TIME?

The gospel that should be preached today is the same message Paul committed his life to preach. He solemnly warned the church not to tamper with that gospel or alter it in any way (Gal. 1:6–9). Church history is strewn with examples of those who thought they could mold the message for their own time—but ended up corrupting the truth and damning themselves. Most of those seeking to make the church "user-friendly" have no intention of perverting the gospel in such a way. But they need to recognize that their desire for a pleasing, attractive mes-sage is utterly incompatible with the true gospel. As their movement gathers momentum, it is becoming more and more clear that they are heading down the same road traveled by the modernists of a hundred years ago.

If church history teaches us anything, it is that different times do *not* require different messages. Those who preach anything other than the unadulterated gospel forfeit the power of God in their ministries.

Charles Spurgeon said the modernists of his day were trying to devise "a faith fashioned for the present century—perhaps we ought rather to say, for the present month."[14] He wrote,

> The idea of a progressive gospel seems to have fascinated many. To us that notion is a sort of cross-breed between nonsense and blasphemy. After the gospel has been found effectual in the eternal salvation of untold multitudes, it seems rather late in the day to alter it; and, since it is the revelation of the all-wise and unchanging God, it appears somewhat audacious to attempt its improvement. When we call up before our mind's eye the gentlemen who have set themselves this presumptuous task, we feel half inclined to laugh; the case is so much like the proposal of moles to improve the light of the sun . . .
>
> Do men really believe that there is a gospel for each century? Or a religion for each fifty years?[15]

Spurgeon clearly understood that those who desired to be embraced as "relevant" by a changing world could not and would not long remain faithful to the unchanging Word of God. He quoted approvingly from a letter written by Henry Varley to the editor of *Word and Work*. Varley wrote, "Revelation, which is unchanging, is not fast enough for an age of which it may be said, 'Change is its fashion.' All the more necessary, therefore, does it become to 'hold fast the form of sound words,' and contend earnestly . . . 'for the faith once for all delivered to the saints.'"[16]

If change was the fashion of the nineteenth century, how much more true is that today? More than any preceding generation of Christians we must be careful to guard the treasure that has been entrusted to us (2 Tim. 2:14). Let's not exchange it for the fads and fancies of a vacillating world.

The gospel is to be preached persuasively, earnestly, and clearly. There certainly is a crucial need for preachers and witnesses for Christ with unique intellectual and creative gifts to apply their communication abilities to the careful presentation of the gospel. It is certainly not wrong to want to be fresh, resourceful, persuasive, and interesting. Any preacher who is truly excited about and committed to the gospel will naturally display those attributes. But keep the focus on the message, not the style. We must make the gospel our one message to the world. After all, it is the gospel—not human inventiveness, not "user-friendliness," not clever techniques or modern methodology—that is the power of God unto salvation to all who believe.

8

HACKING AGAG TO PIECES[1]

Mortification abates [sin's] force, but doth not change its nature. Grace changeth the nature of man, but nothing can change the nature of sin . . . Destroyed it may be, it shall be, but cured it cannot be . . . If it be not overcome and destroyed, it will overcome and destroy the soul.

And herein lies no small part of its power . . . It is never quiet, [whether it is] conquering [or] conquered.

. . . .

Do you mortify; do you make it your daily work; be always at it whilst you live; cease not a day from this work; be killing sin or it will be killing you.

JOHN OWEN[2]

I f sin is a defeated enemy, how can it cause us so much trouble? If sin's dominion has been broken, why does sin so often seem to dominate us?

Every honest Christian will testify that the tendency to sin is not erased by becoming a believer. We still derive pleasure from sin. We still struggle with sinful habits. Some of those habits are so deeply ingrained that we still battle them after years of spiritual warfare against them. We fall into appalling, shameful sins. The truth is, we sin daily. Our thoughts are not what they ought to be. Our time is often wasted on frivolous and worldly pursuits. From time to time our hearts grow cold to the things of God. Why does all this happen if sin's dominion is broken?

GOD'S ANGER AGAINST AMALEK

An Old Testament illustration may help to shed light on our relationship to sin. In 1 Samuel 15, we read that Samuel anointed Saul and solemnly gave him these instructions from the Lord: "Now go and strike Amalek and utterly destroy all that he has, and do not spare him; but put to death both man and woman, child and infant, ox and sheep, camel and donkey" (v. 3).

God's command was clear. Saul was to deal ruthlessly with the Amalekites, killing even their infant children and animals. Their whole tribe was to be utterly and mercilessly leveled—no hostages taken.

What would make a God of infinite love mete out such a severe judgment? The Amalekites were an ancient nomadic race, descendants of Esau (Gen. 36:12). They inhabited the southern part of Canaan and were perennial enemies of the Israelites. They were the same tribe that viciously attacked Israel at Rephidim shortly after the Exodus, in the famous battle when Aaron and Hur had to support Moses' arms (Ex. 17:8–13). They ambushed Israel from behind, massacring the stragglers who were most weary (Deut. 25:18). It was a cowardly attack by the most powerful and savage tribe in the whole region. God supernaturally delivered Israel that day, and the Amalekites fled into hiding. At the conclusion of that skirmish, God swore to Moses, "I will utterly blot out the memory of Amalek from under heaven" (Ex. 17:14). He actually made it a point of the Mosaic law that Israel was to destroy Amalek:

> Remember what Amalek did to you along the way when you came out from Egypt, how he met you along the way and attacked among you all the stragglers at your rear when you were faint and weary; and he did not fear God. Therefore it shall come about when the LORD your God has given you rest from all your surrounding enemies, in the land which the LORD your God gives you as an inheritance to possess, you shall blot out the memory of Amalek from under heaven; *you must not forget.* (Deuteronomy 25:17–19, emphasis added).

The Amalekites were fearful warriors. Their intimidating presence was one of the reasons the Israelites disobeyed God and balked at entering the promised land at Kadesh-barnea (Num. 13:29).

God's anger burned against the Amalekites for their wickedness. He constrained even the corrupt prophet Balaam to prophecy their doom: "Amalek was the first of the nations, but his end shall be destruction" (Num. 24:20). The Amalekites used to harass Israel by coming into the land after crops had been sown and moving through the farmland with their tents and livestock, razing everything in their path (Judg. 6:3–5). They hated God, detested Israel, and seemed to delight in wicked and destructive acts.

God's instructions to Saul, therefore, fulfilled the vow He swore to Moses. Saul was to wipe out the tribe forever. He and his armies were the instrument through which a righteous God would carry out His holy judgment on a sinister people.

THE FOLLY OF PARTIAL OBEDIENCE

But Saul's obedience was only partial. He won a crushing defeat against the Amalekites, routing them "from Havilah as you go to Shur, which is east of Egypt" (1 Sam. 15:8). As commanded, he killed all the people, but "he captured Agag the king of the Amalekites alive" (v. 8). "Saul and the people spared Agag and the best of the sheep, the oxen, the fatlings, the lambs, and all that was good, and were not willing to destroy them utterly; but everything despised and worthless, that they utterly destroyed" (v. 9). In other words, motivated by covetousness, they kept all the best possessions of the Amalekites, collecting the spoils of victory, willfully disobeying the Lord's instructions.

Why did Saul spare Agag? Perhaps he wanted to use the humiliated king of the Amalekites as a trophy to display his own power. Saul seemed motivated only by pride at this point; he even set up a monument to himself at Carmel (v. 12). Whatever his reasons, he disobeyed the clear command of God and allowed Agag to live.

The sin was so serious that God immediately deposed Saul and his descendants forever from the throne of Israel. Samuel told him, "Because you have rejected the word of the LORD, He has also rejected you from being king" (v. 23).

Then Samuel said, "Bring me Agag, the king of the Amalekites" (v. 32).

Agag, evidently thinking that his life had been spared and feeling pretty confident, "came to him cheerfully." "Surely the bitterness of death is past," he said (v. 32).

But Samuel was not amused. He told Agag, "As your sword has made women childless, so shall your mother be childless among women." Scripture simply says, "And Samuel hewed Agag to pieces before the LORD at Gilgal" (v. 33).

Our minds instinctively recoil from what seems a merciless act. But it was *God* who commanded that this be done. This was an act of divine judgment to show the holy wrath of an indignant God against wanton sin. Unlike his countrymen and their king, Samuel was determined to carry out the Lord's command entirely. As it was, the battle that was supposed to exterminate the Amalekites forever ended before the goal was accomplished. Scripture records that only a few years later, the reinvigorated tribe raided the southern territory and took all the women and children captive—including David's family (1 Sam. 30:1–5).

When David found the marauding Amalekites, "Behold, they were spread over all the land, eating and drinking and dancing because of all the great spoil that they had taken from the land of the Philistines and from the land of Judah" (v. 16). He slaughtered them from twilight until the next evening, killing all but four hundred who escaped on camels (v. 17).

The Amalekites make a perfect illustration of the sin that remains in the believer's life. That sin—already utterly defeated—must be dealt with ruthlessly and hacked to pieces, or it will revive and continue to plunder and pillage our hearts and sap our spiritual strength. We cannot be merciful with Agag, or he will turn and try to devour us. In fact, the remaining sin in us often becomes more fiercely determined after it has been overthrown by the gospel.

Scripture commands us to deal with our sin by putting it to death: "Mortify therefore your members which are upon the earth; fornication, uncleanness, inordinate affection, evil concupiscence, and covetousness, which is idolatry: for which things' sake the wrath of God cometh on the children of disobedience" (Col. 3:5–6 KJV). We cannot obey partially or halfheartedly as we seek to eliminate sin from our lives. We cannot stop while the task remains incomplete. Sins, like Amalekites, have a way of escaping the slaughter, breeding, reviving, regrouping, and launching new and unexpected assaults on our most vulnerable areas.

LIFE IN THE SPIRIT

In Romans 8:13 Paul also wrote of "putting to death the deeds of the body." After declaring victory over sin in Romans 6, then describing the ongoing struggle with sin in chapter 7, he describes the triumphant experience of life in the Spirit throughout chapter 8. In the midst of that chapter, the apostle declares that the distinctive behavior of those who are led by the Spirit is that they continually put their evil deeds to death.

It is significant that the Holy Spirit is mentioned only once in the introduction to the epistle (1:4, "the spirit of holiness"), then not mentioned again until Romans 8:1. In Romans 8 alone there are at least twenty references to the Holy Spirit.

Romans 8 portrays the Holy Spirit as the divine agent who frees us from sin and death (vv. 2–3), enables us to live righteously (4–13), assures and comforts us in our affliction (14–19), preserves and sustains us in Christ (20–28), and guarantees our final victory in eternal glory (29–39). Right in the context of this profound teaching about the Holy Spirit's role in the Christian's life, Paul has some important things to say about mortifying sin. He begins by contrasting life in the spirit with life in the flesh and under the law. It is important to understand these truths in their proper context:

> What the Law could not do, weak as it was through the flesh, God did: sending His own Son in the likeness of sinful flesh and as an offering for sin, He condemned sin in the flesh, in order that the requirement of the Law might be fulfilled in us, who do not walk according to the flesh, but according to the Spirit. Those who are according to the flesh set their minds on the things of the flesh, but those who are according to the Spirit, the things of the Spirit. For the mind set on the flesh is death, but the mind set on the Spirit is life and peace, because the mind set on the flesh is hostile toward God; for it does not subject itself to the law of God, for it is not even able to do so; and those who are in the flesh cannot please God. *However, you are not in the flesh but in the Spirit, if indeed the Spirit of God dwells in you.* But if anyone does not have the Spirit of Christ, he does not belong to Him. And if Christ is in you, though the body is dead because of sin, yet the spirit is alive because of righteousness. But if the Spirit of Him who raised Jesus from the dead dwells in you, He who raised Christ Jesus from the dead will also give life to your mortal bodies through His Spirit who indwells you. (vv. 3–11, emphasis added)

In other words, life in the Spirit is markedly different from the life of the unbeliever. *All* true Christians are "in the Spirit." They "do not walk according to the flesh, but according to the Spirit." Those who walk according to the flesh are unbelievers, and Paul is quite definite in making that clear: "If anyone does not have the Spirit of Christ, he does not belong to Him" (v. 9). Later he adds, "For all who are being led by the Spirit of God, these are sons of God" (v. 14).

In other words, there are only two kinds of people in the world—those who are in accord with the flesh, and those who are in accord with the Spirit. Of course, there are in-the-Spirit people at many different levels of spiritual maturity. In-the-flesh people also come in varying degrees of wickedness. But everyone is either "in the flesh" (v. 8) or "in the Spirit" (v. 9). There is no category called "in between."

What Paul is suggesting is that the Holy Spirit changes our basic disposition when we are born again. He brings us into accord with Himself. He actually indwells us (vv. 9, 11). We become partakers of the divine nature (2 Peter 1:4). Our orientation to God changes. Where there was enmity, there is now love (cf. Rom. 8:28). In the flesh we could not please God (v. 8) but now the righteous requirement of the law is fulfilled in us (v. 4). Central to all of this is the reality that our whole mind-set is new. Whereas the mind set on the flesh meant death, the mind set on the things of the Spirit results in life and peace (v. 6).

If your mind-set—the fundamental orientation of your understanding, its bent, its thought patterns—did not change when you made a profession of faith in Christ, something is seriously wrong. That is not to suggest that Christians cannot fall into old patterns and habits. But it *does* mean that our thoughts toward God, sin, and righteousness are radically different now that we are "in the Spirit" from when we were "in the flesh." We have new holy affections and longings for godliness. We have a love for God that transcends our attachment to this world (James 4:4). We can no longer blithely "indulge the flesh in its corrupt desires" (2 Peter 2:10). We no longer have anything in common with those "who set their minds on earthly things. For our citizenship is in heaven" (Phil. 3:19–20). And it is toward heaven that our minds are now inclined. We set our minds on the things of the Spirit (Rom. 8:5). Even when we fail or fall to earthly temptations, we "joyfully concur with the law of God in the inner man" (7:22). That is our basic orientation and mind-set.

In contrast, "the mind set on the flesh is death" (v. 6). Paul does not say that the mind set on the flesh *causes* death. He declares that it *is* death. The state of mind that is dominated by fleshly desires is a condition of spiritual death. In other words, those whose thoughts and desires are altogether fleshly are *already* "dead in [their] trespasses and sins" (Eph. 2:1). This cannot be a description of the true believer in Christ.

Christians are no longer "in the flesh": "You are not in the flesh but in the Spirit, if indeed the Spirit of God dwells in you. But if anyone does not have the Spirit of Christ, he does not belong to Him" (Rom. 8:9). The Greek word translated "dwells" is *oikeō*, which means "to inhabit." Paul is saying that the very Spirit of God indwells every person who trusts in Jesus Christ. The Spirit is in us, and we are "in the Spirit." We are not "in the flesh."

DEATH IN THE PHYSICAL BODY

But we are still "of flesh," and therefore our physical bodies deteriorate and die. The germ of death inhabits us all. Because of the curse of sin, we begin to die as soon as we are born.

For the Christian, however, there is more to this earthly life than death: "If Christ is in you, though the body is dead because of sin, yet the spirit is alive because of righteousness" (v. 10). In other words, the human body is subject to death (and is already dying) because of sin, but the believer's spirit is already alive in Christ. Eternal life is our present possession. Though the body is dying, the spirit is already endowed with incorruptibility.

Here the word "body" clearly refers to the actual physical body (not "the flesh"—that principle of sinfulness that Paul frequently spoke of), and the expression "dead" speaks of physical death. Notice that verses 10 and 11 use the word "body" (*sōma*) instead of "flesh" (*sarx*)—the word Paul used throughout the first nine verses. By contrasting "the body" and "the spirit" in this way, he makes his meaning inescapable. In verse 10, "the spirit is alive" refers to the human spirit, the immaterial part of our being. The body may be dying because of sin, but the believer's spirit is fully alive and thriving "because of righteousness"—because we are justified and therefore already have "passed out of death into life" (John 5:24). Paul is simply saying here what he also told the Corinthians: "Though our outer man is decaying, yet our inner man is being renewed day by day" (2 Cor. 4:16).

In fact, the indwelling Spirit also promises "life to [our] mortal bodies" in a future resurrection with a glorified body (v. 11).

Paul's point is that the body apart from the Spirit of God has no future. It is subject to death. Therefore we have no duty to the mortal side of our beings: "So then, brethren, we are under obligation, not to the flesh, to live according to the flesh—for if you are living according to the flesh, you must die; but if by the Spirit you are putting to death the deeds of the body, you will live" (Rom. 8:12–13). Again Paul uses the word *sarx* ("flesh") in the sense of "sin principle"—and equates it with "the deeds of the body." If you live in accord with the flesh—if you live in response to bodily impulses—you "must die."

Paul is once more drawing the line of distinction as clearly as possible between Christians and non-Christians. He is by no means warning believers that they might lose their salvation if they live according to the flesh. He has already made the point that true believers do not and *cannot* live in accord with the sin principle (vv. 4–9). Besides, Paul began this chapter with the statement, "There is therefore now no condemnation for those who are in Christ Jesus" (8:1). He will end it with the promise that nothing can separate us from the love of God in Christ Jesus (vv. 38–39). A warning of the possibility of falling away would contradict the very purpose for which he was writing.

Paul is simply reiterating what he says again and again throughout his New

Testament epistles—that those whose lives and hearts are altogether fleshly are not true Christians. They are already spiritually dead (v. 6), and unless they repent they are headed for eternal death. Meanwhile, their earthly lives are a kind of abject bondage to sin. They are enslaved to their own flesh, constrained to cater to its sensual desires.

WHAT IS MORTIFICATION?

Christians, on the other hand, have a different obligation—not to the flesh, but to the new principle of righteousness embodied in the Holy Spirit. Therefore they labor by the power of the Spirit to mortify sin in the flesh—to "[put] to death the deeds of the body." If you are doing this, he says, "you will live" (v. 13).

Of course Paul is not suggesting that anyone can obtain life or merit God's favor by the process of mortification. He is saying it is characteristic of true believers that they put to death the deeds of the body. Nothing is more natural than for people "led by the Spirit of God" (v. 14) to mortify their sin. One of the proofs of our salvation is that we do this. It is expected of believers. It is the expression of the new nature.

In other words, the true believer is not like Saul, who wanted to pamper and preserve Agag, but like Samuel, who hacked him to pieces without mercy and without delay. Saul may have wanted to make a lapdog of Agag, but Samuel knew that was utterly impossible. Similarly, we will never tame our flesh. We cannot mollycoddle our sin. We must deal with it quickly and severely.

It was Jesus who said,

> If your right eye makes you stumble, tear it out, and throw it from you; for it is better for you that one of the parts of your body perish, than for your whole body to be thrown into hell. And if your right hand makes you stumble, cut it off, and throw it from you; for it is better for you that one of the parts of your body perish, than for your whole body to go into hell. (Matthew 5:29–30)

Jesus was not speaking in literal terms, of course, though many have misunderstood this passage. No less than the great theologian Origen had himself castrated in a misguided effort to fulfill this command literally. Jesus was *not* calling for self-mutilation, but for mortification of the deeds of the body. Mortification, in the words of Puritan John Owen, means that "'The old man,' with his faculties, and properties, his wisdom, craft, subtlety, strength; this, says the apostle, must be killed, put to death, mortified,—that is, *have its power, life, vigour, and strength, to produce its effects, taken away by the Spirit.*"[3]

Romans 8:12–13, the verses where Paul introduces the idea of mortifying sin, signal a major turning point in the logical thread that runs through this chapter. Martyn Lloyd-Jones said,

> It is here for the first time, in this chapter, that we come to the realm of practical application. All we have had up to this point has been a general description of the Christian—his character, his position. But now the Apostle has really come explicitly to the doctrine of sanctification. *Here we are told exactly how, in practice, the Christian becomes sanctified.* Or, to state it differently, here we are told in detail and in practice how the Christian is to wage the battle against sin.[4]

Paul does not promise immediate freedom from sin's harassment. He does not describe a crisis-moment sanctification, where the believer is immediately made perfect. He does not tell the Romans to "let go and let God" take over while they sit idle. He does not suggest that a turning-point "decision" will solve the matter once and for all. On the contrary, he speaks of a continuous struggle with sin, where we are persistently, perpetually "putting to death the deeds of the body."

The language is often misunderstood. Paul is not calling for a life of self-flagellation. He is not saying believers should starve themselves, wear camel-hair shirts, or deprive themselves of life's basic needs. He is not telling them to mutilate themselves or live monastic lives or anything of the sort. The mortification Paul speaks of has nothing to do with external self-punishment. It is a spiritual process accomplished "by the Spirit."

Paul is describing a way of life where *we seek to throttle sin and crush it from our lives, sapping it of its strength, rooting it out, and depriving it of its influence.* That is what it means to mortify sin.

HOW DO WE MORTIFY SIN?

Mortification involves the cultivation of new habits of godliness, combined with the elimination of old sinful habits from our behavior. It is a constant warfare that takes place within the believer. Although we should expect our triumph over sin to be ever increasing, our mortification can never be wholly complete before we are glorified. We are to remain perpetually committed to the task. We must see sin as a sworn enemy and commit ourselves to slaying it wherever and whenever it rears its head.

Obviously, mortification is the work of believers only. Unbelievers are called to repent and flee to Christ. Those still enslaved to sin have no means by which to put sin to death. The Holy Spirit—the agent of mortification—does not indwell them. Their only hope is the salvation that is offered to those who will trust Jesus Christ and entrust themselves to Him. No one can mortify sin who is not "in Christ" and "in the Spirit."

Scripture offers several practical means whereby believers can mortify their sin. Our growth in grace depends on our obedience to these duties. Not one of them is a fleshly or mechanical formula. They are not religious activities or rituals. John Owen observed that most of the Roman Catholic religious system consists of "mistaken ways and means of mortification . . . Their vows, orders, fastings, penances, are all built on this ground; they are all for the mortifying of sin. Their preachings, sermons, and books of devotion, they look all this way."[5]

But sin cannot be annihilated through legalism, monasticism, pietism, asceticism, Pharisaism, celibacy, self-flagellation, confessional booths, rosary beads, Hail Marys, or any other external means. The instrument of mortification is the Holy Spirit, and His power is the energy that works in us to carry out the process. All the means of mortification are simple commands of Scripture that we are to obey. I want to highlight some of the key ones:

ABSTAIN FROM FLESHLY LUSTS

Peter wrote, "Beloved, I urge you as aliens and strangers to abstain from fleshly lusts, which wage war against the soul" (1 Peter 2:11). In other words, stop lusting. Abstain from it. Stay away from it. "Flee immorality" (1 Cor. 6:18). What could be more direct?

Do you want to put to death the lusts in your heart? Then stop entertaining them. Peter does not prescribe a program of therapy. He does not suggest that it be treated as an addiction. He simply says abstain. Quit doing it. You have no business indulging such thoughts. Put them away at once. *You yourself* must do this; it cannot be done for you. There is no point waiting for some heavenly power to erase this sin automatically from your life. You are to stop it, and stop it immediately. Martyn Lloyd-Jones said,

I do not know of a single scripture—and I speak advisedly—which tells me to take my sin, the particular thing that gets me down, to God in prayer and ask him to deliver me from it and then trust in faith that he will.

Now that teaching is also often put like this: you must say to a man who is constantly defeated by a particular sin, "I think your only hope is to take it to Christ and Christ will take it from you." But what does Scripture say in Ephesians 4:28 to the man who finds himself constantly guilty of stealing, to a man who sees something he likes and takes it? What am I to tell such a man? Am I to say, "Take that sin to Christ and ask him to deliver you"? No, what the apostle Paul tells him is this: "Let him that stole, steal no more." Just that. Stop doing it. And if it is fornication or adultery or lustful thoughts, again: Stop doing it, says Paul. He does not say, "Go and pray to Christ to deliver you." No. You stop doing that, he says, as becomes children of God.[6]

Here is perhaps the most straightforward, obvious means of mortifying our sin: *stop doing it.* Too many people think they must wait for an extraordinary experience, a miracle from heaven, a sign from the Lord, or whatever. They think some special divine intervention is necessary to free them from a sinful practice or pattern of thinking. No, that is precisely the error Romans 6 refutes. You *are* free from sin; now stop doing it. "Abstain." Reckon yourself dead to sin, and don't do it anymore. "Resist the devil and he will flee from you" (James 4:7). It is as simple as that.

MAKE NO PROVISION FOR THE FLESH

In Romans 13:14 Paul writes, "Put on the Lord Jesus Christ, and make no provision for the flesh in regard to its lusts." In other words, simply refuse to accommodate fleshly lusts. If you struggle with gluttony, don't load up on junk food when you shop at the market. If you are tempted with sexual desire, don't fill your mind with images that feed your lust. If you don't want to fall, don't walk where it is slippery. Refuse to furnish your mind with the means to entertain evil thoughts. Make no preparations for the possibility of sin. Thus you can slay sin before it breeds.

FIX YOUR HEART ON CHRIST

The apostle John wrote, "We know that, when He appears, we shall be like Him, because we shall see Him just as He is. And everyone who has this hope fixed on Him purifies himself, just as He is pure" (1 John 3:2–3). It is an inexorable spiritual law that you become like the object of your worship. Psalm 135 says,

> The idols of the nations are but silver and gold,
> The work of man's hands.
> They have mouths, but they do not speak;
> They have eyes, but they do not see;
> They have ears, but they do not hear;
> Nor is there any breath at all in their mouths.
> *Those who make them will be like them,*
> Yes, everyone who trusts in them. (vv. 15–18, emphasis added)

If the heathen become like the lifeless gods they worship, how much more will we be made like Christ, who have the Holy Spirit in us working to accomplish that very goal? As we fix our hearts on Christ, we discover our worship has the effect of conforming us to His image: "But we all, with unveiled face beholding as in a mirror the glory of the Lord, are being transformed into the same image from glory to glory, just as from the Lord, the Spirit" (2 Cor. 3:18).

MEDITATE ON GOD'S WORD

The psalmist wrote, "Thy word I have treasured in my heart, that I may not sin against Thee" (Ps. 119:11). The Lord told Joshua, "This book of the law shall not depart from your mouth, but you shall meditate on it day and night, so that you may be careful to do according to all that is written in it; for then you will make your way prosperous, and then you will have success" (Josh. 1:8). Do you want to have success in the battle against sin? Familiarize yourself with the Word of God. Meditate on it "day and night" (cf. Ps. 1:2). Let it be a lamp to your feet and a light to your path (Ps. 119:105). As the truth begins to penetrate our hearts and minds, it will confront and attack our sin.

Jesus prayed, "Sanctify them in the truth; Thy word is truth" (John 17:17). The truth of God's Word is the medium the Holy Spirit uses in our sanctification. Load your mind with it. Fill your heart with it. Ponder it carefully and let it direct your walk. "Whatever is true, whatever is honorable, whatever is right, whatever is pure, whatever is lovely, whatever is of good repute, if there is any excellence and if anything worthy of praise, let your mind dwell on these things" (Phil. 4:8). "Let the word of Christ richly dwell within you" (Col. 3:16). You will discover that "the sword of the Spirit, which is the word of God" (Eph. 6:17) is the most effective weapon for hacking the flesh to pieces.

Pray Without Ceasing

On the night Jesus was betrayed, He took His disciples with Him to Gethsemane and told them, "Pray that you may not enter into temptation" (Luke 22:40). Later He found them sleeping and rebuked them for their prayerlessness. He told them, "Keep watching and praying, that you may not enter into temptation; the spirit is willing, but the flesh is weak" (Matt. 26:41).

"Lead us not into temptation" was part of the model prayer He gave the disciples (Luke 11:4). Prayer is an effective and necessary means for heading off sinful temptations *before* they can attack. Look at prayer as a preemptive strike against fleshliness. By drawing us near to the Lord and focusing our thoughts on Him, prayer both steels us against fleshly temptation and weakens the temptations when they come.

Watch and pray. Identify the circumstances that lead you into sin, and pray specifically for strength to face those situations. Pray for a holy hatred of sin. Pray that God will show you the real state of your sinful heart. The psalmist prayed this prayer for sanctification:

> Who can discern his errors? Acquit me of hidden faults.
> Also keep back Thy servant from presumptuous sins;
> Let them not rule over me;
> Then I shall be blameless,
> And I shall be acquitted of great transgression.
> Let the words of my mouth and the meditation of my heart
> Be acceptable in Thy sight,
> O LORD, my rock and my Redeemer. (Psalm 19:12–14)

Prayer must include confession and repentance if it is to be effective in mortifying our sin. John wrote, "If we confess our sins, He is faithful and righteous to forgive us our sins and to cleanse us from all unrighteousness" (1 John 1:9). And the writer of Hebrews says, "Let us therefore draw near with confidence to the throne of grace, that we may receive mercy and may find grace to help in time of need" (Heb. 4:16).

Exercise Self-Control

Self-control is a fruit of the Spirit (Gal. 5:23)—and it is also one of the means through which the Spirit enables us to mortify the deeds of the body. Paul wrote,

Everyone who competes in the games exercises self-control in all things. They then do it to receive a perishable wreath, but we an imperishable. Therefore I run in such a way, as not without aim; I box in such a way, as not beating the air; but I buffet my body and make it my slave, lest possibly, after I have preached to others, I myself should be disqualified. (1 Corinthians 9:25–27)

The word "buffet" in that passage is a translation of the Greek word *hupōpiazō*, meaning "to strike under the eye." Athletes discipline their bodies for mere earthly prizes. If they are willing to do that, shouldn't we also be willing to exercise a similar kind of self-control for the heavenly prize?

Paul is not speaking here of punishing the body through self-flagellation or neglect. He certainly is not advocating anything that would physically weaken or injure the body. No athlete would do such things.

I once met a man who wore a belt studded with nails that constantly tore at his flesh. He felt he was punishing his body and atoning for his own sins. Lots of misguided people over the ages have attempted similar means of dealing with the body. Martin Luther almost destroyed his body with excessive fasting as a young monk before he discovered that God's Word says, "The just shall live by faith" (Rom. 1:17 KJV). In the Philippines at Easter each year, there are men who actually have themselves crucified in a bloody ritual that they believe makes them holy.

That is not at all the spirit of what Scripture calls for. It is a watchful self-discipline that refuses to pander to the appetites of the body at the soul's expense. Jesus said, "Be on guard, that your hearts may not be weighted down with dissipation and drunkenness and the worries of life, and [the Day of the Lord] come on you suddenly like a trap" (Luke 21:34).

BE FILLED WITH THE HOLY SPIRIT

"Do not get drunk with wine, for that is dissipation," Paul wrote, "but be filled with the Spirit" (Eph. 5:18). To be Spirit-filled is to be controlled by the Holy Spirit, just as to be drunk is to be under the influence of alcohol. Believers are to be utterly yielded to the Spirit's control.

Now this brings us full circle to where we began in Romans 8:13. We mortify sin "by the Spirit." It is the Holy Spirit's power in us that actually does the work of mortification in those who are yielded to Him. I must emphasize again, however, that this does not mean we are passive in the process. As John Owen wrote,

He doth not so work our mortification in us as not to keep it still an act of our *obedience.* The Holy Ghost works in us and upon us, as we are fit to be wrought in and upon; that is, so as to preserve our own liberty and free obedience. He works upon our understandings, wills, consciences, and affections, agreeably to their own natures; he works *in us* and *with us*, not *against us* or *without us*, so that his assistance is an encouragement as to the facilitating of the work, and no occasion of neglect as to the work itself.[7]

In other words, as we have noted repeatedly, we cannot abandon our own responsibility and passively wait for God to mortify sin on our behalf. The Spirit-filled life is an active, vigorous, working endeavor, where we work out our own salvation with fear and trembling (Phil. 2:12). When we obey, we then discover it is actually God who is at work in us "both to will and to work for His good pleasure" (v. 13). In other words, God both molds our wills to obey and then gives us the energy to work according to whatever pleases Him. That is the Spirit-filled life.

There are many more duties related to mortifying sin—such as clothing oneself with humility (1 Peter 5:5); having the mind of Christ (Phil. 2:5); putting away spiteful feelings toward others (Eph. 4:31–32); putting on the armor of God (Eph. 6:11–17); laying aside sinful attitudes (Col. 3:8–9); adding the graces of spiritual growth to one's life (2 Peter 1:5–7); following the *know, reckon, yield, obey, serve* pattern of Romans 6—and many similar responsibilities the New Testament assigns to believers. These may *all* be subsumed under this basic category of being filled with the Spirit.

It is really as simple as this: "Walk by the Spirit, and you will not carry out the desire of the flesh" (Gal. 5:16). The fruit of the Spirit will overgrow and choke out the works of the flesh.

"Let us [therefore] cleanse ourselves from all defilement of flesh and spirit, perfecting holiness in the fear of God" (2 Cor. 7:1).

STRIKE SIN AT ITS HEAD

John Owen wrote, "He that is appointed to kill an enemy, if he leave striking before the other ceases living, doth but half his work."[8] We must be always at the task of mortifying sin. We may slaughter a whole tribe of Amalekites, but if we deliberately permit one Agag to escape, God will not be pleased with our efforts.

The flesh is very subtle and deceptive, as we know. A particular sin may leave us alone for a while to make us think we are rid of it. But it can come back with a hellish fury if we are not on our guard. Sin perpetually stalks us; we must be continually mortifying it. This is a duty we cannot rest from until we rest in glory.

Give sin an inch, it will take a mile. If it can gain a footing in our lives, it will send forth roots and grow like kudzu. It will use us and abuse us and inflict as much disaster as possible. Owen wrote,

> Every unclean thought or glance would be adultery if it could; every covetous desire would be oppression, every thought of unbelief would be atheism, might it grow to its head . . . It proceeds toward its height by degrees, making good the ground it hath got by hardness . . . Now nothing can prevent this but mortification; that withers the root and strikes at the head of sin every hour, so that whatever it aims at it is crossed in. *There is not the best saint in the world but, if he should give over this duty, would fall into as many cursed sins as ever did any of his kind.*[9]

Later, he added, "Sin sets itself against every act of holiness, and against every degree we grow to. Let not that man think he makes any progress in holiness while he walks not over the bellies of his lusts."[10]

We are not ignorant of Satan's devices, the apostle declares (2 Cor. 2:11). Neither should we be naive about the subtleties of our own flesh. When Agag comes to us cheerfully, saying, "Surely the bitterness of death is past" (1 Sam. 15:32); when he wants to make friends and declare an end to hostilities—that is when it is most imperative that we turn on him and cut him ruthlessly to pieces before the Lord.

SIN IS NOT MORTIFIED WHEN IT IS MERELY COVERED UP

You can obscure your sin from others' sight, but that is not the same as mortification. If a sin has simply been papered over with hypocrisy, what good is there in that? If conscience has only been daubed, we are in a much more dangerous state than before. "He who conceals his transgressions will not prosper, but he who confesses and forsakes them will find compassion" (Prov. 28:13). You have not done your duty with regard to your sin until you have confessed and forsaken it.

SIN IS NOT MORTIFIED WHEN IT IS ONLY INTERNALIZED

If you forsake the outward practice of some evil yet continue to ruminate on the memory of that sin's pleasures, beware. You may have moved your sin into the privacy of your imagination, where it is known only to you and to God. But that sin has not been mortified. If anything it has been made more deadly by being married to pretended righteousness. Jesus rebuked the Pharisees for this very thing. They avoided murder but tolerated hate. They refrained from fornication but indulged in lustful thoughts. Jesus declared them worthy of eternal hell (Matt. 5:21–28).

SIN IS NOT MORTIFIED WHEN IT IS EXCHANGED FOR ANOTHER SIN

What good is it to trade the lust of the flesh for the lust of the eyes? That lust has not been mortified; it has only changed form. Puritan Thomas Fuller said, "Some think themselves improved in piety, because they have left prodigality and reel into covetousness."[11] If you succumb to this tactic, your heart is in danger of being hardened by the deceitfulness of sin (Heb. 3:13).

SIN IS NOT MORTIFIED UNTIL THE CONSCIENCE HAS BEEN APPEASED

The goal is "love from a pure heart and a good conscience and a sincere faith" (1 Tim. 1:5). As long as the conscience remains defiled, it affects our testimony.

> Sanctify Christ as Lord in your hearts, always being ready to make a defense to everyone who asks you to give an account for the hope that is in you, yet with gentleness and reverence; *and keep a good conscience* so that in the thing in which you are slandered, those who revile your good behavior in Christ may be put to shame. (1 Peter 3:15–16, emphasis added)

Part of the process of mortification is working through the issue of our guilt. Those who attempt to evade the guilt have not properly confessed their sin; therefore they cannot be cleansed and fully forgiven.

If you want to mortify sin, John Owen wrote, "*Load thy conscience with the guilt of it.*"[12] Contrary to the popular wisdom of our day, he believed the pangs of guilt were a natural and healthy consequence of wrongdoing. "Be ashamed," he wrote,[13] for he saw shame as an advantage in the mortification of sin. He correctly understood Paul's meaning in 2 Corinthians 7:10: "The sorrow that is according to the will of God produces a repentance without regret."

Those who give a nod of the head to their guilt, claim the promise of forgiveness, quickly reassure themselves, and then think no more of their wrongdoing are subjecting themselves to the heart-hardening deceit of sin—

especially when the sin threatens to become a habit. Let sorrow do its full work in your heart to produce a deep, honest repentance, and those sins will be severely weakened.

SIN IS NOT MORTIFIED WHEN IT IS MERELY REPRESSED

Some people use diversions to avoid dealing with their sin. They try to drown their consciences with alcohol or drown out their guilt with entertainment and other distractions. When temptation surfaces they do not give a biblical answer, as Jesus did (Matt. 4:4, 7, 10). Instead they seek a fleshly escape route. Of this tendency Martyn Lloyd-Jones said,

> If you merely repress a temptation or this first motion of sin within you, it will probably come up again still more strongly. To that extent I agree with the modern psychology. Repression is always bad. "Well, what do you do?" asks someone. I answer: When you feel that first motion of sin, just pull yourself up and say, "Of course I am not having any dealings with this at all." Expose the thing and say, "This is evil, this is vileness, this is the thing that drove the first man out of Paradise." Pull it out, look at it, denounce it, hate it for what it is; then you have really dealt with it. You must not merely push it back in a spirit of fear, and in a timorous manner. Bring it out, expose it, and analyse it; and then denounce it for what it is until you hate it.[14]

That is sound advice. We should deal with our sin courageously, striking at its head. Subduing it a little bit is not enough. We need to exterminate it, hack it in pieces—seek by the means of grace and the power of the Spirit to wring the deadly life from it.

It is a lifelong task, in which our progress will always be only gradual. That may make the fight seem daunting at first. But as soon as we set ourselves to the work, we discover that sin shall *not* be master over us, for we are under grace (Rom. 6:14). That means it is God who is at work in us both to will and to work for His good pleasure (Phil. 2:13). And having begun His good work in us, He "will perfect it until the day of Christ Jesus" (1:6).

9

WHAT HEAVEN WILL BE LIKE[1]

Gustav Mahler's Fourth Symphony is based on a poem that describes heaven from a child's point of view. The music certainly *sounds* heavenly. The symphony's fourth movement features a soprano singing the German words to the poem *"Das himmlische Leben"*—"The Heavenly Life." English listeners might simply be moved by the serene beauty of the music. But the German words paint a peculiar picture of heaven.

In the first place, the inhabitants of this heaven are voracious carnivores. The poem speaks of Herod as a butcher who kills unsuspecting little lambs so that the inhabitants of heaven can eat all they like. And the oxen are so plentiful that the apostle Luke slaughters them "without giving it a thought."

The lyrics also have the inhabitants of heaven jumping and skipping and singing—but mostly gorging themselves on an endless supply of food. Peter catches fish, and Martha cooks them. So this child's vision of heaven turns out to be another "paradise" where earthly appetites are indulged.

I'm intrigued by the way the unbelieving world portrays heaven. At one end of the spectrum is this view that heaven exists to gratify earthly lusts. At the other is a cynical suspicion that heaven will be unbearably monotonous. The classic caricature pictures heaven's inhabitants sitting on clouds and playing harps. I don't know if anyone really imagines heaven will be like that, but I have no doubt that many people think of heaven as a bland, boring place with nothing enjoyable to do.

A skeptic once told me, "I'd rather be in hell with my friends than in heaven with all the church people." Such a flippant attitude betrays a tragic lack of regard for the horrors of hell. It also grossly underestimates the blessedness of heaven.

This deep-seated suspicion that heaven may be an eternal bore reflects the sinful thinking of man. As sinners we are naturally prone to think a little sin is surely more enjoyable than perfect righteousness. It is hard for us to imagine a realm wholly devoid of sin and yet filled with endless pleasures.

But that is exactly how heaven will be. We will bask in the glory of God, realizing at last our chief end—to glorify God and to *enjoy* Him forever. The psalmist wrote, "In thy presence is fulness of joy; at thy right hand there are pleasures for evermore" (Ps. 16:11 KJV).

Such a thought is unfathomable to our finite minds. But Scripture repeatedly makes clear that heaven is a realm of unsurpassed joy, unfading glory, undiminished bliss, unlimited delights, and unending pleasures. Nothing about it can possibly be boring or humdrum. It will be a perfect existence. We will have unbroken fellowship with all heaven's inhabitants. Life there will be devoid of any sorrows, cares, tears, fears, or pain: "And God shall wipe away all tears from their eyes; and there shall be no more death, neither sorrow, nor crying, neither shall there be any more pain: for the former things are passed away. And he that sat upon the throne said, Behold, I make all things new" (Rev. 21:4–5 KJV).

The best of our spiritual experiences here are only small samples of heaven. Our highest spiritual heights, the profoundest of all our joys, and the greatest of our spiritual blessings will be normal in heaven. As we live now in the heavenlies, we are merely tasting the glories of the life to come. When we consider that Christ prayed for all who know Him to spend eternity with Him in unbroken fellowship (John 17:24), our hearts should overflow with gratitude and expectation.

The preacher of Ecclesiastes said, "The day of one's death is better than the day of one's birth" (7:1). He was merely being cynical about the meaninglessness and futility of this earthly life, but there is a valid sense for the Christian in which it is true that our death ushers us into an infinitely greater glory than our birth ever did. The confidence that heaven awaits us should fill us with a glorious hope. Paul said, "For to me to live is Christ, and to die is gain" (Phil. 1:21). The prospect of heaven made him joyful even in the face of death.

ABSENT FROM THE BODY, PRESENT WITH THE LORD

Paul also said he was "willing rather to be absent from the body, and to be present with the Lord" (2 Cor. 5:8 KJV). This was not a morbid death wish on Paul's part. He was not saying he was fed up with living and eager to die. Rather, he was expressing his confidence that earthly existence is not the end of life at all for the Christian. Death immediately ushers the believer into a fuller, higher realm of more abundant life—in the very presence of the Lord.

If you are a Christian, trusting Christ *alone* for your salvation, Scripture promises that the moment you leave this life you go to heaven. To be absent from the body is to be present with the Lord. To depart this life is to be "with Christ" (Phil. 1:23). "To live is Christ, and to die is gain" (v. 21).

We need to have the heart of Paul—yearning to be clothed with our heavenly form and to exchange this transient world for eternal joy. He wrote, "This corruptible must put on incorruption, and this mortal must put on immortality" (1 Cor. 15:53 KJV). Our mortality will be swallowed up by a more abundant life (2 Cor. 5:4).

Someone inevitably asks about the state of believers who die between now and the final consummation of all things. Are there compartments within heaven? Where did Old Testament believers go when they died? Do believers who die receive temporary bodies between now and the Resurrection? What is the intermediate state like? And what about purgatory?

SOME WRONG VIEWS

A number of speculative views have been proposed to attempt to answer those questions. With regard to the state of Old Testament believers, for example, some teach that in the Old Testament, hades (the realm of the dead) was divided into two sections—one for the wicked and one for the righteous. They suggest that Old Testament saints who died went to the realm called "Abraham's bosom" (cf. Luke 16:22–23)—a sort of holding tank. According to this theory, these believers were not brought into heaven until Christ conquered death in His resurrection.

Most of that is sheer conjecture with little if any real biblical support. Wilbur Smith writes, "However abundant the Scriptural data might be regarding the resurrection of believers and their life in heaven, the state of the soul between death and resurrection is rarely referred to in the Bible."[2] Scripture simply does not give much information about the intermediate state. But what we do know from Scripture is enough to debunk some of the wrong theories.

Soul sleep. One view held by many is that the soul of a believer who dies remains unconscious until the resurrection. This view is found in some of the noncanonical writings of the early church. Its best-known advocates today are the Seventh-day Adventists. They point out that the word "sleep" is often used in Scripture as a synonym for death. For example, Jesus told the disciples, "Our friend Lazarus sleepeth; but I go, that I may awake him out of sleep" (John 11:11 KJV). And Paul described the dead in Christ as "them also which sleep in Jesus" (1 Thess. 4:14 KJV).

But the "sleep" referred to in such imagery has to do with the body, not the soul. In his account of the Crucifixion, Matthew wrote of a great earthquake: "And the graves were opened; and many bodies of the saints which slept arose" (Matt. 27:52 KJV). It is the *body*, not the soul, that "sleeps" in death. The body lies in rest, utterly devoid of any sensation or awareness. But the soul enters the very presence of the Lord. This was affirmed again and again by the apostle Paul in the verses I just cited, as he described his desire to be absent from the body, so that he could be "present with the Lord" (2 Cor. 5:8 KJV).

The souls of the departed enter into their rest. But it is a rest from labor and strife, not a rest of unconsciousness. The apostle John was told to write, "Blessed are the dead which die in the Lord from henceforth: Yea, saith the Spirit, that they may rest from their labours" (Rev. 14:13 KJV). Yet he is clearly not describing a "rest" of unconscious sleep; in the scene John witnessed in heaven, the souls of the redeemed were there, actively singing and praising God (vv. 1–4).

Everything Scripture says about the death of believers indicates that they are immediately ushered consciously into the Lord's presence. In the words of the Westminster Confession of Faith,

> The bodies of men after death return to dust, and see corruption; but their souls, (which neither die nor sleep,) having an immortal subsistence, immediately return to God who gave them. The souls of the righteous, being then made perfect in holiness, are received into the highest heavens, where they behold the face of God in light and glory, waiting for the full redemption of their bodies. (32.1)

Purgatory. The Roman Catholic doctrine of purgatory is nowhere taught in Scripture. It was devised to accommodate Catholicism's denial of justification by faith alone. Here's why:

Scripture very clearly teaches that an absolutely *perfect* righteousness is necessary for entry into heaven. Jesus said, "I say unto you, That except your righteousness shall exceed the righteousness of the scribes and Pharisees, ye shall in no case enter into the kingdom of heaven" (Matt. 5:20 KJV). He then added, "Be ye therefore perfect, even as your Father which is in heaven is perfect" (v. 48 KJV)— thus setting the standard as high as it can possibly be set.

Later in Jesus' ministry, when the rich young ruler approached Him, asking how he might enter heaven, Jesus upheld this same standard of absolute perfection. He began by declaring that "there is none good but one, that is, God" (Matt. 19:17 KJV)—not disclaiming sinless perfection for Himself, but plainly pointing out that such perfection is impossible for sinful humanity. Then, however, Jesus told the young man that in order to obtain eternal life, he must have a track record of perfect obedience to the law (vv. 17–21). Again and again, He made the required standard of righteousness impossibly high for all who would seek to earn God's favor on their own.

The young ruler clearly did not understand or acknowledge his own sinfulness. He assured Jesus that he had indeed kept the law from his youth up (v. 20).

Jesus subtly pointed out the young man's covetousness, which was a violation of the tenth commandment. From the outset of His conversation with the young man, the Lord was prodding him to confess that no one but God Himself is truly *good.* But the rich young ruler was unwilling to face his own sin, and so he finally went away without salvation.

The disciples marveled at this. The young man was evidently—from the human perspective—one of the most righteous individuals they knew. Notice that no one disputed his claim that he had obeyed the Law. There must have been no overt sins in his life that anyone could point to. He was the best of men. So the disciples were floored when he walked away with no assurance of eternal life from Jesus. In fact, Jesus told them, "Verily I say unto you, That a rich man shall hardly enter into the kingdom of heaven" (v. 23 KJV).

Again, He was setting the standard at an impossible height. He was saying that the most fastidious legal observance is not enough. The most flawless external righteousness is not enough. All the worldly advantages of wealth are of no help. Only *absolute perfection* is acceptable to God. Our Lord kept underscoring these things because He wanted people to see the utter futility of seeking to earn righteousness by any system of works.

The disciples got the message. They asked, "Who then can be saved?" (v. 25 KJV).

And Jesus replied, "With men this is impossible; but with God all things are possible" (v. 26 KJV).

We know from Paul's treatise on justification in Romans 4 that God saves believers *by imputing to them the merit of Christ's perfect righteousness*—not in any sense because of their own righteousness. God accepts believers "in Christ." He clothes them with the perfect righteousness of Christ. He declares them perfectly righteous because of Christ. Their sins have been imputed to Christ, who has paid the full penalty. His righteousness is now imputed to them, and they receive the full merit for it. That is what justification by faith means.

In other words, God does not first make us perfect, then accept us on that basis. He *first* justifies us by imputing to us an alien righteousness, *then* perfects us by conforming us to the image of Christ. He justifies the ungodly (Rom. 4:5).

Paul wrote, "Therefore being justified by faith, we have peace with God through our Lord Jesus Christ" (Rom. 5:1). And "there is therefore now no condemnation to them which are in Christ Jesus" (Rom. 8:1 KJV). Those verses describe our justification as something already accomplished. They speak of it in the past tense. Jesus Himself described justification as an immediate event when He told how the repentant publican was saved after begging God for mercy: "This man went down to his house justified" (Luke 18:14 KJV). Justification is thus a completed fact for the believer; it is not an ongoing process. We stand before God fully acceptable to Him because of Christ's righteousness—not our own.

Roman Catholic doctrine denies all that. Catholicism teaches that justification is an ongoing process that depends on the degree of real, personal righteousness we achieve. According to Rome, Christ's merit imputed to us is not enough to save; we must earn merit of our own through the sacraments and other good works we do. Righteousness is infused into us, then perfected by our own efforts. According to Catholic teaching, this real, personal righteousness that resides in us is the necessary ground on which God accepts us. And our justification is not complete until we are perfect. This reverses the order, suggesting that we must *first* be perfected, and only *then* is our justification complete.

The Catholic view of justification poses an obvious dilemma. We know too well that even the best Christians fall far short of perfection. No one (Catholic teaching actually says *almost* no one) achieves absolute perfection in this life. And if our own perfection is a prerequisite to heaven, it would seem no one could enter heaven immediately upon death. Any remaining imperfections would need to be worked out first.

The doctrine of purgatory is necessary to solve this dilemma. Deny that we are justified by faith alone, and you must devise an explanation of how we can make the transition from our imperfect state in this life to the perfect state of heaven. Purgatory is where Roman Catholics believe most people go after death to be finally purged of their sins and gain whatever merit they may be lacking to enter heaven. Catholicism teaches that this will involve intense pain and suffering.

Oddly enough, although Catholic doctrine denies that the imputed righteousness of Christ is sufficient to save sinners in this life, it does allow the imputation of righteousness from earthly sinners to those in purgatory. Masses are said for the dead, and supposedly the righteousness earned via the sacrament is imputed to the person in purgatory, and that shortens his or her stay there.

THE BIBLICAL RESPONSE

Of course, none of this is taught in Scripture. The sufferings of Christ were fully sufficient to atone for our sins. Our own sufferings can add nothing to the merit of Christ. As the writer of Hebrews says, there is no efficacious sacrifice for sin other than what Christ has provided; if Christ's sacrifice is not sufficient, or if we willfully turn away from it, "there remaineth no more sacrifice for sins, but a certain fearful looking for of judgment and fiery indignation, which shall devour the adversaries" (Heb. 10:26–27 KJV).

For all believers, because we are fully justified, there can be no condemnation. No postmortem suffering is necessary to atone for remaining sin; *all* our sins are covered by the blood of Christ. No merit is lacking that must be made up. Every believer will be able to say with the prophet Isaiah, "I will greatly rejoice in the LORD, my soul shall be joyful in my God; for he hath clothed me with the garments of salvation, he hath covered me with the robe of righteousness, as a bridegroom decketh himself with ornaments, and as a bride adorneth herself with her jewels" (Isa. 61:10 KJV).

Some claim that 1 Corinthians 3 describes purgatory, where the believer is put through a fiery judgment to purge out the dross of sin. But read that passage again. It describes the judgment of the believer's works, to see if they are "wood, hay, stubble" or "gold, silver, precious stones" (v. 12 KJV). At issue is whether our works endure or are burned up. And it is the works, not the saints themselves, that are tested in the purging fire. This is the judgment that will take place in the eschatalogical future at the *bema* of Christ, not an ongoing state of purgatory that believers pass through on their way to heaven:

> Every man's work shall be made manifest: for the day shall declare it, because it shall be revealed by fire; and the fire shall try every man's work of what sort it is. If any man's work abide which he hath built thereupon, he shall receive a reward. If any man's work shall be burned, he shall suffer loss: *but he himself shall be saved; yet so as by fire.* (vv. 13–15 KJV, emphasis added)

Notice again, that only the works, not the believers themselves, must go through the fire. Also note that rewards are what is at issue—not entrance to heaven.

Everything in Scripture indicates that the believer's entrance to heaven occurs immediately upon death. Let's examine a few key passages:

Psalm 16. Here we find the psalmist hopeful even as he faced death: "For thou wilt not leave my soul in hell [Hebrew, *sheol*, the realm of the dead]; neither wilt thou suffer thine Holy One to see corruption. Thou wilt shew me the path of life: in thy presence is fulness of joy; at thy right hand there are pleasures for evermore" (vv. 10–11 KJV). The psalmist anticipated that when he left this world, he would enter the presence of God, finding pleasure and fullness of joy. He had no fear of purgatorial sufferings. And he left no place for the notion of soul sleep.

Psalm 23. The final verse of this familiar psalm says, "Surely goodness and mercy shall follow me all the days of my life: and I will dwell in the house of the LORD for ever" (KJV). David was certain that once his life was over, he would dwell in the house of the Lord forever (which can refer only to heaven). Notice that he goes immediately from "all the days of my life" to "dwell[ing] in the house of the LORD." The hope he expresses here is exactly the same as Paul's: "to be absent from the body and to be at home with the Lord" (2 Cor. 5:8).

Luke 16. When the beggar Lazarus died, Jesus says he "was carried by the angels into Abraham's bosom" (v. 22). As we noted earlier, some think this expression "Abraham's bosom" describes a sort of holding tank where Old Testament saints went while awaiting heaven. I believe both Abraham and Lazarus were in the presence of God. In any case, this account rules out both soul sleep and purgatory.

To shed light on the expression "Abraham's bosom," we turn to a parallel expression that occurs in John 13. This is part of the apostle John's description of that final Passover celebration in the Upper Room. He writes, "Now there was leaning on Jesus' bosom one of his disciples, whom Jesus loved" (v. 23 KJV). The scene is a low table, where guests had to recline. This disciple (who was John himself—John 21:20, 24) was in a position so that his head was near Jesus' chest. They positioned themselves that way so they could converse while they ate with a free hand.

So when Jesus says Lazarus was carried to "Abraham's bosom" He indicates that the former beggar was reclining at a banquet table in a celebration of joy, next to Abraham, the father of the faithful. In other words, Lazarus was in the position of a guest of honor. Imagine the dismay of the Pharisees when Jesus portrayed an ordinary beggar reclining at the table next to the greatest of the Jewish Fathers!

Again, I believe this is heaven, not some intermediate state. Scripture never suggests Old Testament believers went to a special compartment where they had to wait for Christ to carry them into glory. In fact, the evidence points to a different conclusion.

Matthew 17. For example, when Christ was transfigured, Moses and Elijah appeared with Him (v. 3). Although Christ's death and resurrection hadn't yet occurred, Moses and Elijah were summoned from the realm of departed saints to the Mount of Transfiguration, where they conversed with Jesus about "His departure which He was about to accomplish at Jerusalem" (Luke 9:31). It seems obvious that they had not been shut away for ages in some intermediate compartment of hades, but that they were intimately familiar with Christ, partakers of His glory, and knowledgeable enough about His earthly work to discuss the details of what He was about to do. This is an amazing passage, a clear window into the kind of close fellowship we will share with Christ in eternity.

Luke 23. This familiar passage describes that touching moment during the crucifixion when one of the thieves next to Jesus repented. "He said unto Jesus, Lord, remember me when thou comest into thy kingdom. And Jesus said unto him, Verily I say unto thee, Today shalt thou be with me in paradise" (vv. 42–43 KJV).

"Paradise" is the same word the apostle Paul used to describe being caught up into the "third heaven" in 2 Corinthians 12:4. Paradise is a synonym for heaven. It cannot be a reference to purgatory. And the promise of paradise *today* rules out not only purgatory, but soul sleep as well.

If anyone were a candidate for purgatory, this thief would be. Moments before, he had taunted Christ along with the unrepentant thief (Mark 15:32). His repentance was a last-minute change—while he was literally in his death throes. Yet Jesus promised to see him that very day in Paradise.

BIBLICAL GLIMPSES OF HEAVEN

Scripture contains many descriptions of heaven. Some of them are cast in apocalyptic language filled with symbolism and mystery. Apocalyptic symbolism in Scripture always means something of great consequence is under discussion. Don't make the error of thinking symbolic language means the thing described is unreal. As we have already established, the Bible asserts that heaven is a real place. And the descriptions of heaven, even the most apocalyptic ones, describe a real place.

EZEKIEL'S WHEEL

One of the most dramatic descriptions of heaven in all Scripture comes from the prophet Ezekiel. Ezekiel was wonderfully transported to the very heart of heaven in a vision, and he describes in vivid detail what heaven and the throne room of God are like.

Ezekiel 1:4–28 says this:

> And as I looked, behold, a storm wind was coming from the north, a great cloud with fire flashing forth continually and a bright light around it, and in its midst something like glowing metal in the midst of the fire. And within it there were figures resembling four living beings. And this was their appearance: they had human form. Each of them had four faces and four wings. And their legs were straight and their feet were like a calf's hoof, and they gleamed like burnished bronze. Under their wings on their four sides were human hands. As for the faces and wings of the four of them, their wings touched one another; their faces did not turn when they moved, each went straight forward. As for the form of their faces, each had the face of a man, all four had the face of a lion on the right and the face of a bull on the left, and all four had the face of an eagle. Such were their faces. Their wings were spread out above; each had two touching another being, and two covering their bodies. And each went straight forward; wherever the spirit was about to go, they would go, without turning as they went. In the midst of the living beings there was something that looked like burning coals of fire, like torches darting back and forth among the living beings. The fire was bright, and lightning was flashing from the fire. And the living beings ran to and fro like bolts of lightning.
>
> Now as I looked at the living beings, behold, there was one wheel on the earth beside the living beings, for each of the four of them. The appearance of the wheels and their workmanship was like sparkling beryl, and all four of them had the same form, their appearance and workmanship being as if one wheel were within another. Whenever they moved, they moved in any of their four directions, without turning as they moved. As for their rims they were lofty and awesome, and the rims of all four of them were full of eyes round about. And whenever the living beings moved, the wheels moved with them. And whenever the living beings rose from the earth, the wheels rose also. Wherever the spirit was about to go, they would go in that direction. And the wheels rose close

beside them; for the spirit of the living beings was in the wheels. Whenever those went, these went; and whenever those stood still, these stood still. And whenever those rose from the earth, the wheels rose close beside them; for the spirit of the living beings was in the wheels.

Now over the heads of the living beings there was something like an expanse, like the awesome gleam of crystal, extended over their heads. And under the expanse their wings were stretched out straight, one toward the other; each one also had two wings covering their bodies on the one side and on the other. I also heard the sound of their wings like the sound of abundant waters as they went, like the voice of the Almighty, a sound of tumult like the sound of an army camp; whenever they stood still, they dropped their wings. And there came a voice from above the expanse that was over their heads; whenever they stood still, they dropped their wings.

Now above the expanse that was over their heads there was something resembling a throne, like lapis lazuli in appearance; and on that which resembled a throne, high up, was a figure with the appearance of a man. Then I noticed from the appearance of His loins and upward something like glowing metal that looked like fire all around within it, and from the appearance of His loins and downward I saw something like fire; and there was a radiance around Him. As the appearance of the rainbow in the clouds on a rainy day, so was the appearance of the surrounding radiance. Such was the appearance of the likeness of the glory of the LORD. And when I saw it, I fell on my face.

That is Ezekiel's description of God's throne in heaven. We can't fully understand all he described, and neither did he. But under the inspiration of the Holy Spirit he attempted to describe what he saw: blazing light reflected off polished jewels and colored wheels of light mingled with angelic beings (the "living beings"). Around the throne of the eternal, glorious God, he saw a flashing, sparkling, spinning rainbow of brilliance.

How do we interpret such symbolism? Some strive to find meaning in every facet of Ezekiel's vision. (One source I consulted, for example, explains the faces of the angelic creatures like this: The lion refers to majesty and power; the man represents intelligence and will; the ox stands for patient service, and the eagle speaks of swift judgment.) But we must be cautious not to get carried away reading meaning into symbols that are not explained to us. This is not a secret message to be decoded; it is a large picture designed to display the sovereignty, majesty, and glory of God and the incredible beauty, symmetry, and perfection of His heaven. Although it's impossible to interpret the specifics definitively, we *can* understand that Ezekiel's aim was to put the glory of heaven on display. The wheels that moved in concert, the flashing lightning, the sparkling jewels, and the brilliant light—all picture God's glory.

So although Ezekiel's picture of heaven may be beyond our ability to fathom, we can certainly grasp the main idea: heaven is a realm of inexpressible glory.

JOHN'S APOCALYPSE

John's extended vision of heaven is described throughout the book of Revelation. The Greek word translated "heaven" occurs more than fifty times in the book. Twice God is called "the God of heaven" (11:13; 16:11). The entire book is written from a heavenly perspective, though it deals largely with events that occur on earth.

There are many striking similarities between John's vision and Ezekiel's. John's is a fuller account, of course, but it blends beautifully with what Ezekiel described. In chapter 4, for example, John recounts being caught up into heaven:

> After this I looked, and, behold, a door was opened in heaven: and the first voice which I heard was as it were of a trumpet talking with me; which said, Come up hither, and I will show thee things which must be hereafter. And immediately I was in the spirit: and, behold, a throne was set in heaven, and one sat on the throne. (vv. 1–2 KJV)

Notice that Ezekiel ended his vision of heaven with a description of God's throne and the inexplicable glory of heaven. John *begins* by describing that same throne. Repeatedly in this passage he mentions the throne, which is the center of heaven and the focal point of God's presence. From the throne of God emanates all the glory of heaven.

Verse 3 says, "He who was sitting was like a jasper stone." Jasper is an opaque, translucent crystalline quartz of differing colors, especially shades of green. (But the jasper of ancient times may actually have been a transparent stone.) Verse 3 adds that God was like "a sardius in appearance." Some suggest that the red sardius may speak of God as Redeemer, the one who provided a blood sacrifice—thus stressing the glory of God's redemptive character. Jasper and sardius were also the first and last of the twelve stones on the breastplate of the high priest (Ex. 28:17, 20 KJV).

It's impossible to ignore the fact that both Ezekiel and John are describing a scene of breathtaking glory and dazzling beauty—surpassing the limits of human language. John, like Ezekiel, is painting a big picture that portrays heaven as a realm of inexpressible glory. Again, let's not get so caught up in trying to read meaning into the symbols that we miss that rather obvious point.

Language fails when men try to describe divine glory, so John is using these comparisons to precious jewels to picture the breathtaking beauty of heavenly glory. The jewels he mentions were the most stunning, glorious images he could picture, so he resorts to them to make his point. Remember, though, that he is actually describing a glory that far exceeds that of any jewel. If the scene is hard for you to visualize, that's fine. John is purposely painting a picture of glory that exceeds our ability to imagine.

Sounding much like Ezekiel, John continues, "There was a rainbow around the throne, like an emerald in appearance . . . And from the throne proceed flashes of lightning and sounds and peals of thunder" (vv. 3, 5). Again the imagery is designed to inspire awe and fear. It speaks of an immeasurable glory, power, and majesty.

The thunder and lightning are reminiscent of another scene in Scripture: Mount Sinai, where God came down to give the Law. The Israelites saw the divine glory in the form of thundering and lightning (Ex. 19:16). This language seeks to describe the indescribable. The sense it conveys is an awe that transcends any earthly awe.

John continues his description of the scene around the throne, giving another detail we ought to note carefully: "There were seven lamps of fire burning before the throne, which are the seven Spirits of God" (v. 5).

That verse confuses a lot of people. It does not suggest that there are seven Holy Spirits. The apostle Paul makes that clear in 1 Corinthians 12:4: "There are diversities of gifts, but the same Spirit" (KJV; cf. v. 11)—and in Ephesians 4:4: "There is one body, and *one* Spirit" (KJV, emphasis added; cf. Eph. 2:18). So this cannot be a reference to seven distinct Spirits of God. Obviously, that would violate what Scripture teaches elsewhere about the personality of the Holy Spirit.

The expression "seven spirits" is therefore to be understood as apocalyptic symbolism. John links it to seven lamps, which echo the lampstands of the churches in Revelation 2–3. And those in turn seem to have some relationship to the seven lamps in the original tabernacle (cf. Ex. 25:31–37). These were actually seven candles atop a *single* gold lampstand. The imagery the seven lamps conveys is therefore that of a sevenfold menorah. And the reference to "seven spirits" should be interpreted as a reference to the one, albeit "sevenfold," Spirit of God.

In what sense is the Spirit "sevenfold"? This could be a reference back to the Spirit's sovereignty over the seven churches in chapters 2–3. It could also be a reference to Isaiah 11:2 (KJV), which describes "The spirit of [1] the LORD . . . the spirit of [2] wisdom and [3] understanding, the spirit of [4] counsel and [5] might, the spirit of [6] knowledge and of [7] the fear of the LORD." Whatever it means, it does not suggest that there is more than "one Spirit" by whom we are baptized into the body of Christ (1 Cor. 12:13). That would run counter to the rest of Scripture (cf. also Eph. 2:18; John 14:16–17).

Look again at Revelation 4. Verse 6 says, "Before the throne there was, as it were, a sea of glass like crystal." Picture the beauty of that scene: a brilliant rainbow and the flashing colors of emerald, sardius, and jasper all splashing off a sea of crystal!

Again, all this color, light, and crystal reflect the splendor and majesty of the throne of God. This is familiar imagery in Scripture. In Exodus 24, we read: "Moses went up with Aaron, Nadab and Abihu, and seventy of the elders of Israel, and they saw the God of Israel; and under His feet there appeared to be a pavement of sapphire, as clear as the sky itself" (vv. 9–10). The flashing and sparkling light of God's glory is reflected by the crystal clear, brilliant, sparkling sea of glass. Notice that the crystal sea is described as "pavement of sapphire" in Exodus 24—possibly because of the color reflecting off it. But both passages speak of its extraordinary "clearness." Ezekiel described it as "like the awesome gleam of crystal" (1:22). Again, it pictures heaven as a realm of unimaginable beauty, where every element of everything is designed as a backdrop to reflect the divine glory.

All this emphasis on brightness and clarity suggests that heaven is not a land of shadows and mists. Instead, everything is described in terms of light and brilliance and clarity!

Even when John describes the other inhabitants of heaven, the focus remains on the glory of God. The seats of twenty-four "elders"—no doubt representing the whole body of the redeemed church—encircle the throne (Rev. 4:4). Verse 6 adds that four living creatures also encircled the throne—undoubtedly a reference to angelic creatures, perhaps the cherubim. So surrounding the throne are the angelic host and the church; occupying the throne is God Himself in all the glory of His majestic revelation.

It is significant that the book of Revelation alone mentions the throne of

God at least thirty-nine times. All activity in heaven focuses this direction, and all the furnishings of heaven reflect the glory that emanates from here.

IS THERE A TEMPLE IN HEAVEN OR NOT?

In the ancient world, the two most important buildings of any national capitol were the palace and the temple. They represented civil and spiritual authority. In heaven the centrality of the throne of God emphasizes both His sovereignty and His worthiness to be worshiped. All heaven is His palace, and all heaven is His temple.

In Revelation 3:12 Christ says, "Him that overcometh [in Johannine writings this refers to every true believer] will I make a pillar in the temple of my God, and he shall go no more out" (KJV). In Revelation 7:15 one of the twenty-four elders, speaking of saints who have come out of the Great Tribulation, tells the apostle, "Therefore are they before the throne of God, and serve him day and night in his temple: and he that sitteth on the throne shall dwell among them" (KJV).

In other words, those verses teach that Christians will serve God forever in a heavenly temple. Other passages also speak of a temple in heaven. For example, Revelation 11:19 speaks of "The temple of God which is in heaven" and "the ark of His covenant . . . in His temple." Later John describes "the temple of the tabernacle of the testimony in heaven" (15:5). Those passages make it clear that there is a temple in heaven.

In Revelation 21:22, however, describing New Jerusalem, John writes, "And I saw no temple therein: for the Lord God Almighty and the Lamb are the temple of it" (KJV). Attempting to reconcile Revelation 21:22 with the rest of Revelation, some interpreters argue that presently there *is* a temple in heaven, but when God constructs the new heavens and earth, there *won't be*. That does not seem to capture the most obvious meaning of John's description. The temple in heaven is not a building; it is the Lord God Almighty Himself. Revelation 7:15 implies this when it says, "He who sits on the throne shall spread His tabernacle over them." And Revelation 21:23, continuing the thought of *no temple*, adds, "The city had no need of the sun, neither of the moon, to shine in it: for the glory of God did lighten it, and the Lamb is the light thereof" (KJV).

In other words, the glory of God both illuminates heaven and defines the boundaries of its temple. One might say all heaven is the temple, and the glory and presence of the Lord permeate it. Or, as John writes, "the Lord God Almighty and the Lamb *are* the temple of it" (v. 22 KJV, emphasis added).

A misunderstanding of these verses, unfortunately, has contributed to the notion that heaven is a dull, monotonous place. After all, who wants to be a pillar in a temple we can never leave? (cf. Rev. 3:12). But don't miss the import of what John is saying here. The point is not that we become immovable support posts in a building, but that we enter the very presence of the Lord and never again leave *Him*. Remember, *He* is the temple of which we are pillars. The imagery is tremendously rich, echoing Jesus's promise, "I will come again, and receive you unto myself; that where I am, there ye may be also" (John 14:3 KJV)—and the apostle Paul's great hope, "So shall we ever be with the Lord" (1 Thess. 4:17 KJV). Our place will forever be in the very presence of God.

Bear in mind that both Ezekiel and the apostle John are struggling to describe the indescribable. Even if God had revealed all the details about heaven, we wouldn't be able to know or understand them. It's unlike anything we know. But in Ephesians 2, Paul gives some insight into heaven from a slightly different perspective. Here Paul is describing our utter dependence on God for salvation, saying we were dead in our trespasses and sins (v. 1), by nature children of wrath (v. 3). Then he describes God's mercy and love toward us in saving us from our sins. The thought of God's grace reaching out to save us, when we deserved the opposite, ought to overwhelm us with gratitude and humility.

Now notice what Paul says in Ephesians 2:7: God saved us so "that in the ages to come he might show the exceeding riches of his grace in his kindness toward us through Christ Jesus" (KJV). That verse won't satisfy people curious to understand what heaven *looks* like, but note the vivid description of what heaven will *be* like: it is a place where the riches of God's grace shine even more brightly than they do here on earth. That is what makes me long for heaven most.

Stop and think of it. Every good thing we know here on earth is a product of God's grace (cf. James 1:17). And we who know Christ are going to heaven for this express purpose: so that God can showcase the infinite riches of His grace by showering His goodness on us endlessly. Does that not make your heart prefer the riches of heaven to the meager pleasures of earth?

10

JUST AS GOD HAS FORGIVEN YOU[1]

Forgiving each other, just as God in Christ also has forgiven you.

EPHESIANS 4:32

It was Monday, December 1, 1997. About a dozen students were huddled to pray—as they did every morning—in the hallway outside the administration office at Heath High School, Paducah, Kentucky. Classes would start in a few minutes, so someone closed in prayer.

The final amen still hung in the air. Students had not yet begun to move away to their classes. Suddenly, the sound of gunshots shattered the peace of the moment. A fourteen-year-old freshman had walked up to the group with a .22-caliber automatic pistol and was firing into the prayer circle, calmly shooting students one at a time.

When it was over, three students were dead and five others seriously wounded. The story made headlines for weeks. What was so astonishing was that by all accounts, the students in the prayer circle had done nothing to provoke the boy who did the shooting. In fact, several of them had previously befriended him. The secular media were at a loss to explain how anyone so young could commit such a heinous act of pure evil.

Another aspect of the story also caught the media's eye: the amazing forgiveness immediately extended by the survivors and their loved ones. Many relatives of the victims were interviewed by the press in the days and weeks following the shooting. Despite the utter senselessness of the crime, no one spoke with bitterness or a desire for vengeance. Churches in Paducah, while ministering to the victims and their loved ones, also reached out to the shooter and his family. One of the injured girls was fifteen-year-old Melissa Jenkins. As she lay in the hospital less than a week after the shootings, fully aware the damage to her spinal cord was so severe that she would be a paraplegic for the rest of her life, she nonetheless sent a message through a friend to the boy who had deliberately shot her: "Tell him I forgive him."

How can someone who has been so grievously wounded forgive so freely and so quickly? Apart from Christ it is well nigh impossible. "But we have the mind of Christ" (1 Cor. 2:16). The Holy Spirit indwells and empowers us. Therefore Christians are capable of superhuman acts of forgiveness.

One of the earliest examples of this sort of forgiveness is Stephen, the first martyr. While he was being stoned, with large rocks battering his body, breaking his bones, causing him to bleed and ultimately die—in the midst of all that trauma—he found strength to pray for his killers. Scripture says, "Falling on his knees, he cried out with a loud voice, 'Lord, do not hold this sin against them!' Having said this, he fell asleep" (Acts 7:60). Despite the violence of the moment, his death was so peaceful that Scripture portrays him as simply drifting into a tranquil slumber.

The natural tendency in such situations is to pray for vengeance. In fact, the death of Old Testament prophet Zechariah makes an interesting contrast with that of Stephen. Like Stephen, Zechariah was stoned, but notice the marked difference in his dying prayer:

> So they conspired against him and at the command of the king they stoned him to death in the court of the house of the LORD. Thus Joash the king did not remember the kindness which his father Jehoiada had shown him, but he murdered his son. And as he died he said, "May the Lord see and avenge!" (2 Chronicles 24:21–22)

We cannot fault Zechariah for praying for vengeance. He recognized, of course, that vengeance belonged to God, and he properly left the matter with God. His praying this way should not be regarded as a sin.

In fact, there's a legitimate sense in which all martyrs are entitled to plead for vengeance against their persecutors. Revelation 6:10 gives us a look behind the curtains of the cosmic drama. There we learn that the perpetual cry of the martyrs of all ages is "How long, O Lord, holy and true, will You refrain from judging and avenging our blood on those who dwell on the earth?"

There's certainly no sin in crying for justice like that. God *will* avenge His people, and when His vengeance is finally administered, no one will be able to complain that it is unjust. In fact, we will simply marvel at the longsuffering of God that restrained vengeance for so long.

But for now, in the bright light of the new covenant, while the fullness of divine vengeance is restrained and the gospel is being proclaimed to the world, there's a higher good than vengeance to plead for—forgiveness and reconciliation with those who persecute us. Jesus said, "Love your enemies, do good to those who hate you, bless those who curse you, pray for those who mistreat you" (Luke 6:27–28). Christ Himself gave us the example to follow when He died at the hands of evil men, praying for their forgiveness. Stephen obviously got the message.

What about justice? It is natural, and even right, to want to see justice fulfilled and divine vengeance administered. But for the Christian there is a much higher priority. Justice will come, but in the meantime our thoughts and actions toward others are to be driven by a nobler principle. As Christians, we should be obsessed with forgiveness, not vengeance.

THE VOICE OF THE BLOOD

There's a clear illustration of this in the book of Hebrews. The writer of Hebrews makes repeated references to Abel, Adam's secondborn, who was killed unjustly by his own elder brother. Abel is listed in Hebrews 11 as the first member of the famous "Hall of Faith" found in that chapter. Hebrews 11:4 says this about Abel: "By faith Abel offered unto God a more excellent sacrifice than Cain, by which he obtained witness that he was righteous, God testifying of his gifts: and by it he being dead yet speaketh" (KJV).

That phrase "he being dead yet speaketh" is a familiar one, but have you ever realized what it refers to? It is an allusion to Genesis 4:10, where God said to Cain, "What have you done? The voice of your brother's blood is crying to Me from the ground." Though he was dead, he still spoke, through his innocent blood, crying out for mercy.

Those were figurative terms, of course. Abel's blood did not literally cry out. But the violent and unjust manner of his death—brutal murder at his own brother's wicked hand—fairly screamed for vengeance. Justice needed to be done. A crime had been committed for which severe punishment was in order. Abel's blood, spilled on the ground, was a testimony against Cain. In metaphorical terms, Abel's blood was crying for vengeance.

Abel was the first martyr, and the blood of every martyr since has joined the cry for justice against the persecutors of God's people. In that sense, they *all* still speak, though they are dead. They are the very ones pictured in Revelation 6:10, under the altar, calling for God to glorify Himself in the execution of justice.

But Hebrews 12:24 makes an interesting contrast. There the writer mentions *Jesus'* blood, "which speaks better than the blood of Abel." The meaning is clear: whereas Abel's blood (and the blood of other martyrs) screams for vengeance, Christ's blood pleads for mercy.

Jesus' blood, shed as an atonement for sins, appeals for *forgiveness* on behalf of sinners. This is a remarkable truth. All the blood of all the martyrs of all time cries out for justice and vengeance and retribution. But Christ's blood "speaks better."

Again, there is nothing wrong with desiring justice. It is certainly legitimate to want to see wrongs made right and evildoers recompensed for their wickedness. But the longing for forgiveness is better still. Christians are to be characterized by a desire for mercy, compassion, and forgiveness—even for their enemies.

How do we develop such a state of mind? How can a Christian, badly hurt by the offenses of another, learn to forgive "from [the] heart" the way Jesus commanded (Matt. 18:35)? What about the commands in Scripture to confront those who sin against us? How do we know when to confront, and when to overlook an offense?

Furthermore, how can we forgive those who have not repented? Doesn't God Himself withhold forgiveness from the unrepentant? If we are to forgive in the same way we have been forgiven, don't we first need to require the repentance of the offender?

Those are all excellent questions. Does the Bible offer answers? I believe it does. Let's begin by exploring what Scripture means when it commands us to forgive in the same way God forgives.

GOD'S FORGIVENESS/OUR FORGIVENESS

How can forgiveness between fellow sinners be compared to the forgiveness of an offended deity? There must be some similarities, because Scripture instructs us to forgive in the same manner as we have been forgiven. This idea occurs in two verses, Ephesians 4:32 ("forgiv[e] each other, just as God in Christ also has forgiven you") and Colossians 3:13 ("just as the Lord forgave you").

Some take the position that this teaches forgiveness should always be conditional. Their rationale goes like this: God forgives only those who repent. Therefore, if we are going to forgive in the same manner as we have been forgiven, we should withhold forgiveness from all who are unrepentant. Some fine teachers hold this view. For example, Jay Adams writes,

It should go without saying that since our forgiveness is modeled after God's (Eph. 4:32), it must be conditional. Forgiveness by God rests on clear, unmistakable conditions. The apostles did not merely announce that God had forgiven men . . . Paul and the apostles turned away from those who refused to meet the conditions, just as John and Jesus did earlier when the scribes and the Pharisees would not repent.[2]

There is some merit in Adams's position. There are times when forgiveness *must* be conditional, and we shall discuss that issue before the close of this chapter. I have great respect for Adams and have recommended his book on forgiveness as a helpful study of the subject. On this issue, however, I must disagree with the position he takes.

To make conditionality the gist of Christlike forgiving seems to miss the whole point of what Scripture is saying. When Scripture instructs us to forgive in the manner we have been forgiven, what is in view is not the idea of *withholding* forgiveness until the offender expresses repentance.

Listen carefully to what these verses are saying:

- *Matthew 6:12, 14–15:* "And forgive us our debts, as we forgive our debtors . . . For if ye forgive men their trespasses, your heavenly Father will also forgive you: but if ye forgive not men their trespasses, neither will your Father forgive your trespasses" (KJV).

- *James 2:13:* "For judgment will be merciless to one who has shown no mercy; mercy triumphs over judgment."

- *Matthew 18:35:* "So likewise shall my heavenly Father do also unto you, if ye from your hearts forgive not every one his brother their trespasses" (KJV).

- *Luke 6:36–38:* "Be merciful, just as your Father is merciful. Do not judge, and you will not be judged; and do not condemn, and you will not be condemned; pardon, and you will be pardoned. Give, and it will be given to you. They will pour into your lap a good measure— pressed down, shaken together, and running over. For by your standard of measure it will be measured to you in return" (KJV).

The emphasis is on forgiving freely, generously, willingly, eagerly, speedily— and from the heart. The attitude of the forgiver is where the focus of Scripture lies, not the terms of forgiveness.

Most of those who hold that all forgiveness is conditional portray forgiveness as a formal transaction, where the forgiven one must repent, and the offended party promises in return never to bring up the sin again. If this transaction has not occurred, they say, real forgiveness has not yet taken place. In some cases the offender repents and asks forgiveness without prompting, and forgiveness should be granted on the spot. But in most cases, particularly when the offender is ignorant of having committed a wrong, the offended party must first confront the offender and formally solicit repentance before he or she can forgive. In short, no act of forgiveness can occur until the offender asks for forgiveness.

Sadly, I have seen people who hold this opinion become obsessive confronters and ultimately make themselves odious to friend and foe alike. Others nurse grudges, refuse to relinquish bitterness, and even sever friendships over relatively petty offenses—justifying such attitudes because they are convinced they have no duty to forgive an offender until the offender repents.

While it is often true that forgiveness involves a two-way transaction, it is not true of *all* forgiveness. There are times when forgiveness *should* be unconditional and unilateral, and there are other times when forgiveness must be withheld until the offender repents. The biblical principles governing these different kinds of forgiveness are clear.

CONDITIONAL FORGIVENESS/ UNCONDITIONAL FORGIVENESS

It is obvious from Scripture that sometimes forgiveness must be conditional. In certain cases the offender is to be confronted and ultimately even excommunicated from the church if he or she refuses to repent (Luke 17:3; Matt. 18:17).

But does *every* offense call for confrontation, possibly leading to formal church discipline? Is there no place for simply granting unilateral forgiveness for petty offenses? Is there no time when the offended party should simply overlook a transgression, choosing to suffer wrong—and forgive without being asked or without formally confronting the offender?

Obviously, these questions have important practical ramifications. If you had a friend who scrupulously tried to confront you every time you committed a petty offense, wouldn't the friendship grow tedious pretty quickly? And if marriage partners saw it as their solemn duty to confront each other for every offense, wouldn't such a mind-set make the marriage relationship practically impossible to endure?

It is a mistake to assume that verses like Luke 17:3 ("If your brother sins, rebuke him") and Matthew 18:15 ("If your brother sins, go and show him his fault") are absolute prescriptions for every kind of transgression. If we were obligated to confront one another for every paltry misdeed, we would be doing little else.

Indeed, Scripture gives us another principle for dealing with the vast majority of petty infractions: overlook the offense. Forgive unilaterally, unconditionally. Grant pardon freely and unceremoniously. Love demands this: "Keep fervent in your love for one another, because love covers a multitude of sins" (1 Peter 4:8). "Hatred stirs up strife, but love covers all transgressions" (Prov. 10:12). "He who conceals a transgression seeks love" (Prov. 17:9). Love "does not take into account a wrong suffered . . . [but] bears all things, believes all things, hopes all things, endures all things" (1 Cor. 13:5, 7). The New International Version renders 1 Corinthians 13:5 this way: "[Love] keeps no record of wrongs."

Jay Adams recognizes the Christian's duty to overlook petty offenses, citing some of these same texts. "But," he writes, "it is not . . . forgiveness."[3] Having defined forgiveness as a two-way transaction, he has no room in his system for unilateral or unconditional forgiveness. So he draws a distinction between forgiveness and overlooking another's transgression. If true, that would mean all the petty offenses we choose to overlook (or "cover," in biblical terminology) are not really to be regarded as forgiven.

But the Bible itself makes no such distinction. Covering another's transgression is the very essence of forgiveness. Speaking of God's forgiveness, Psalm 32:1 equates the concepts of forgiveness and the covering of sin: "How blessed is he whose transgression is forgiven, whose sin is covered!" This is a Hebrew parallelism, employing the two different expressions to designate the same concept. To cover someone else's sin is the very essence of forgiveness.

Psalm 85:2 draws the same parallel: "You forgave the iniquity of Your people; You covered all their sin."

James 5:20 also equates forgiveness with the covering of sin: "He who turns a sinner from the error of his way will save his soul from death and will cover a multitude of sins."

Furthermore, Scripture also teaches that forgiveness can be unilateral and unconditional. Mark 11:25–26 clearly speaks of this kind of forgiveness and even makes it a condition for receiving God's forgiveness: "Whenever you stand praying, forgive, if you have anything against anyone, so that your Father who is in heaven will also forgive you your transgressions. But if you do not forgive, neither will your Father who is in heaven forgive your transgressions."

That speaks of a forgiveness granted to the offender with no formal transaction required. It necessarily describes a pardon that is wholly unilateral, because it takes place *while the forgiver stands praying*.[4] "Forgive" is the clear command of that verse, and it is to take place on the spot. There is no mention of confrontation. There is no command to seek the offender's repentance. The forgiveness of Mark 11:25 is therefore different from the forgiveness of Luke 17:3. *This* forgiveness is to be granted unconditionally and unilaterally.

UNCONDITIONAL FORGIVENESS:
WHAT DOES IT MEAN?

What does unilateral forgiveness entail? If there's no transaction, no seeking of forgiveness, no formal granting of pardon, no words exchanged between the two parties—then what, exactly, is accomplished by this sort of forgiveness?

Its chief effects are wrought in the heart of the forgiver. This kind of forgiveness involves a deliberate decision to cover the other person's offense. "Forgive" in Mark 11:25 is an imperative, a command. The forgiveness called for here is necessarily a volitional matter. In other words, it is a choice, not a feeling or an involuntary response.

It is, as Matthew 18:35 suggests, *from the heart*—but even that does not place forgiveness primarily in the realm of feeling. "Heart" in Scripture normally designates the seat of the intellect (cf. Prov. 23:7; Luke 9:47). So this speaks of a deliberate and rational decision. It is a choice made by the offended party to set aside the other person's transgression and not permit the offense to cause a breach in the relationship.

In effect, the person who chooses to forgive resolves not to remember the offense, refuses to hold a grudge, relinquishes any claim on recompense, and resists the temptation to brood or retaliate. The offended party simply bears the insult. The offense is set aside, lovingly covered for Christ's sake. For petty and unintentional offenses, this is the proper and loving way to forgive—unilaterally, without confrontation and without stirring any strife.

This, I believe, is what Scripture refers to most often when it calls us to forgive one another. The heavy emphasis on forgiveness in Scripture is not meant to make us more confrontational, but quite the opposite. When Scripture calls us to have an attitude of forgiveness, the emphasis is always on long-suffering, patience, benevolence, forbearance, kindness, and mercy—not confrontation.

To deny that forgiveness can ever be unilateral is in my view a potentially serious mistake. It places too much stress on confrontation. And that tends to produce more conflict than it avoids. People who insist on confronting every wrong often simply stir strife—the antithesis of what Jesus' teaching on forgiveness was intended to produce. Real love should *cover* the vast majority of transgressions, not constantly haul them out in the open for dissection (1 Peter 4:8).

TO CONFRONT, OR NOT TO CONFRONT?

All of this calls for some careful distinctions. Obviously there *are* times when confrontation is essential. How do we identify those situations? Are there clear biblical principles that teach us when to confront, and when to forgive unilaterally?

I believe there are. Here are some guidelines to help you in drawing the distinction:

Wherever possible, especially if the offense is petty or unintentional, it is best to forgive unilaterally. This is the very essence of a gracious spirit. It is the Christlike attitude called for in Ephesians 4:1–3: "Therefore I, the prisoner of the Lord, implore you to walk in a manner worthy of the calling with which you have been called, with all humility and gentleness, with patience, showing tolerance for one another in love, being diligent to preserve the unity of the Spirit in the bond of peace."

That calls for a gracious forbearance ("tolerance") of others' faults. This is necessary for the sake of maintaining peace.

In other words, believers are supposed to have a sort of mutual immunity to petty offenses. Love "is not easily provoked" (1 Cor. 13:5 KJV). If *every* fault required formal confrontation, the whole of our church life would be spent confronting and resolving conflicts over petty annoyances. So for the sake of peace and to preserve the unity of the Spirit, we are to show tolerance wherever possible.

This, then, is the governing rule: unless there is some reason an offense *requires* confrontation, unconditional, unilateral forgiveness should cover the transgression. The offended party, in suffering the offense, is following in the footsteps of Christ (1 Peter 2:21–25).

If you are the only injured party, even if the offense was public and flagrant, you may choose to forgive unilaterally. Examples of this abound in Scripture. Joseph, for example, was the victim of a grievous wrong at the hands of his brothers. They plotted to kill him, then sold him into slavery.

But he held no grudge. Years later, when famine drove the wicked brothers to Egypt in search of food, Joseph recognized them and freely forgave them, even without any expression of repentance on their part. Before they even realized who he was, he was moved to tears with compassion for them. Finally revealing his true identity to them, he said, "I am your brother Joseph, whom you sold into Egypt. Now do not be grieved or angry with yourselves, because you sold me here, for God sent me before you to preserve life" (Gen. 45:4–5). His forgiveness was unconditional, unilateral, not predicated on any expression of remorse from them.

In fact, as far as we know from Scripture, the closest these brothers ever came to formally declaring their repentance was after Jacob died. Now that their father was no longer there to stay Joseph's hand, they imagined their offended brother might unleash vengeance against them. The brothers, knowing the gravity of their sin, were evidently unable to believe his charity toward them was well meant. They feared he might still secretly harbor a wish for vengeance. So they told Joseph that it was *their father's* wish that he grant them forgiveness (Gen. 50:16–17). They did not formally admit their wrong and express repentance, though it is quite clear that they were humbled men by now.

But all their pleading was wholly unnecessary. Joseph had forgiven them long before. Having seen undeniable evidence that the hand of divine Providence was working good in his life through the evil that was done to him, Joseph had long since forgiven his brothers fully, freely, and unconditionally. His perspective? "You meant evil against me, but God meant it for good" (Gen. 50:20). The knowledge that God had a good purpose in his sufferings made it impossible for Joseph to harbor a grudge.

There are other examples of unilateral forgiveness in Scripture, even when the offense was public and pronounced. For example, on at least one significant occasion, David unilaterally and unconditionally forgave the most humiliating kind of public insult.

It occurred during Absalom's rebellion against David. David was forced to flee Jerusalem so that his defiant son would not destroy the city in his zeal to overthrow David's throne. During that agonizing and painful exodus from Jerusalem, a worthless character named Shimei publicly taunted the already heartbroken David, trying to humiliate him further. Second Samuel 16:5–8 records what happened:

[Shimei] came out cursing continually as he came. He threw stones at David and at all the servants of King David; and all the people and all the mighty men were at his right hand and at his left. Thus Shimei said when he cursed, "Get out, get out, you man of bloodshed, and worthless fellow! The LORD has returned upon you all the bloodshed of the house of

Saul, in whose place you have reigned; and the LORD has given the kingdom into the hand of your son Absalom. And behold, you are taken in
your own evil, for you are a man of bloodshed!

Abishai, one of David's companions, wanted justice on the spot: "Why should
this dead dog curse my lord the king? Let me go over now and cut off his head"
(v. 9).

But David's response was a godly forbearance:

If he curses, and if the LORD has told him, "Curse David," then who shall
say, "Why have you done so?" . . . Behold, my son who came out from
me seeks my life; how much more now this Benjamite? Let him alone and
let him curse, for the LORD has told him. Perhaps the LORD will look on
my affliction and return good to me instead of his cursing this day. (vv.
10–12)

Even though Shimei continued to run along the hillside next to David, cursing
and throwing rocks and dirt at the king, David bore the insults with grace and
forbearance—even though under the circumstances it would have been perfectly appropriate for David, a sitting king, to demand that he be punished.

Later, after David was victorious over the rebels, Shimei made a show of
remorse, begging David's mercy. David, still over the protest of his men, reaffirmed his forgiveness to Shimei (2 Sam. 19:18–23). Having already forgiven the
initial offense unilaterally, David now forgave Shimei formally.

Stephen's prayers for those who stoned him are another example of unilateral, unconditional forgiveness. The fact that Stephen prayed for God's mercy for
his murderers shows that he had already forgiven them in his own heart. It is true
that *God's* forgiveness was not to be granted apart from their repentance, but
Stephen himself had already made that deliberate, conscious choice to relinquish
the right to retribution. He had forgiven them in his heart.

This brings up an important point. Even after we have forgiven offenders for
their transgressions against us, God Himself may exact justice for their sins
against *Him*. We can forgive an offense against us. But we cannot grant forgiveness for a sin against God. "Who can forgive sins, but God alone?" (Luke 5:21).
To forgive someone is not to convey some priestly absolution, clearing him of sin
before God. Those whom we forgive must still give account to God.

For example, Stephen's forgiving his killers did not assure that their sins
would go unpunished if they did not also seek *God's* forgiveness. In the case of

Saul of Tarsus (who stood by the garments of Stephen's killers—consenting to the martyr's death—Acts 7:58; 8:1), his offense was completely blotted out when he fully repented. We are never told what became of those who threw the stones, but if they never embraced Christ as Lord and Savior, they will suffer the wrath of God for the sin of killing Stephen. Stephen forgave the offense against Him; the sin against God still must be reckoned with.

Shimei is another case in point. David kept his promise not to kill Shimei, but Shimei remained an unregenerate and worthless man to the end of his life. Knowing this, on his deathbed, David instructed Solomon how to deal with Shimei: "Do not let him go unpunished, for you are a wise man; and you will know what you ought to do to him, and you will bring his gray hair down to Sheol with blood" (1 Kings 2:9).

This is a difficult command to explain, until you realize that David, as the divinely appointed king, was responsible to see that God's glory was not besmirched in Israel. He had kept his promise to Shimei: he did not kill him for his insult. As far as David was concerned, the personal offense against him was forgiven. But Shimei's act also involved the most wretched kind of blasphemy against God. And since Shimei remained in wanton rebellion against God, divine justice still had a claim on him. For the sake of the nation's purity, this needed to be dealt with. It was now time for the account to be settled—for the sake of *God's* glory, not David's. David could overlook a personal transgression against him; he could not ultimately overlook a public act of overt hostility to God. As Puritan commentator Matthew Henry wrote, David's instructions to Solomon "proceeded not from personal revenge, but a prudent zeal for the honour of the government and the covenant God had made with his family, the contempt of which ought not to go unpunished."[5] Surely that is why David waited until he was on his deathbed to order that Shimei be punished. This way, no one could say that David did it to preserve his own honor.

And Solomon, wisely, honored David's forgiveness of Shimei's insult. Instead of summarily executing him for that past offense, Solomon imposed a restriction on Shimei, forbidding him ever to set foot outside the city of Jerusalem. As long as he stayed in the city, under the king's supervision, he could move about freely in perfect safety. But the day he set foot across the Kidron Valley, he would be killed. Shimei agreed to the terms, which were gracious (1 Kings 2:36–38). But because he was a wicked man, Shimei broke his word. He left the city in search of some runaway slaves, and when Solomon found out, he summoned him and said,

Did I not make you swear by the LORD and solemnly warn you, saying, "You will know for certain that on the day you depart and go anywhere, you shall surely die"? And you said to me, "The word which I have heard is good." Why then have you not kept the oath of the LORD, and the command which I have laid on you? . . . You know all the evil which you acknowledge in your heart, which you did to my father David; therefore *the LORD* shall return your evil on your own head. (vv. 42–44, emphasis added)

In other words, Shimei's death was the Lord's, *not David's,* reprisal for Shimei's sin. David forgave the man and kept his promise not to retaliate. But in the end, given Shimei's refusal to repent, God Himself demanded justice.

Our forgiving an offense does not guarantee that the offender will receive judicial forgiveness from God. God, who knows the heart, always judges righteously. Our part is to be gracious, and bear the wrong, and pray for the offender's full repentance. God Himself will see to it that justice is done if the offender fails to seek divine forgiveness.

WHEN UNCONDITIONAL FORGIVENESS IS NOT AN OPTION

There are times when it is necessary to confront an offender. In such cases, unconditional forgiveness is not an option. These generally involve more serious sins, not petty or picayune complaints, but soul-threatening sins or transgressions that endanger the fellowship of saints. In such situations Luke 17:3 applies: "If your brother sins, rebuke him; and if he repents, forgive him." And in such cases, if a brother or sister in Christ refuses to repent, the discipline process outlined in Matthew 18 applies.

Here are some guidelines for determining when such confrontation is necessary:

If you observe an offense that is a sin against someone other than you, you must confront. Justice does not permit a Christian to cover a sin against someone else. I can unilaterally and unconditionally forgive a personal offense when I am the victim, because it is I who then bears the wrong. But when I see that someone else has been sinned against, it is my duty to seek justice. (The only exception to this would be when the offended person himself chooses to ignore a personal slight or insult. This was the case when David forbade Abishai to wreak vengeance against Shimei.)

While we are entitled, and even encouraged, to overlook wrongs committed against us, Scripture everywhere forbids us to overlook wrongs committed against another:

- *Exodus 23:6:* "You shall not pervert the justice due to your needy brother in his dispute."

- *Deuteronomy 16:20:* "Justice, and only justice, you shall pursue."

- *Isaiah 1:17:* "Learn to do good; seek justice, reprove the ruthless, defend the orphan, plead for the widow."

- *Isaiah 59:15–16:* "Yes, truth is lacking; and he who turns aside from evil makes himself a prey. Now the LORD saw, and it was displeasing in His sight that there was no justice. And He saw that there was no man, and was astonished that there was no one to intercede."

- *Jeremiah 22:3:* "Thus says the LORD, 'Do justice and righteousness, and deliver the one who has been robbed from the power of his oppressor. Also do not mistreat or do violence to the stranger, the orphan, or the widow; and do not shed innocent blood in this place.'"

- *Lamentations 3:35–36:* "To deprive a man of justice in the presence of the Most High, to defraud a man in his lawsuit—of these things the Lord does not approve."

It is not our prerogative to "forgive" someone for an offense against another. Therefore, those who witness such an offense have a duty to confront the offender with his or her transgression.

When ignoring an offense might be hurtful to the offender, confrontation is required. Sometimes choosing to overlook an offense might actually injure the offender. In such cases it is our duty to confront in love.

Galatians 6:1–2 says, "Brethren, if a man be overtaken in a fault, ye which are spiritual, restore such a one in the spirit of meekness; considering thyself, lest thou also be tempted. Bear ye one another's burdens, and so fulfil the law of Christ" (KJV).

The word translated "overtaken" in that passage literally means "caught." It can signify two things. It might mean that the person was discovered in some secret transgression. Or it could mean that the person is ensnared in some sinful habit. Either way, confrontation is necessary. Overlooking the sin is not an option. Love for the sinning brother requires that you confront and seek to restore. This is an essential part of bearing one another's burdens (v. 2).

Sins that require confrontation because of their potential for harm to the sinning person include serious doctrinal error, moral failure, repeated instances of the same offense, sinful habits or destructive tendencies, or any other transgression that poses a serious danger to the offender's spiritual well-being.

In all such cases, confrontation should be motivated by love and a desire for the offender's good. Such confrontation should never be used to gratify a thirst for personal vengeance, punish the offender, or fulfill any other self-aggrandizing purposes. That is why Galatians 6:1 expressly says those "who are spiritual" should deal with the sinning individual.

Ironically, these are the circumstances in which confrontation is the hardest. We are easily tempted to confront the sins we should overlook and overlook the ones we should confront. But whether the situation calls for forbearance or confrontation, the primary motivation should always be love for the offender.

When a sin is scandalous or otherwise potentially damaging to the body of Christ, confrontation is essential. Some sins have the potential to defile many people. Hebrews 12:15 warns of such dangers: "See to it that no one comes short of the grace of God; that no root of bitterness springing up causes trouble, and by it many be defiled."

The responsibility is incumbent on every member of the body not only to stimulate one another to love and good deeds (Heb. 10:24), but also to exhort one another, so that no one becomes hardened through the deceitfulness of sin (Heb. 3:13).

The apostle Paul rebuked the Corinthians for their failure to confront and deal with scandalous sin among the flock. One of their members was having sexual relations with "his father's wife" (1 Cor. 5:1)—probably his stepmother, but the sin carried such a stigma in the culture that it was tantamount to incest. Such sins did "not exist even among the Gentiles." So even the rankest pagans in Corinth were scandalized by the sin in that church.

Paul rebuked them: "Ye are puffed up, and have not rather mourned" (v. 2 KJV). "Puffed up" is from a Greek expression that literally means "inflated." It bespeaks pride. Perhaps, as is true of many today, their pride was in their tolerance. They may have been boasting in the very fact that they were not so "narrow-minded" as to make an issue out of this man's misdeeds.

Paul rebuked them harshly: "Your boasting is not good. Do you not know that a little leaven leavens the whole lump of dough?" (v. 6). He ordered them to excommunicate the offender, who, he said, needed to be "removed from your midst" (v. 2):

> I, on my part, though absent in body but present in spirit, have already judged him who has so committed this, as though I were present. In the name of our Lord Jesus, when you are assembled, and I with you in spirit, with the power of our Lord Jesus, I have decided to deliver such a one to Satan for the destruction of his flesh, so that his spirit may be saved in the day of the Lord Jesus. (vv. 3–5)

Open sin is *always* a scandal in the church and must be dealt with. It is not our prerogative to "forgive" those intent on living lives of flagrant disobedience. The entire church suffers when this sort of sin is permitted to exist. The sin is like leaven, working its way through a lump of dough. Covering such sins, overlooking the evil, is *never* the right thing in such situations. This sort of sin must be rebuked, and Matthew 18 describes the process by which this is to be done.

Any time an offense results in a broken relationship, formal forgiveness is an essential step toward reconciliation. Any sort of offense that causes a breach in relationships simply cannot be overlooked. Both the offense and the breach must be confronted, and reconciliation must be sought.

Reconciliation is always the goal when we confront someone about a wrong done. Once again, if your confronting aims at punishing the offender, or if it is simply a means of castigation and censure, then you are confronting with the wrong aim in mind. The goal of all righteous confrontation is the repair of a broken relationship and the restoration of the offender.

Whenever there is a broken relationship between Christians, *both* parties have a responsibility to seek reconciliation. If you are the offended party, Luke 17:3 applies: "If your brother sins, rebuke him." You are the one who must go to him. If you are the offender, Matthew 5:23–24 applies: "If you are presenting your offering at the altar, and there remember that your brother has something against you, leave your offering there before the altar and go; first be reconciled to your brother, and then come and present your offering."

A rift in the relationship between Christians rules out the possibility of the kind of forgiveness that simply overlooks a fault. Whether harsh words have been exchanged or an icy silence prevails, if both sides know that a breach exists, the only way to resolve matters is by the formal granting of forgiveness. Sometimes the wrong is one-sided. Other times it involves admission of wrong and the seeking of forgiveness on both sides.

In any case, reconciliation is essential. If you have committed the offense, it is sinful not to make it right. If you are the offended party, you also have a duty to seek reconciliation—to try to win your brother. There is never any excuse for a Christian on either side of a broken relationship to refuse to pursue reconciliation. The only instance where such a conflict should remain unresolved is if all the steps of discipline in Matthew 18 have been exhausted and the guilty party still refuses to repent.

Furthermore, if you are the guilty party, you have a responsibility to pursue reconciliation *quickly.* This is repeatedly emphasized in Scripture. For example, Matthew 5:23–24 (cited previously) suggests that if you are in the middle of an act of worship and then you remember that you have offended a brother, you are to leave your gift at the altar, and *first* be reconciled to your brother. The reconciliation of a broken relationship takes precedence in such a case over worship!

That makes reconciliation a very high priority indeed, for reconciliation even takes precedence over worship offered to the Lord. My book on the subject of worship was titled *The Ultimate Priority,* because worship is normally the supreme priority in the Christian's life. But there is this one exception: when you know you have offended a brother or sister. And then the first priority is the reconciling of the broken relationship.

Matthew 5 continues: "Make friends quickly with your opponent at law while you are with him on the way, so that your opponent may not hand you over to the judge, and the judge to the officer, and you be thrown into prison. Truly I say to you, you will not come out of there until you have paid up the last cent" (vv. 25–26).

In such cases, especially if you have committed a wrong, your duty is to seek reconciliation without delay. Those who delay or impede the reconciliation process will reap additional punishment. The allusion is to divine chastisement, and the verse implies that God Himself will enforce the penalty due those who defer such an urgent duty.

SUFFERING WRONG RATHER THAN CAUSING REPROACH

The presumption in Matthew 5 seems to be that the party who is being handed over to the judge is the guilty party. Since he has committed the wrong, it is therefore incumbent on him more than anyone else to seek to remedy the wrong speedily.

But sometimes it may be even appropriate for the one who has been wronged simply to suffer the wrong, especially if necessary to avoid the dishonor of bringing a dispute before a secular court.

In the church at Corinth, for example, there were believers who, refusing to settle their differences among themselves, were suing one another in pagan courts (1 Cor. 6:1). Paul reminded them that it is better to suffer wrong or be defrauded than to bring a lawsuit against another believer before a pagan judge.

Sadly, I have known of several Christians who were willing to violate that clear command. They always seem convinced that somehow *their* case is the exception to Paul's rule. Give them a chance to explain why they feel they are within their rights to sue a fellow Christian, and inevitably they will explain how they are about to be wronged through some great injustice that only a court can remedy. Surely God does not countenance such gross injustices, they typically plead. He cannot wish that *this* wrong be overlooked, and so on.

Yet Paul *recognizes* that the other person may be wrong. He plainly says it is better to be defrauded than to sue another Christian (1 Cor. 6:7). Lawsuits where a Christian takes another Christian before a secular judge are *never* justifiable.

But what if the offender stubbornly and deliberately refuses to acknowledge the wrong? The church should act as an arbiter, rather than a secular court. Ultimately in such cases, the church may need to institute discipline against the offending member (1 Cor. 6:2).

I'm convinced that if church discipline were more consistently practiced, there would be fewer such conflicts between Christians, and genuine love and harmony would prevail more in the church.

An appalling number of churches refuse to obey the biblical instructions to discipline sinning members. What should someone do who has exhausted every avenue of appeal in the church and still feels an injustice has been done? In such cases, 1 Corinthians 6:7 applies: suffer the wrong for the sake of Christ. If the church you attend is wantonly disobeying Christ's clear instructions about how to deal with sin in the fellowship, you may also need to seek a church where Scripture is more faithfully obeyed.

But some injustices will never be made right this side of eternity. It is clear that the Christian's duty in such cases is to suffer the wrong gracefully, magnanimously, and willingly for the sake of Christ. God Himself will ultimately right all such wrongs. Meanwhile, we must refuse to harbor a grudge. We must never allow a spirit of resentment to stain our character. We must seek to be like Joseph, willing to see the hand of God working good, even in the most unjust circumstances.

WHEN IT IS HARD TO FORGIVE

Such an attitude certainly does not come naturally to the fallen creature. We tend to be driven by too much by our feelings. Those who indulge themselves in bitter feelings will find forgiveness does not easily germinate in such soil. Instead, the root that springs up is a defiling influence. It is hurtful not only to the bitter person, but also to many others as well (Heb. 12:15).

Forgiveness is often frustrated by negative emotions, lingering resentment, and unquenched anger. Some imagine, wrongly, that they *cannot* forgive if they do not "feel" like forgiving.

But as we already noted briefly, forgiveness is not a feeling. Those who insist on being driven by passion will find forgiveness very hard indeed, because forgiveness often involves a deliberate choice that runs contrary to our feelings. Bitter emotions incline us to dwell on an offense. Forgiveness is a voluntary, rational decision to set the offense aside.

"But I cannot do that," someone says. "I *try* to set it aside, but everywhere I go, something reminds me, and I find myself thinking about it, getting upset all over again."

Such thoughts are temptations to sin. Brooding over an offense is no less a sin than lust, or covetousness, or any other kind of heart-sin. A willful choice must be made to turn away from that kind of thinking. Instead we must deliberately cover the offense and refuse to succumb to angry and vengeful thinking—whether we feel like it or not.

Those who forgive even when it's hard invariably find that the proper emotions will follow. "Love your enemies, do good to those who hate you, bless those who curse you, pray for those who mistreat you" (Luke 6:27–28)— those are all willful, deliberate, rational acts, not reflex emotions. Obey Christ's commands to do such things and your anger will eventually give way to meekness; frustration will be overcome by peace; and anxiety will succumb to calm.

Forgiveness results in the lifting of many burdens. To grant someone forgiveness when he or she repents is to lift the burden of guilt from that person. But to forgive, even when forgiveness is unilateral and unconditional, liberates the forgiver to enjoy the even greater mercies given in return by a generous heavenly Father who promises to pour into our laps "a good measure—pressed down, shaken together, and running over" (Luke 6:38).

11

SHADE FOR OUR CHILDREN[1]

Bring them up in the nurture and admonition of the Lord.
EPHESIANS 6:4 (KJV)

An old Chinese proverb says, "One generation plants the trees and another gets the shade." Our generation lives in the shade of many trees that were planted by our ancestors.

In spiritual terms, we derive shade from our parents' and grandparents' ethical standards, their perceptions of right and wrong, their sense of moral duty, and above all, their spiritual commitment. Their ideals determined the kind of civilization we inherited from them, and our generation's ideals will likewise shape tomorrow's culture for our kids.

There's no question that society as a whole is in a serious state of moral and spiritual decline. So the question that faces Christian parents today is whether we can plant some trees that will shade future generations from what may well be the blistering heat of anti-Christian values in an anti-Christian world. Are we planting the right kind of shade trees, or are we leaving our children totally exposed?

THE DEMISE OF MODERN SOCIETY

It should be obvious to anyone who has any commitment to the truth of Scripture that our culture as a whole is rapidly disintegrating morally, ethically, and above all spiritually. The values now embraced by society as a whole are badly out of sync with God's divine order.

For example, the American court system sanctions the wholesale massacring of millions of unborn children annually, but a court in Kansas City recently sentenced one woman to four months in jail for killing a litter of unwanted kittens.[2]

A court in Janesville, Wisconsin, sentenced a man to twelve years in prison for killing five cats "to relieve stress."[3] The case was indeed a heinous example of cruelty to animals. But two days after that man began serving his twelve-year prison sentence, a Delaware court sentenced a woman to only thirty months in prison for killing her newborn infant. The woman had tossed the newborn child out a third-floor motel-room window into garbage bins in the alley below, umbilical cord still attached. Evidence showed the baby was alive when thrown out the window but died of exposure, abandonment, and massive skull fractures.[4]

It is clear that our society as a whole no longer believes humans are made in the image of God, very different from animals.

In fact, the increasing popularity of the animal-rights lobby perfectly illustrates how far our society has moved from the moorings of biblical principles. Even while this movement continues to gain unprecedented popularity, it grows more and more radical, and more and more outspoken against the biblical view of humanity. Ingrid Newkirk, founder of People for the Ethical Treatment of Animals (PETA), says, "There is no rational basis for saying that a human being has special rights. When it comes to having a central nervous system, and the ability to feel pain, hunger, and thirst, a rat is a pig is a dog is a boy."[5] Newkirk sees no difference between the atrocities of World War II and killing animals for food: "Six million Jews died in concentration camps, but six *billion* broiler chickens will die this year in slaughterhouses."[6]

Such ideas are gaining widespread approval in mainstream society. Some of our culture's best-known and most-respected celebrities parrot similar thoughts, usually under the guise of compassion. But such a skewed perspective of "kindness" to animals quickly becomes wanton unkindness to creatures made in God's image. The inevitable impact such thinking will have on the legacy today's parents leave the next generation is hinted at in a remark made by Michael Fox, vice president of the Humane Society of the United States. He says, "The life of an ant and the life of my child should be granted equal consideration."[7] What kind of values will our children's culture have?

Society is full of similar frightening trends. The future is unthinkable for a society without any absolute moral standard by which to determine right and wrong. Already we are willing to sentence people to prison for killing animals while encouraging abortionists to kill children.

Where is our culture going? What kind of value system, what kind of morality, what kind of world are we establishing for the next generation?

And as Christians, are we planting any shade trees for our children? Or are we leaving them totally exposed?

THE DEMISE OF THE FAMILY

We may be watching the death of the germ cell of all civilization, the family. Signs of the family's demise are abundantly clear all around us. Numerous facts confirm the grim prognosis. There's almost no need to cite statistics. For the past forty years or more the signs of the family's collapse have been paraded before us continually: divorce, the sexual revolution, abortion, sterilization, delinquency, infidelity, homosexuality, radical feminism, the "children's rights" movement, together with the normalization of the single-parent home, the decline of the nuclear family, and other similar signs. We have been watching the braiding of an intricate rope that will ultimately strangle the family.

To be perfectly frank, there has been a growing effort for more than a quarter of a century to carve out the tombstone for the family. In his 1971 book, *The Death of the Family*,[8] British psychiatrist Dr. David Cooper suggested that it is time to do away with the family completely. A similar suggestion was made in Kate Millet's 1970 feminist manifesto, *Sexual Politics*.[9] She claimed that families, along with all patriarchal structures, must go because they are nothing more than tools for the oppression and enslavement of women.

Most of the people touting such perspectives are aggressive, angry, and determined to impose their agendas on the rest of society. The most fertile ground for the propagation of such viewpoints is the university campus. Consequently, the proponents of antifamily social engineering are busily reeducating the young people who will soon be the main leaders of society—and the parents of a generation that will probably be even more dysfunctional than the current one.

This sort of indoctrination has been going on for many years, so that some of the most influential people already shaping modern society at the highest levels—from government leaders to those who make network television's programming decisions—are some of the most virulent and outspoken enemies of the traditional family.

Hillary Rodham Clinton, for example, would like to hand over to the federal government some of the rights and responsibilities of child rearing. Mrs. Clinton's book *It Takes a Village*[10] was written to set forth an agenda that would move America closer to state-sponsored parenting. Although she gives lip service to the importance of the parents' and grandparents' roles, she clearly believes that parents should not be permitted to train their own children unsupervised by the secular government. She also suggests that a more socialist approach to parenting should be the new norm—including state-sponsored day-care centers and full-day preschools for children as young as three. It appears that the "village"

Mrs. Clinton envisions is a morass of federally funded programs designed to indoctrinate children with whatever values the state deems acceptable. And if anything has been made clear over the past half century, it is that biblical values are certainly *not* deemed acceptable in any government-sponsored program in America. Therefore Mrs. Clinton's "village" would no doubt indoctrinate children with secular humanism instead.

Other voices are calling for even more radical measures against the traditional family. Ti-Grace Atkinson, former president of the New York chapter of the National Organization for Women, says she would like to eliminate all sex, marriage, motherhood, and love. "Marriage is legalized servitude," she says, "and family relations are the basis for all human oppression."[11]

Gore Vidal, best-selling author and social critic, agrees. He proposes reorganizing society to eliminate the family as we now know it. Instead, he would like to see a central "Authority" with the power to control human population, food distribution, and the use of natural resources.[12]

IS IT TOO LATE TO SAVE THE FAMILY?

Fortunately, the voices calling for such Orwellian alternatives to the family are still in the minority. Even secular sociologists for the most part regard the decline of the family as an unmitigated disaster. Most agree that the family is a crucial building block for civilized society, and they freely admit that if the family does not survive—and thrive—as an institution, the demise of society itself cannot be far behind.

Consequently, in virtually every public forum these days, we're beginning to hear knowledgeable people talk about the need to shore up the family. Sociologists, psychologists, analysts, so-called marriage and family experts, and all the rest are scrambling to come up with solutions for what ails the family. I'm speaking now about secular, non-Christian voices, yet they are expressing concern about the number of families that are breaking up and the inevitable negative effect this has on society. They note with concern the increasing numbers of "latchkey children"—kids who come home daily to unsupervised, parentless homes. They express fears about the dramatic rise in serious crimes committed by young children. They are cautioning us that parental permissiveness, relaxed moral standards, and other liberalizing social influences have already resulted in the demise of many families and some whole communities. And if not corrected, these problems will destroy society as we know it.

Anyone can see that most of these problems are directly related to the breakdown of values once nurtured in the family. It has become painfully obvious that most such ills are not merely social problems, requiring public sector solutions; but they are first of all *family* problems, whose solutions depend on the rescue of the family as an institution.

The problem is that society as a whole has already rejected the biblical values that are necessary for the recovery and preservation of the family. The term "family values" is a scorned and much-abused phrase, derided by some as a propaganda tool, hijacked by others who advocate values that are absolutely detrimental to the family.

But the truth is, the only real "values" that can save the family are rooted in Scripture—they are *biblical* values, not just *family* values. Therefore the future of the family in our society hinges on the success of those who are committed to the truth of Scripture. Various secular experts have been proposing their humanistic "solutions" to society's problems for years, with virtually no impact. The secular experts will never uncover any solution outside Scripture that will heal those woes. No such solution exists.

Meanwhile, as human relationships continue to deteriorate within families, the very fabric of society is being torn apart. (Watch any random episode of *The Jerry Springer Show,* and you're likely to see troubling evidence that this is the case.) Conversely, if society is to grow stronger, the turnaround must begin in our families.

Unfortunately, society itself may pose the biggest obstacle to the reform of the family. Consider the following antifamily values our culture has already canonized. All of these are fairly new developments within the past half-century:

- All taboos have been abolished and replaced with one new taboo:

  No one is permitted to believe that absolute moral standards, instituted by God, revealed in the Bible, should govern all human behavior.

- Divorce is available on demand for any reason, or for no reason at all.

- Since gender differences are supposed to be downplayed and eliminated as much as possible, it's now improper to speak of "headship" in the family as a masculine responsibility.

- Married women with children are encouraged to work outside the home.

- Entertainment, and television in particular, dominates home life.

- Killing a baby seal for fur is criminal; yet killing unborn human infants for any reason whatsoever is defended as a matter of free, personal choice.

- Pornography of the most debauched sort is protected in America under the First Amendment; yet teaching children in public schools that sexual promiscuity is immoral is prohibited as a violation of the Constitution.

Can a society committed to such values save its own failing families? Not much common sense is needed to see that the seeds of the family's destruction are built right into the moral values our culture has embraced over the past generation. It would seem obvious that unless society itself is impacted by the kind of sweeping revival early America experienced during the first Great Awakening, the future for of the family as an institution in this culture is in serious trouble.

WHERE IS THE CHURCH IN ALL OF THIS?

I'm certainly not suggesting that the family might be saved by moral reform in a secular culture. This is not a rallying cry for Christians to be more aggressive in pursuing political action. Far too many of the church's efforts in recent years have been squandered trying to confront antifamily trends such as abortion and homosexuality through legislative efforts alone. Reform is no answer for a culture like ours. *Redemption* is what is needed—and that occurs at the individual, not the societal, level. The church needs to get back to the real task to which we are called: evangelizing the lost. Only when multitudes of individuals in our society turn to Christ will society itself experience any significant transformation.

Meanwhile, Christian families have an obligation to plant shade trees for future generations of children. But, frankly, even in the church, the family's condition looks pretty bleak.

Not that there aren't positive signs. For nearly three decades there has been a tremendous preoccupation among evangelicals with the need to rescue the family. Christian bookstores are well stocked with books on marriage and the family. Christian radio is also crowded with family-oriented programming. For more than two decades running, the most popular Christian broadcast (by far) has been *Focus on the Family.* There is no shortage of Christian programs, seminars, and ministries devoted to the family and parenting.

But despite all the ink and airtime such ministries have devoted to the subjects of parenting and the family, statistics still show that in general, Christian families are not in much better shape than the families of their non-Christian neighbors. According to some pollsters, the divorce rate among evangelicals may actually be a few percentage points *higher* than in the world at large. The percentage of single-parent families is already higher in the church than in the world. Children from Christian families are not immune to the lure of drugs, gangs, promiscuous sex, and all the other evils plaguing the youth of today. By and large, Christian families are suffering from all the same woes as non-Christian families.

Something is clearly wrong.

Part of the problem is that many of the parenting and family programs being labeled "Christian" today are not truly Christian. Some are nothing more than secular behaviorism papered over with a religious veneer—an unholy amalgam of biblical-sounding expressions blended with humanistic psychology. Even some of the better Christian parenting programs focus far too much on relatively petty extrabiblical matters and not enough on the essential biblical principles. One book I consulted spent chapter after chapter on issues like how to make a chore list to hang on the refrigerator, how to organize your child's schedule to limit television time, games to play in the car, and similar "how-to" advice. Such pragmatic concerns may have their place, but they don't go to the heart of what Christian parents in a society like ours need to be concerned with. (That particular book actually had very little that was distinctively Christian, outside the author's preface.)

Some Christian parenting programs seem to begin well, but they quickly move away from biblical principles and into other things. Those "other things" often receive more stress than more vital issues that *are* truly biblical. Parents who sign up for such programs demand detailed, heavily regimented programs or turnkey parenting systems that "work" right out of the box. So that is what the experts try to produce. The resulting lists of rules and "how-tos" quickly supersede the vital biblical principles. The lure in this direction is subtle but strong, and rare is the parenting guru who successfully avoids it.

What is desperately needed is a return to the *biblical* principles of parenting. Christian parents don't need new, shrink-wrapped "programs"; they need to apply and obey consistently the few simple principles that are clearly set forth for parents in God's Word, such as these: Constantly teach your kids the truth of God's Word (Deut. 6:7). Discipline them when they do wrong (Prov. 23:13–14). And don't provoke them to anger (Col. 3:21). Those few select principles alone, if consistently applied, would have a far greater positive impact for the typical struggling parent than hours of discussion about whether babies should be permitted pacifiers, or what age kids should be before they're permitted to choose their own clothes—or dozens of similar issues that consume so much time in the typical parenting program.

Throughout this book we'll be closely examining those biblical parenting principles and others. We begin with four oft-neglected biblical principles that should lay the foundation for the Christian parent's perspective.

CHILDREN SHOULD BE SEEN AS A BLESSING, NOT A HARDSHIP

First, Scripture clearly teaches that children are blessed gifts from the Lord. God designed them to be a blessing. They are supposed to be a joy. They are a benediction from the Lord to grace our lives with fulfillment, meaning, happiness, and satisfaction. Parenthood is God's gift to us.

This is true even in a fallen world, infected with the curse of sin. In the midst of all that's evil, children are tokens of God's loving-kindness. They are living proof that God's mercy extends even to fallen, sinful creatures.

Remember that Adam and Eve ate the forbidden fruit before they had conceived any offspring. Yet God did not simply destroy them and start over with a new race. Instead, he permitted Adam and Eve to fulfill the command given them before the Fall: be fruitful and multiply (Gen. 1:28). And He set in motion a plan of redemption that would ultimately embrace untold numbers of Adam's offspring (Rev. 7:9–10). The children Eve bore therefore embodied the hope that fallen sinners could be redeemed.

And when God cursed the earth because of Adam's sin, He multiplied the *pain* of the childbirth process (Gen. 3:16), but He did not nullify the blessing inherent in bearing children.

Eve recognized this. Genesis 4:1 says, "Now Adam knew Eve his wife, and she conceived and bore Cain, and said, 'I have acquired a man from the LORD'" (NKJV). She clearly recognized that the Lord was the source of this child. She regarded the child as a gift from the hand of the one whom she had sinned against, and she was overjoyed by it. Despite the pain of childbirth, and irrespective of the fallenness of the child himself, she knew that the child was an emblem of God's grace to her.

In verse 25 we read, "And Adam knew his wife again, and she bore a son and named him Seth, 'For God has appointed another seed for me'" (NKJV). Children, Eve knew, are blessed gifts from God.

What of the children of unbelievers? They represent divine blessings too. In Genesis 17:20 God promised to bless Ishmael. How would He bless him? By multiplying his children and descendants. He told Abraham, "And as for Ishmael, I have heard you. Behold, I have blessed him, and will make him fruitful, and will multiply him exceedingly" (NKJV).

Throughout Scripture we find a running theme that highlights children as blessings from the hand of a loving and merciful God. This becomes evident, for example, in the contest between Leah and Rachel for Jacob's affection. Genesis 29:31–33 says:

When the LORD saw that Leah was unloved, He opened her womb; but Rachel was barren. So Leah conceived and bore a son, and she called his name Reuben; for she said, "The LORD has surely looked on my affliction. Now therefore, my husband will love me." Then she conceived again and bore a son, and said, "Because the LORD has heard that I am unloved, He has therefore given me this son also." (NKJV)

Notice that the Lord's compassion for Leah is manifested by His enabling her to bear children. The Lord is the one who opened her womb, and Leah recognized this.

Meanwhile, although Jacob loved Rachel more, Rachel believed her own barrenness somehow implied she was less favored. Scripture says, "Rachel envied her sister, and said to Jacob, 'Give me children, or else I die!'" (Gen. 30:1 NKJV).

Scripture says, "And Jacob's anger was aroused against Rachel, and he said, 'Am I in the place of God, who has withheld from you the fruit of the womb?'" (v. 2 NKJV). He too recognized that only God can give children.

Rachel was so determined to have children that she concocted a wrong-headed scheme by which to have *surrogate* children through her handmaid, Bilhah (v. 3)—thus compounding the already sinful complexities of the polygamous relationship that was the source of her strife with Leah in the first place. In the end, God blessed Rachel with children too—and she praised Him for His goodness to her: "And she conceived and bore a son, and said, 'God has taken away my reproach'" (v. 23 NKJV). Rachel died giving birth to Benjamin, and her midwife offered these words of dying comfort: "Do not fear; you will have this son also" (35:17 NKJV).

Throughout this tale of the parents who gave birth to the various tribes of God's chosen people, one thing is clear: all parties understood that children signify the blessing of the Lord.

By God's gracious design, children are given to bring parents joy, happiness, contentment, satisfaction, and love. Psalm 127:3–5 says so expressly:

> Behold, children are a gift of the LORD,
> The fruit of the womb is a reward.
> Like arrows in the hand of a warrior,
> So are the children of one's youth.
> How blessed is the man whose quiver is full of them;
> They will not be ashamed
> When they speak with their enemies in the gate.

Clearly, in the plan of God, children are meant to be a blessing, not a hardship. And they usually are a blessing when they arrive. But left exposed to this world and unshaded by the proper kind of protection, they will indeed break your heart.

That leads to the second foundational principle:

PARENTING IS SUPPOSED TO BE A JOY, NOT A BURDEN

The parent's task is not a yoke to be borne; it is a privilege to be enjoyed. If God's design in *giving* us children is to bless us, the task He calls us to as parents is nothing more than an extension and magnification of that blessing.

Parenting is hard only to the degree that parents *make* it hard by failing to follow the simple principles God sets forth. To neglect one's duty before God as a parent is to forfeit the blessing inherent in the task—and those who do so take on a burden God never intended parents to bear.

One sure way to fill your life with misery is to abdicate the responsibility God has given you as a parent and steward of the child He has graciously placed into your hands. Conversely, nothing in your life will engender more sheer joy and gladness than bringing up your children in the nurture and admonition of the Lord.

Are there no inherently distasteful aspects to parenting? Of course, none of us takes delight in having to discipline our children. I quickly learned as a parent that what my parents always told me about discipline was right: it usually pains the parent more than it pains the child. But even the discipline process ultimately produces joy when we are faithful to God's instructions. Proverbs 29:17 says, "Correct your son, and he will give you rest; yes, he will give delight to your soul" (NKJV).

There's a refreshing, exhilarating wealth of rich joy in godly parenting that cannot be acquired by any other means. God has graciously designed into the parenting process a fountain of delight, if we abide by His principles.

Does Scripture guarantee that our parenting will succeed if we follow God's plan? Consider this third foundational point:

SUCCESS IN PARENTING IS MEASURED BY WHAT THE PARENTS DO, NOT BY WHAT THE CHILD DOES

If we measure our "success" as parents solely by what our children become, there is no inviolable guarantee in Scripture that we will experience absolute "success" on those terms. Sometimes children raised in fine Christian families grow up to abandon the faith. On the other hand, the Lord graciously redeems many children whose parents are utter failures. The outcome of the child, as a factor taken by itself, is no reliable gauge of the parents' success.

However, the *true* measure of success for Christian parents is the parents' own character. To the degree that we have followed God's design for parenting, we have succeeded as parents before God.

Invariably parents ask about Proverbs 22:6: "Train up a child in the way he should go, and when he is old he will not depart from it." Isn't that a biblical promise that if we raise our children right, we can guarantee they will walk faithfully with the Lord?

But that notion is based on a misunderstanding of the nature of the Proverbs. These are wise sayings and truisms—not necessarily inviolable rules. For example, two verses earlier, we read, "By humility and the fear of the LORD are riches and honor and life" (v. 4). That is certainly not a blanket promise that everyone who is humble and fears the Lord will always be rich and receive honor. Too many other verses also teach us that the righteous are inevitably persecuted (2 Tim. 3:12) and often poor (James 2:5).

Furthermore, Proverbs 10:27 says, "The fear of the LORD prolongs days, but the years of the wicked will be shortened" (NKJV). We know that this principle does not hold true in every case. It cannot be claimed as if it were a binding promise from God to all who fear the Lord.

Likewise, Proverbs 22:6 is a principle that is generally true. The same principle would be true if applied to soldiers, carpenters, teachers, or any other form of training. How a person is trained determines what he becomes. In Jesus' words, "Everyone, after he has been fully trained, will be like his teacher" (Luke 6:40). The same principle applies to children, who are also, normally, products of their training. This is an axiomatic, or self-evident, truism.

But Proverbs 22:6 is not a promise for Christian parents to claim that will guarantee their children will never depart from the way of truth. The great Puritan commentator Matthew Henry made these remarks about the truism of Proverbs 22:6:

> When they *grow up,* when they *grow old,* it is to be hoped, they *will not depart from it.* Good impressions made upon them then will abide upon them all their days. Ordinarily the vessel retains the savour with which it was first seasoned. Many indeed have departed from the good way in which they were trained up; Solomon himself did so. But early training may be a means of their recovering themselves, as it is supposed Solomon did. At least the parents will have the comfort of having done their duty and used the means.[13]

As a general rule, parents who follow biblical principles in bringing up their children *will* see a positive effect on the character of their children. From a purely statistical point of view, children who grow up in Christ-honoring homes are more likely to remain faithful to Christ in adulthood than kids growing up in homes where the parents dishonor the Lord. The truism of Proverbs 22:6 does apply. We're certainly not to think that God's sovereignty in salvation means the way we raise our kids is immaterial. God often uses faithful parents as instruments in the salvation of children.

Ultimately, however, your children's salvation *is* a matter to be settled between them and God. Nothing you can do will *guarantee* your kids' salvation. To that end you should be praying to God and instructing your child—using all available means to impress the truths of the gospel perpetually on the child's heart. But ultimately a grown child's spiritual fitness alone is not necessarily a reliable gauge of the parents' success.

Having said that, I want to stress that sometimes—I should say *often*—parents *are* partly to blame for their wayward children's rebellion. And it has been my observation over the years that parents are generally more to blame for wayward kids than society, or peers, or any of the other influences parents tend to blame. I occasionally encounter parents who have violated nearly every biblical principle of parenting, who nonetheless come to the pastor seeking some kind of absolution from the responsibility for their children's defiance. They want verbal assurance that they are in no way to blame; someone else is.

God Himself has given the responsibility for raising children to parents— not to schoolteachers, peers, child-care workers, or other people outside the family—and therefore it is wrong for parents to attempt to unload that responsibility or shift the blame when things go wrong. This is the fourth foundational principle:

A CHILD'S MOST IMPORTANT INFLUENCES COME FROM PARENTS, NOT PEERS

God has solemnly charged parents with the duty of raising their children in the nurture and admonition of the Lord. It is not the parents' prerogative to delegate that duty to others. Parents must involve themselves in their children's lives enough to ensure that *no other influence* takes precedence. To parents who complain that their kids' failures are the kids' friends' fault, my inevitable reply is that ultimately the parents themselves must therefore be to blame, because they were the ones who allowed peers to have more input into their kids' lives than they have themselves.

Some parents will no doubt cynically roll their eyes at that and insist that it is unrealistic in this day and age to expect parents to influence their kids more than peers, the culture, television, schoolteachers, and all the other factors that vie for a controlling interest in the typical child's life.

A similar cynicism is expressed in a recently published book, *The Nurture Assumption: Why Children Turn Out the Way They Do,*[14] by Judith Rich Harris, a New Jersey-based grandmother and author of several psychology textbooks. She insists that virtually nothing parents can do will make any significant difference in their child's temperament, personality, or character. "Parenting has been oversold," she says. "You have been led to believe that you have more of an influence on your child's personality than you really do."[15] According to Harris, our children's peer groups, not their parents, determine what kind of people they will grow up to be. She gives an amazing array of evidence ranging from technical research data to anecdotal testimony, all arguing persuasively that this is the case.

At first glance, the notion that parents have little influence on their kids' character seems contrary to everything we believe about parenting. But those who read the book may find Harris's theory more than plausible—even convincing.

Still, a moment's reflection will reveal *why* parents in our culture have less influence on their kids than peer groups do: most parents have simply abdicated the parental role. They have turned their kids over to their peers. They have invested less time in teaching their kids than the amount of time they permit the kids to watch television. In the worst cases, they have permitted all their children's spiritual, moral, and ethical instruction to come from television, movies, music, and other children. Even in the best cases, parents rely too much on schoolteachers, Sunday-school teachers, and youth leaders—all influences outside the purview of the family.

Parents must realize that character is neither inbred by genetics nor picked up by osmosis. Children are *taught* to be what they become. If they become something other than what the parents hoped for, it is usually because they have simply learned from those who were there to teach them in their parents' absence.

In other words, the parents, not the kids—and not even the peer groups— are ultimately to blame for the parents' diminishing influence in our culture. Whenever outside influences shape a child's character more than the parents, the parents have failed in their duties. It is as simple as that.

Christian parents today desperately need to own this simple principle. Before the throne of God *we* will be held accountable if we have turned our children over to other influences that shape their character in ungodly ways. God has placed in *our* hands the responsibility of bringing our children up in the nurture and admonition of the Lord, and we will give account to God for our stewardship of this great gift. If others have more influence on our children than we, we are *culpable,* not excusable, on those grounds.

God has made parenting a full-time responsibility. There are no coffee breaks from our parental duties. This principle was even built into the Law at Sinai. God prefaced His instructions to the Israelites with this solemn charge: "These words, which I am commanding you today, shall be on your heart. You shall teach them diligently to your sons and shall talk of them when you sit in your house and when you walk by the way and when you lie down and when you rise up" (Deut. 6:6–7).

That is God's own definition of the parents' task. It means parenting is a full-time assignment in every sense of the expression. No phase of life is exempt. Not one hour of the day is excluded. There is no time-out for the parent who wants to be faithful to this calling.

Some parents think they can compartmentalize their children's lives, assign a set number of hours per week to spend on parenting, and then fulfill their duties as parents by making sure the hours they put into the task are "quality time." That whole philosophy is contrary to the spirit of Deuteronomy 6:7, and it is a sure way to guarantee that outside influences will have more effect than the parents in shaping the child's character.

The history of Old Testament Israel is an object lesson about the dangers of neglecting this vital principle. The Israelites failed miserably when it came to the duty of teaching their children about God's righteousness. Consider these telling verses about the generation of Israelites who first entered the promised land. And note that this was merely one generation after God had first given the law at Sinai:

> The people served the LORD all the days of Joshua, and all the days of the elders who outlived Joshua, who had seen all the great works of the LORD which He had done for Israel . . . When all that generation had been gathered to their fathers, another generation arose after them who did not know the LORD nor the work which He had done for Israel. (Judges 2:7, 10 NKJV)

In other words, that whole generation of Israelites failed in their responsibility. They neglected to teach their children about the things God had done for Israel. And as a consequence, the next generation turned away from the Lord *en masse:*

> Then the children of Israel did evil in the sight of the LORD, and served the Baals; and they forsook the LORD God of their fathers, who had brought them out of the land of Egypt; and they followed other gods from among the gods of the people who were all around them, and they bowed down to them; and they provoked the LORD to anger. They forsook the LORD and served Baal and the Ashtoreths. (vv. 11–13 NKJV)

The children turned to the evil gods of the Canaanites. Their environment influenced them more than their parents did—because the parents abdicated the parental role. The result was idolatry, chaos, and destruction. "Everyone did what was right in his own eyes" (21:25 NKJV).

The same pattern was repeated again and again throughout Israel's history. Whenever a generation of parents neglected to plant the seeds that would provide shade trees for subsequent generations, the children suffered the spiritual famine that inevitably followed.

The same thing is still occurring to this day. Right now the outlook for the next generation is as bleak as it has ever been. And there will be no turnaround unless this generation of Christian parents resumes the full-time work of planting spiritual shade trees.

For many parents, the first step toward getting back on track must be a fresh commitment to the things of God for themselves. If our own priorities in life are askew, there's no hope of teaching our children what they need to learn.

Parent, take inventory in your own heart. Do you thirst for God as the deer pants after the water? Or is your own life sending your children a message of hypocrisy and spiritual indifference? Is your own commitment to Christ what you hope to see in your children's lives? Is your obedience to His Word the same kind of submission you long to see from your own kids? These are crucial questions each parent must face if we really want to be successful parents and good role models for our children. Parents who are lax in these areas virtually guarantee that their sons and daughters will fail spiritually. For parents to be derelict in their own spiritual lives is tantamount to cutting down all the shade trees for the next generation in their family.

12

WHY CHRIST MUST RETURN[1]

Scripture predicted a time when skeptics would mock the very notion of Christ's return: "Scoffers will come in the last days, walking according to their own lusts, and saying, 'Where is the promise of His coming?'" (2 Peter 3:3–4 NKJV). There is no shortage of voices raising that chorus today.

For example, one group of self-styled authorities on Scripture claims to have discovered (using the techniques of modern literary criticism) that Christ did not even actually say the great majority of things attributed to Him by the New Testament. The so-called Jesus Seminar, a group of two hundred liberal Bible scholars, was convened to try to reach consensus about which sayings of Christ are "authentic." This was deemed necessary because these particular scholars had already concluded that most of the words attributed to Christ in Scripture are spurious additions to the gospel accounts. Their collective final decisions about which sayings are authentic were made by majority vote. The seminar's verdict was no surprise to anyone familiar with liberal theology's approach to Scripture. These "scholars" concluded that of the more than seven hundred sayings attributed to Jesus in the gospels, only thirty-one are unquestionably authentic—and more than half of those are actually duplicate statements from parallel passages. So all told, according to the Jesus Seminar scholars, only about fifteen of the New Testament sayings attributed to Jesus represent words He actually said.[2]

In addition to the few statements they accepted as authentic, the scholars of the Jesus Seminar listed several more sayings they regarded as questionable but possibly authentic. They flatly rejected more than 80 percent of the words of Christ in Scripture—including, of course, all the major passages where Christ promised His second coming.

"Where is the promise of His return?" According to the Jesus Seminar scholars, Jesus made no such promise in the first place.

That kind of hard-core skepticism under a scholarly veneer is being mass-marketed widely these days. And the doctrine of the Second Coming is a particular target. One author writes,

> Jesus says: "Verily I say unto you, This generation shall not pass, till all these things be fulfilled."

> How could Jesus have been wrong about his return? A group of bible scholars known as the "Jesus Seminar" have studied the sayings of Jesus using the most recently discovered copies of ancient biblical manuscripts, other historical writings directly related to the times of Jesus and the early Christian church, scientific writing-style analysis, and other tools. After years of intense study and debate this group has come to the general consensus that over 80% of the words attributed to Jesus in the New Testament were not His words at all, but the interpretations and additions of early believers.

> It is very important to remember that nothing Jesus said was written down for at least an entire generation after his death. Stories of his words and ministry were circulated solely by word of mouth. This historical fact of the Oral Period is not disputed by any reputable bible scholar . . . As difficult as it may be for bible-believers to accept, objective scholarly analysis has shown that the words of Jesus have been highly corrupted by the beliefs and words of early Christian believers.[3]

In the first place, that author misrepresents and grossly overstates the significance of the Jesus Seminar's work. The seminar's findings have absolutely no "scientific" authority. They are merely the pooling of liberal opinion—little more than sheer conjecture grounded in sinful unbelief and skepticism. And it is misleading in the extreme to suggest that the liberal conclusions of the Jesus Seminar are "not disputed by any reputable bible scholar." The statement itself betrays the circular reasoning and closed-mindedness that is so typical of liberal "scholarship"; any scholar who disputes their theories is *automatically* regarded as "not reputable."

Nonetheless, multitudes have bought such lies—and chiefly, it seems, many are clergymen. A few years ago I read about a survey given to a group of Protestant pastors at a church convention in Evanston, Illinois. Ninety percent said they have no expectation whatsoever that Christ will ever really return to earth.

The result of all this skepticism from so many scholars and clergy is that a whole segment of society regards the hope of the Second Coming as unenlightened nonsense and mindless fundamentalist fantasy. The arrogance of the scoffers has practically gained the status of conventional wisdom.

But Scripture is neither vague nor equivocal on the promise of Christ's return. A large proportion (by some accounts, as much as one-fifth) of Scripture is prophetic, and perhaps a third or more of the prophetic passages refer to the second coming of Christ or events related to it. It is a major theme of both Old Testament and New Testament prophecy.

And regardless of what the scoffers say, Jesus is coming. World history is barreling toward a conclusion, and the conclusion has already been ordained by God and foretold in Scripture. It could be soon, or it could be another thousand years (or more) away. Either way, God is not slack concerning His promise. Christ *will* return.

One ironic thing is that we live in a time when even the scoffers are in a state of rather fearful expectation. The frightening potential of worldwide destruction exists on several levels. Even the most impassioned secularists must acknowledge the very real potential that the world as we know it could end at any time—through nuclear war, a nuclear accident, an energy crisis, various ecological disasters, killer viruses like AIDS (or worse), or even a cosmic collision of some kind. In fact, most people recognize that this world *cannot* exist forever. And we face constant reminders of this. For nearly the whole of the twentieth century, an unremitting string of books, articles, scientific studies, and even Hollywood productions assaulted the public consciousness, warning us that if we do not collectively change the way we're living, we're going to go out of existence along with our little planet. In fact, the most vocal doomsayers today are not people who expect the return of Christ, but secularists who have recognized that this world and all life on it inevitably *will* end someday. They are right. It will end, but not because of ecological irresponsibility or human destructiveness.

How will it end? Can we know? Yes we can. The Bible gives a very clear direct answer. The world as we know it will end with the return of Jesus Christ. The history of the world will climax in His literal, bodily return to the earth.

This is as certain as any truth in Scripture. Here are nine reasons we can know from Scripture that Christ is coming again:

THE PROMISE OF GOD DEMANDS IT

The Old Testament was full of messianic promise. In fact, it's fair to say that the coming Messiah was the main focus of the Old Testament. The first hint of a messianic Redeemer came in Genesis 3, right after Adam's fall, when God promised that the Seed of the woman would crush the serpent's head (Gen. 3:15). In the closing chapter of the final book of the Old Testament, God promised that "The Sun of Righteousness shall arise with healing in His wings" (Mal. 4:2 NKJV). And between those two promises, the entire Old Testament is filled with prophecies of the coming deliverer—at least 333 distinct promises, by one count.

More than a hundred of those prophecies were literally fulfilled at the first advent of Christ. Here are some key ones:

- Isaiah prophesied that he would be born of a virgin (Isa. 7:14; Matt. 1:18, 24–25).

- Micah foresaw that Bethlehem would be His birthplace (Mic. 5:2; Matt. 2:1).

- The experience of Old Testament Israel graphically foreshadowed Him as being called out of Egypt (Hos. 11:1;[4] Matt. 2:13–15).

- Isaiah foretold that he would be a descendant of Jesse (King David's father), and that He would be uniquely anointed with the Spirit of God (Isa. 11:1–5; Matt. 3:16–17).

- Zechariah prophesied that He would enter Jerusalem riding on a colt, the foal of a donkey (Zech. 9:9; Luke 19:35–37).

- Psalm 41:9 predicted that He would be betrayed by a familiar friend with whom he had shared a meal (cf. Matt. 10:4).

- Zechariah prophesied that He would be stricken and His sheep scattered, anticipating that He would be forsaken by his own closest disciples (Zech. 13:7; Mark 14:50).

- Zechariah also foretold the exact price of Judas's betrayal (thirty pieces of silver), as well as what would become of the betrayal money (Zech. 11:12–13; Matt. 26:15; 27:6–7).

- Isaiah foretold many details of the crucifixion (Isa. 52:14–53:12; Matt. 26:67; 27:29–30, 57–60).

- David foretold many additional details of the tortures Christ endured at the cross, including His last cry to the Father, the piercing of His hands and feet, and the parting of His garments (Ps. 22; Matt. 27:35, 42–43, 46; John 19:23–24).

- David also prophetically foretold that none of His bones would be broken (Ps. 34:20; John 19:33).

- And elsewhere David alluded to the Resurrection (Ps. 16:10; cf. Acts 2:28; 13:35–37).

All the prophecies dealing with the first advent of Christ were fulfilled precisely, literally. His riding on a donkey, the parting of His garments, the piercing of His hands and feet, and the vivid prophecies of His rejection by men in Isaiah 53—all these *might* have been interpreted symbolically by Old Testament scholars before Christ. But the New Testament record repeatedly reports that such things were fulfilled in the most literal sense, so "that the Scriptures of the prophets might be fulfilled" (NKJV) (Matt. 26:56; cf. 2:15; 4:14–15; 8:17; 12:17–18; 13:35; 21:4–5; 27:35; John 12:38; 15:25; 19:24, 28).

In some cases Old Testament prophecies about Christ were fulfilled with a literalism that could not even have been anticipated by even the most careful Old Testament scholars. For example, Psalm 69 seems to be a lament from David while he was under attack from his enemies and in deep distress. Nothing in the psalm itself gives us a clue that any prophesies are contained in it. In fact, in verse 5, David refers to his own foolishness and sins. So these words came from the heart of David to describe his own anguish at being hated without a cause. Yet there is a deeper, prophetic meaning. Typologically, David prefigured the Redeemer. And the New Testament indicates that certain phrases in this psalm refer to Christ in an even greater way than they referred to David. "Zeal for Your house has eaten me up" (v. 9 NKJV) is shown to be a prophecy that was literally fulfilled by Christ in Mark 11:15–17. Verse 21, "They also gave me gall for my food, and for my thirst they gave me vinegar to drink" (NKJV), turns out to be a prophecy that was literally fulfilled on the cross (Matt. 27:34).

It stands to reason, then, that the remaining two-thirds of Old Testament messianic prophecies will also be fulfilled literally. And that requires the return of Jesus Christ to this earth.

When Christ took up the scroll in His hometown synagogue at Nazareth and began to read, in God's perfect timing, the scheduled reading for that week came from Isaiah 61. Luke 4 records the incident:

And He was handed the book of the prophet Isaiah. And when He had opened the book, He found the place where it was written:

"The Spirit of the LORD is upon Me,
Because He has anointed Me
To preach the gospel to the poor;
He has sent Me to heal the brokenhearted,
To proclaim liberty to the captives
And recovery of sight to the blind,
To set at liberty those who are oppressed;
To proclaim the acceptable year of the LORD."

Then He closed the book, and gave it back to the attendant and sat down. And the eyes of all who were in the synagogue were fixed on Him. And He began to say to them, "Today this Scripture is fulfilled in your hearing." (vv. 17–21 NKJV)

If we compare the text with Isaiah 61, we see that Christ stopped reading abruptly in the middle of a sentence. Here's the full text of Isaiah 61:1–3:

The Spirit of the Lord GOD is upon Me,
Because the LORD has anointed Me
To preach good tidings to the poor;
He has sent Me to heal the brokenhearted,
To proclaim liberty to the captives,
And the opening of the prison to those who are bound;
To proclaim the acceptable year of the LORD,
And the day of vengeance of our God;
To comfort all who mourn,
To console those who mourn in Zion,
To give them beauty for ashes,
The oil of joy for mourning,
The garment of praise for the spirit of heaviness;
That they may be called trees of righteousness,
The planting of the LORD,
That He may be glorified. (NKJV, emphasis added)

The rest of the chapter from Isaiah goes on to describe the blessings of the millennial kingdom, when "the earth brings forth its bud, as the garden causes the things that are sown in it to spring forth, so the LORD God will cause righteousness and praise to spring forth before all the nations" (v. 11 NKJV).

Christ deliberately stopped reading mid-sentence because "the day of vengeance of our God" pertains to His second advent, not His first. Many Old Testament prophecies seemed to telescope messianic events this same way, so that it was not always immediately obvious when one portion of a prophecy referred to the first coming of Christ, while another portion referred to His second coming. Employing the Old Testament alone, anyone would have found it very difficult to discern any distinction between the two classes of messianic prophecies.

But here are some familiar Old Testament prophecies about Christ that await fulfillment at His second coming:

PSALM 2

We know this speaks of Christ. Verse 7 is quoted several times in the New Testament and applied to Him: "You are My Son, today I have begotten You" (NKJV; cf. Acts 13:33; Heb. 1:5; 5:5). Yet many aspects of this psalm await future fulfillment: verse 6 suggests an earthly reign that is yet to be realized: "Yet I have set My King on My holy hill of Zion" (NKJV). The kingdom and the judgment described in verses 8–9 also have yet to be fulfilled literally:

> I will give You
> The nations for Your inheritance,
> And the ends of the earth for Your possession.
> You shall break them with a rod of iron;
> You shall dash them to pieces like a potter's vessel.

ISAIAH 9:6–7

This familiar passage also seems to have both the first and second comings of Christ in view: "For unto us a Child is born, unto us a Son is given . . ." That plainly refers to His first advent, anticipating the angel's promise to Mary in Luke 1:35. But the rest of Isaiah 9:6–7 (NKJV) describes Him as a king in glory on David's throne:

> And the government will be upon His shoulder.
> And His name will be called
> Wonderful, Counselor, Mighty God,
> Everlasting Father, Prince of Peace.
> Of the increase of His government and peace
> There will be no end,
> Upon the throne of David and over His kingdom,

To order it and establish it with judgment and justice
From that time forward, even forever.

Christ Himself pointed to His second coming as the time when He would
assume that throne in a literal sense: "When the Son of Man comes in His glory,
and all the holy angels with Him, *then* He will sit on the throne of His glory"
(Matt. 25:31 NKJV, emphasis added).

MICAH 4:3

This passage echoes the promise of a kingdom of peace under His rule:

He shall judge between many peoples,
And rebuke strong nations afar off;
They shall beat their swords into plowshares,
And their spears into pruning hooks;
Nation shall not lift up sword against nation,
Neither shall they learn war anymore. (NKJV)

Again, the literal fulfillment of that prophecy awaits a second advent of the
Savior.

JEREMIAH 23:5

Here the Word of God expressly states that the future kingdom of Christ
is to be an earthly one: "'Behold, the days are coming,' says the LORD, 'That I
will raise to David a Branch of righteousness; a King shall reign and prosper,
and execute judgment and righteousness *in the earth*'" (NKJV, emphasis added).
He must return to establish that kingdom on earth.

ZECHARIAH 14:4–9

Zechariah describes the Second Coming graphically:

And in that day His feet will stand on the Mount of Olives,
Which faces Jerusalem on the east.
And the Mount of Olives shall be split in two,
From east to west,
Making a very large valley;
Half of the mountain shall move toward the north
And half of it toward the south.

Then you shall flee through My mountain valley,
For the mountain valley shall reach to Azal.
Yes, you shall flee
As you fled from the earthquake
In the days of Uzziah king of Judah.
Thus the LORD my God will come,
And all the saints with You.
It shall come to pass in that day
That there will be no light;
The lights will diminish.
It shall be one day
Which is known to the LORD—
Neither day nor night.
But at evening time it shall happen
That it will be light.
And in that day it shall be
That living waters shall flow from Jerusalem,
Half of them toward the eastern sea
And half of them toward the western sea;
In both summer and winter it shall occur.
And the LORD shall be King over all the earth.
In that day it shall be—
"The LORD is one,"
And His name one. (NKJV)

That describes the glorious appearing of Christ, which is yet to come, when He returns to set all things right. Nothing like that occurred at His first coming. Like much that pertains to messianic prophecy in the Old Testament, it awaits future fulfillment at the second coming of Christ.

Scripture says God cannot lie, and He will not change His mind (Titus 1:2; Num. 23:19). What He has promised, He will do. And much of what He promised about Christ requires that the Savior return to earth in triumph in order to bring it to pass. The truthfulness of the Bible is at stake.

THE TEACHING OF CHRIST DEMANDS IT

Christ's own words also make it clear that He will return. His earthly teaching was filled with references to His second coming. Many of His parables spoke of it. In fact, the gospels include entire chapters dealing with events related to the Second Coming (Matt. 24–25; Luke 21).

On the night of His betrayal, Christ told the disciples, "I go to prepare a place for you. And if I go and prepare a place for you, I will come again and receive you to Myself" (John 14:2–3 NKJV). Not only is the credibility of God at stake in the Second Coming, but so is the credibility of His Son. *If Jesus doesn't return, He's a liar.*

But His own words are a divine guarantee that He *will* be back. "Indeed, let God be true but every man a liar" (Rom. 3:4 NKJV).

Christ, on trial for His life, defended His own deity with a bold declaration of the Second Coming in the most triumphant terms. He told the High Priest, "You will see the Son of Man sitting at the right hand of the Power, and coming with the clouds of heaven" (Mark 14:62 NKJV).

And a short time before that, as Christ had unfolded the panorama of future events to His disciples on the Mount of Olives, He told them, "As the lightning comes from the east and flashes to the west, so also will the coming of the Son of Man be" (Matt. 24:27 NKJV). He added this vivid description:

> The sign of the Son of Man will appear in heaven, and then all the tribes of the earth will mourn, and they will see the Son of Man coming on the clouds of heaven with power and great glory. And He will send His angels with a great sound of a trumpet, and they will gather together His elect from the four winds, from one end of heaven to the other. (vv. 30–31 NKJV)

Several of the parables Christ told to illustrate His kingdom emphasized the truth of the Second Coming. He did this "because [the disciples] thought the kingdom of God would appear immediately" (Luke 19:11 NKJV)—and so He stressed repeatedly that the aspect of His kingdom in operation since His first coming until now is spiritual and invisible (Luke 17:20–21), whereas the visible, earthly aspect of His kingdom pertained to His second coming. So His parables often pictured a ruler who, having gone to a far-off country, returns to rule in person. The parable in Luke 19:12–27 expressly pictures "a certain nobleman [who] went into a far country to receive for himself a kingdom and to return" (v. 12 NKJV). And upon returning, "having received the kingdom" (v. 15), He executes judgment and distributes joint rulership in His kingdom to His servants who were faithful in His absence (vv. 15–19 NKJV).

Similarly, three parables in the Olivet Discourse—the parable of the two servants (Matt. 24:45–51), the parable of the ten virgins (Matt. 25:1–13), and the parable of the talents (vv. 14–30)—all underscore the certainty of Christ's return.

Nor is that all. In the book of Revelation, Christ repeatedly said, "Surely I am coming quickly" (Rev. 22:20 NKJV; cf. 2:5, 16; 3:11; 22:7, 12). The Revelation unfolds "the things which will take place after this" (1:19 NKJV; 4:1). And the crown and culmination of it all is Christ's triumphant return, described in chapter 19.

So Christ has repeatedly assured us of His return. He made these promises during His earthly ministry, just before His return to heaven, and even in a vision to John from His throne in heaven. He wanted both friends and enemies to know that He would be back. His very credibility depends on the Second Coming.

THE TESTIMONY OF THE HOLY SPIRIT DEMANDS IT

God cannot lie (Titus 1:2), so His promise guarantees Christ's return. Jesus is truth incarnate (John 14:6), so His teaching also infallibly confirms the fact of the Second Coming. The Holy Spirit, who is called "the Spirit of truth" (John 14:17; 15:26 NKJV) also testifies of the second coming of Christ.

The apostle Paul wrote these words under the Holy Spirit's inspiration in 1 Corinthians 1:4–7:

> I thank my God always concerning you for the grace of God which was given to you by Christ Jesus, that you were enriched in everything by Him in all utterance and all knowledge, even as the testimony of Christ was confirmed in you, so that you come short in no gift, eagerly waiting for the revelation of our Lord Jesus Christ. (NKJV)

Paul meant to make clear that it was the Holy Spirit who confirmed the testimony of Christ in them, and it was the Holy Spirit who gave them their expectancy for Christ's coming. Moreover, the Holy Spirit as the divine author of Scripture thereby confirms the promise of Christ's coming (2 Peter 1:20–21).

He confirmed the same promise through several of the New Testament authors. Elsewhere Paul wrote, "Our citizenship is in heaven, from which we also eagerly wait for the Savior, the Lord Jesus Christ" (Phil. 3:20 NKJV). He encouraged the Colossians with this: "When Christ who is our life appears, then you also will appear with Him in glory" (Col. 3:4 NKJV). And he had much to say about the Lord's return in his epistles to the Thessalonians. Here's a sample:

For the Lord Himself will descend from heaven with a shout, with the voice of an archangel, and with the trumpet of God. And the dead in Christ will rise first. Then we who are alive and remain shall be caught up together with them in the clouds to meet the Lord in the air. And thus we shall always be with the Lord. (1 Thessalonians 4:16–17 NKJV)

The Holy Spirit further confirmed the promise of Christ's return through the writer of Hebrews. Hebrews 9:28 says, "So Christ was offered once to bear the sins of many. To those who eagerly wait for Him He will appear a second time" (NKJV).

You'll find the promise reiterated in the epistle of James: "Therefore be patient, brethren, until the coming of the Lord. See how the farmer waits for the precious fruit of the earth, waiting patiently for it until it receives the early and latter rain. You also be patient. Establish your hearts, for the coming of the Lord is at hand" (James 5:7–8 NKJV).

Peter penned similar Spirit-inspired promises. Here's one: "Gird up the loins of your mind, be sober, and rest your hope fully upon the grace that is to be brought to you at the revelation of Jesus Christ" (1 Peter 1:13 NKJV). And another: "When the Chief Shepherd appears, you will receive the crown of glory that does not fade away" (5:4 NKJV).

The Spirit also confirmed this truth through the apostle John. First John 3:2 is one of the most blessed promises in Scripture: "Beloved, now we are children of God; and it has not yet been revealed what we shall be, but we know that when He is revealed, we shall be like Him, for we shall see Him as He is" (NKJV).

Again and again, the Holy Spirit testifies through the writers of the New Testament that Christ is coming a second time. His testimony, through the pens of the men whom He employed as instruments to write the inspired Word of God, adds a third infallible witness to that of the Father and the Son. Through the inerrant Scriptures, the Holy Spirit is still testifying that Jesus is coming.

THE PROGRAM FOR THE CHURCH DEMANDS IT

God's plan for the church also demands the return of Christ. He is currently "visit[ing] the Gentiles to take out of them a people for His name" (Acts 15:14 NKJV). He is gathering His elect into one great body, the church. And the church's role is to be like a pure bride for God's own Son, ready to be presented to Him at His second coming.

And that is precisely the imagery the apostle Paul uses in 2 Corinthians 11:2.

He writes to the church at Corinth: "I am jealous for you with godly jealousy. For I have betrothed you to one husband, that I may present you as a chaste virgin to Christ" (NKJV).

Scripture repeatedly portrays Christ at His second coming as a bridegroom coming to claim his bride. The apostle John's vision of heaven included a vivid description of the wedding supper:

> And I heard, as it were, the voice of a great multitude, as the sound of many waters and as the sound of mighty thunderings, saying, "Alleluia! For the Lord God Omnipotent reigns! Let us be glad and rejoice and give Him glory, for the marriage of the Lamb has come, and His wife has made herself ready." And to her it was granted to be arrayed in fine linen, clean and bright, for the fine linen is the righteous acts of the saints. Then he said to me, "Write: 'Blessed are those who are called to the marriage supper of the Lamb!'" And he said to me, "These are the true sayings of God." (Revelation 19:6–9 NKJV)

That symbolism is based on the pattern that was in vogue for Oriental weddings during New Testament times. In fact, that pattern was based on ancient traditions that reached far back into Old Testament history. Every marriage had three vital elements, each symbolized in the relationship of Christ with His church:

THE BRIDAL PRICE

In New Testament times, marriages were arranged by parents. Parents would get together and agree by contract to have their children marry one another— sometimes before the bride and bridegroom had even met. These marriage contracts were binding, and to seal the contract, the husband-to-be or his father had to pay a bridal price, or dowry.[5] This ensured the bride's financial security. The money, though paid to the bride's father, was meant to be kept for her in case her husband died or deserted her (cf. Gen. 31:15). The bridal price also included gifts for the bride (cf. Gen. 24:53; Judg. 1:15). Once the dowry was paid, the union contract was recognized by law and could only be terminated by divorce—even before any wedding vows were exchanged and the physical union was consummated (cf. Matt. 1:18–19).

The New Testament employs this imagery to describe the relationship between Christ and the church. When He died on the cross, the price He paid with His own blood was like a legal payment for His marriage to His church— the dowry. Paul repeatedly referred to the church as a purchased possession of the heavenly Bridegroom. The symbolism was so vital that Paul even employed it to teach what a godly marriage should be. He instructed husbands,

> Love your wives, just as Christ also loved the church and gave Himself for her, that He might sanctify and cleanse her with the washing of water by the word, that He might present her to Himself a glorious church, not having spot or wrinkle or any such thing, but that she should be holy and without blemish. (Ephesians 5:25–27 NKJV)

Paul's farewell speech to the Ephesian elders included this charge: "Shepherd the church of God which He purchased with His own blood" (Acts 20:28 NKJV). That was, by the way, the highest dowry ever paid. And although the marriage has not yet been consummated, it is legally in effect and will be binding forever. That is the very thing that guarantees our security. Nothing can separate us from the love of Christ.

THE BETROTHAL

The betrothal in an ancient marriage was officially marked by a ceremony where the bride and the bridegroom met in the presence of witnesses and gave gifts to each other. This ceremony would have looked very similar to a modern wedding ceremony, except that it took place long before the marriage could be consummated—sometimes a year or more in advance. Then the bride and her husband-to-be would return to their respective homes. During the period between the betrothal and the consummation of the marriage, he was occupied with preparing a place for his bride. This usually meant building an addition or an attachment to his father's house, so that the new couple would have a secure place to begin their lives together. Joseph and Mary had entered such a betrothal before Gabriel brought her the heavenly message about the miracle of virgin conception and birth (Luke 1:26–36; Matt. 1:19–25).

Again this beautifully pictures Christ and His church. He has given her gifts (Eph. 4:8), and He has gone to prepare her a place in His Father's house (John 14:2). This entire age between His first and second comings is therefore like the betrothal period. The church is espoused to Christ. The bridal price has been paid; gifts have been given. The union is forever binding. But it awaits a final consummation.

THE MARRIAGE FEAST

The final phase of a marriage occurred when the bridegroom and his friends would go to the bride's house for a marriage ceremony and a great feast.

This event is depicted in the story of the marriage at Cana (John 2:1–11) and the parable of the virgins (Matt. 25:1–13).

Likewise, the marriage supper of the Lamb and His bride will signal the consummation of God's plan for the church. That feast cannot occur until Christ returns for His bride (Rev. 19:6–16). And that is precisely God's plan for the church. Therefore Christ *must* return.

The institution of marriage itself is a beautiful metaphor that pictures Christ's love for His church. And if He were not going to return to claim her, it would spoil the whole point. So God's program for the church demands the return of Jesus Christ.

THE CORRUPTION IN THE WORLD DEMANDS IT

Here's another reason Christ must return: to judge the world. In Matthew 16:27, Jesus said, "The Son of Man will come in the glory of His Father with His angels, and then He will reward each according to his works" (NKJV). Scripture portrays the return of Christ as the blessed hope of the church (Titus 2:13). But for the world of unbelievers, the return of Christ is a terrifying prospect, because His coming means immediate judgment on them. In John 5:25–29, He promised this coming judgment:

> Most assuredly, I say to you, the hour is coming, and now is, when the dead will hear the voice of the Son of God; and those who hear will live. For as the Father has life in Himself, so He has granted the Son to have life in Himself, and has given Him authority to execute judgment also, because He is the Son of Man. Do not marvel at this; for the hour is coming in which all who are in the graves will hear His voice and come forth—those who have done good, to the resurrection of life, and those who have done evil, to the resurrection of condemnation. (NKJV)

Scripture repeatedly associates Christ's return with final, comprehensive judgment. Jude 14–15 says, "Behold, the Lord comes with ten thousands of His saints, to execute judgment on all, to convict all who are ungodly among them of all their ungodly deeds which they have committed in an ungodly way, and of all the harsh things which ungodly sinners have spoken against Him" (NKJV).

Paul told the Thessalonian believers,

> The Lord Jesus [will be] revealed from heaven with His mighty angels, in flaming fire taking vengeance on those who do not know God, and on

those who do not obey the gospel of our Lord Jesus Christ. These shall be punished with everlasting destruction from the presence of the Lord and from the glory of His power, when He comes, in that Day, to be glorified in His saints and to be admired among all those who believe, because our testimony among you was believed. (2 Thessalonians 1:7–10 NKJV)

Scripture tells us all judgment has been committed to Christ (John 5:22). And Scripture repeatedly portrays His returning to earth in order to carry out that judgment. The consummate picture of this is Revelation 19:11–16:

Now I saw heaven opened, and behold, a white horse. And He who sat on him was called Faithful and True, and in righteousness He judges and makes war. His eyes were like a flame of fire, and on His head were many crowns. He had a name written that no one knew except Himself. He was clothed with a robe dipped in blood, and His name is called The Word of God. And the armies in heaven, clothed in fine linen, white and clean, followed Him on white horses. Now out of His mouth goes a sharp sword, that with it He should strike the nations. And He Himself will rule them with a rod of iron. He Himself treads the winepress of the fierceness and wrath of Almighty God. And He has on His robe and on His thigh a name written:

KING OF KINGS AND LORD OF LORDS. (NKJV)

Jesus *must* return, in order to execute just retribution on sinners and carry out the judgment He has promised.

THE FUTURE OF ISRAEL DEMANDS IT

So it is clear that God's dealings with the church and the world both necessitate the return of Christ. Did you realize His plan for Israel also demands the Second Coming?

Zechariah 12:10 includes this promise: "I will pour on the house of David and on the inhabitants of Jerusalem the Spirit of grace and supplication; then they will look on Me whom they pierced. Yes, they will mourn for Him as one mourns for his only son, and grieve for Him as one grieves for a firstborn" (NKJV). That salvation of Israel has not yet happened, but it will. "In that day a fountain shall be opened for the house of David and for the inhabitants of

Jerusalem, for sin and for uncleanness" (13:1 NKJV). The whole of Zechariah 14 goes on to detail that great day of salvation for Israel, which occurs at the Lord's return.

Romans 11:25–27 says this:

Blindness in part has happened to Israel until the fullness of the Gentiles has come in. And so all Israel will be saved, as it is written:

"The Deliverer will come out of Zion,
And He will turn away ungodliness from Jacob;
For this is My covenant with them,
When I take away their sins." (NKJV)

Paul was clearly describing a future reality. He was looking forward to a time when "all Israel will be saved." He pictured the people of God as an olive tree. Israel, the natural branches of the domestic tree, failed to produce fruit, so God broke the branches off and grafted in branches from a wild olive tree, representing the elect Gentiles. Apparently in Paul's day Gentiles were already being added to the church in greater numbers than Jewish converts. And Paul reminded the Gentile converts: "You, being a wild olive tree, were grafted in among them, and with them became a partaker of the root and fatness of the olive tree" (v. 17 NKJV). But a time is coming when the natural branches will be grafted back into the olive tree (vv. 23–24). And Paul expressly connects that phenomenon with the return of Christ, the Deliverer who will come out of Zion (v. 26).

THE VINDICATION OF CHRIST DEMANDS IT

Here's another important reason Christ must return: it is inconceivable that the last public view the world would have of Jesus Christ might be the view of a bleeding, dying, crucified criminal, covered with blood, spit, and flies, hanging naked in a Jerusalem twilight. Did you realize that after His resurrection, He never appeared in a public venue before unbelievers? Plenty of *believers* saw Him, touched Him, spoke to Him, and gave unanimous testimony that He was risen from the dead. But there is no record that unbelievers ever saw Him. If they did, they no doubt became believers immediately. Believers who saw Him certainly had all their doubts dispelled, as illustrated in Thomas's encounter with the risen Christ (cf. John 20:25–29).

In 1 Corinthians 15:5–8, Paul lists those who witnessed the risen Lord:

He was seen by Cephas, then by the twelve. After that He was seen by over five hundred brethren at once, of whom the greater part remain to the present, but some have fallen asleep. After that He was seen by James, then by all the apostles. Then last of all He was seen by me also, as by one born out of due time. (NKJV)

Notice that there is not an unbeliever in the group.

So the last time the world saw Him on display, He was humiliated, suffering, and hanging on the cross. His glory has not yet been displayed to the world.

But the world *will* see it. Scripture says, "Christ was offered once to bear the sins of many. To those who eagerly wait for Him He will appear a second time" (Heb. 9:28 NKJV). "He is coming with clouds, and every eye will see Him, even they who pierced Him. And all the tribes of the earth will mourn because of Him" (Rev. 1:7 NKJV). "As the lightning comes from the east and flashes to the west, so also will the coming of the Son of Man be" (Matt. 24:27 NKJV).

A couple of important passages of Scripture set prophecies about His humiliation and His subsequent public exaltation side by side, suggesting that one cannot occur without the other. Psalm 22:16–18 prophesied in detail the treatment He would receive at the hands of those who put Him to death:

Dogs have surrounded Me;
The congregation of the wicked has enclosed Me.
They pierced My hands and My feet;
I can count all My bones.
They look and stare at Me.
They divide My garments among them,
And for My clothing they cast lots. (NKJV)

But the climax of that same psalm anticipates the glory that will be on display when He returns to earth:

All the ends of the world
Shall remember and turn to the LORD,
And all the families of the nations
Shall worship before You.
For the kingdom is the LORD's,
And He rules over the nations. (vv. 27–28 NKJV)

Matthew 26 also sets His first advent suffering and His second coming glory alongside one another. Matthew 26:67–68 describes the treatment Christ received at the hands of those who arrested Him: "They spat in His face and beat Him; and others struck Him with the palms of their hands, saying, 'Prophesy to us, Christ! Who is the one who struck You?'" (NKJV). They mocked Him. Played games with Him. Plucked His beard. Humiliated Him. And ultimately they executed Him. Is that how Jesus is to be remembered in the eyes of the world? Is that His last public appearance on earth?

In this very context, Jesus Himself indicated that it would not be. "The high priest . . . said to Him, 'I put You under oath by the living God: Tell us if You are the Christ, the Son of God!' Jesus said to him, 'It is as you said. Nevertheless, I say to you, hereafter you will see the Son of Man sitting at the right hand of the Power, and coming on the clouds of heaven'" (vv. 63–64 NKJV). And thus the promise of future exaltation was expressed graphically by Jesus Himself, in the midst of His own humiliation.

The indignity and shame of the crucifixion took place in full view of a scoffing crowd. How public will the display of His glory be? "Every eye will see him" (Rev. 1:7 NKJV).

> There will be signs in the sun, in the moon, and in the stars; and on the earth distress of nations, with perplexity, the sea and the waves roaring; men's hearts failing them from fear and the expectation of those things which are coming on the earth, for the powers of heaven will be shaken. Then they will see the Son of Man coming in a cloud with power and great glory. (Luke 21:25–27 NKJV)

The Savior who was humiliated and taunted and put to death in a public display of humanity's hatred of God will return as conquering Lord in view of the entire world. He *must* return.

THE DESTRUCTION OF SATAN DEMANDS IT

There is still another vital reason Christ must return: to destroy the devil. Satan, though an already defeated foe as far as Christians are concerned, still exercises a kind of dominion over this world. Three times in the gospel of John, Christ referred to the devil as "the ruler of this world" (12:31; 14:30; 16:11 NKJV). In 2 Corinthians 4:4 the apostle Paul calls Satan "the god of this age" (NKJV). In Ephesians 2:2 he calls him "the prince of the power of the air, the spirit who now works in the sons of disobedience" (NKJV). And in Ephesians 6:12 he refers to Satan's hierarchy of evil spirits as "principalities . . . powers . . . the rulers of the darkness of this age . . . spiritual hosts of wickedness in the heavenly places" (NKJV). First John 5:19 says, "The whole world lies under the sway of the wicked one" (NKJV).

There's a sense in which Satan still runs the world. How did he gain this power? At creation, God gave dominion over all creation to Adam. And when Adam succumbed to Satan's enticements, obeying the devil rather than God, Adam in effect abdicated his place of dominion and left that authority to the devil. Satan has been the ruler of this world ever since. He has no legal right to rule. He's a usurper. Yet God allows him to remain in power.

When Christ atoned for sin, He dealt Satan the crushing blow, redeeming Adam's fallen race and destroying Satan's claim to world dominion. "Therefore God also has highly exalted Him and given Him the name which is above every name, that at the name of Jesus every knee should bow, of those in heaven, and of those on earth, and of those under the earth, and that every tongue should confess that Jesus Christ is Lord, to the glory of God the Father" (Phil. 2:9–11 NKJV). Christ is the only rightful Ruler of this world, and when he returns He will overthrow and destroy Satan completely.

Revelation 5 pictures this drama in graphic terms. The apostle John describes his vision of heaven, where God was seated on his throne, holding a scroll that had seven seals. The scroll also had writing on the inside and back (v. 1).

That is a description of this world's title deed. In biblical times, as is true even today, title deeds were vital records that proved who owned a piece of property. In the Old Testament era, land could not permanently change ownership. Tracts of land could be used temporarily as collateral for a loan or given away for a period of time in payment of a debt. But land could not be sold permanently (Lev. 25:23). During the Jubilee year (which occurred every fifty years) all land that had changed hands was to be returned to the family of its rightful owner (v. 10). Even between Jubilee years, those wishing to recover their families' lands could redeem their property for a fair price. Jeremiah redeemed some of his family's land by these means (Jer. 32:6–7), and he describes how the transaction was carefully recorded in a title deed:

> I signed the deed and sealed it, took witnesses, and weighed the money on the scales. So I took the purchase deed, both that which was sealed according to the law and custom, and that which was open; and I gave the purchase deed to Baruch the son of Neriah, son of Mahseiah, in the

presence of Hanamel my uncle's son, and in the presence of the witnesses who signed the purchase deed, before all the Jews who sat in the court of the prison. (vv. 10–12 NKJV)

Those signatures would have been recorded with seals, so a typical title deed would have multiple seals, just like the scroll in Revelation 5. And the typical first-century reader of John's vision would have understood this scroll as a legal document, a title deed. It is, I believe, the very title deed to this earth.

No one could lawfully open a title deed except the rightful heir designated by the deed itself. That is why there was writing on the outside of the scroll. The writing on the outside was a summary of what was in the document, identifying who had the right to open it. Jewish deeds were, by law, witnessed by at least three signatures, with three seals—and sometimes more, depending on the importance of the document.

The seven-sealed scroll in Revelation 5 is clearly a document of monumental importance, and the fact that God Himself was holding the scroll while angels were loudly seeking someone worthy to open it (vv. 2–3) suggests that whoever was qualified to open the scroll must be someone very worthy indeed.

The situation seemed such a dilemma to John that he started crying: "I wept much, because no one was found worthy to open and read the scroll, or to look at it" (v. 4 NKJV). But there was no question in heaven about who had authority to open that title deed. "One of the elders said to me, 'Do not weep. Behold, the Lion of the tribe of Judah, the Root of David, has prevailed to open the scroll and to loose its seven seals'" (v. 5 NKJV). Christ as Son of God was the legitimate Heir to all creation (Ps. 2:6–8; Heb. 1:1–2). And He also earned the right to the title deed of the earth, because He redeemed the world from the dominion of Satan.

And having already paid the redemption price, Christ *must* return to earth to establish His dominion here. Revelation 6–7 describes the opening of the seven seals, each one resulting in a unique judgment. The final seal brings utter silence in heaven, followed by seven trumpet blasts. And again, each of the seven blasts unleashes a new wave of judgment (chapters 8–11). Following the trumpets, seven vials representing seven final judgment plagues are poured out on the earth (chapter 16). Finally, after one last-ditch effort by Satan to retain his unlawful dominion over the earth, Christ Himself returns. Revelation 19 describes the scene, in which He comes suddenly and destroys His enemies. In chapter 20, Satan is chained and thrown into a bottomless pit and then finally confined forever to an eternal lake of fire. With that, Christ's final victory over Satan is complete.

Scripture consistently portrays Christ's return to earth as the necessary prelude to Satan's ultimate doom. Therefore Christ *must* return to earth to accomplish the final destruction of His archenemy.

THE HOPE OF THE SAINTS DEMANDS IT

And here's a final reason the Lord must return to earth: only His glorious, triumphant return can fulfill the hope of the saints. God is not in the business of giving false hope. He knows what we are waiting for. He knows the longing of our hearts. His Word gives us every reason to long for the appearing of our Lord Jesus Christ—and He will not disappoint that blessed hope.

Peter saw the promise of Christ's return as a great comfort for the people of God in their times of trial—"that the genuineness of your faith, being much more precious than gold that perishes, though it is tested by fire, may be found to praise, honor, and glory at the revelation of Jesus Christ" (1 Peter 1:7 NKJV).

Paul encouraged believers to have that same hope:

> We ourselves boast of you among the churches of God for your patience and faith in all your persecutions and tribulations that you endure, which is manifest evidence of the righteous judgment of God, that you may be counted worthy of the kingdom of God, for which you also suffer; since it is a righteous thing with God to repay with tribulation those who trouble you, and to give you who are troubled rest with us when the Lord Jesus is revealed from heaven with His mighty angels. (2 Thessalonians 1:4–7 NKJV)

All true believers long for the day when Jesus will return to earth. Paul characterizes all Christians as those who "love his appearing" (2 Tim. 4:8 KJV). John adds, "Now we are children of God; and it has not yet been revealed what we shall be, but we know that when He is revealed, we shall be like Him, for we shall see Him as He is" (1 John 3:2 NKJV). In other words, the return of Christ will instantly usher in the fullness of our glorification.

For all these reasons, Christ *must* return. We are taught throughout the New Testament to look for His coming, to long for it, and to wait patiently and expectantly for it. This has been the blessed hope of every true child of God since the beginning of the age. And the fulfillment of that hope is now closer than it has ever been.

The apostle John added these words: "And everyone who has this hope in Him purifies himself, just as He is pure" (v. 3 NKJV). This is the test of a healthy eschatology: Is your hope a sanctifying influence on your soul? Rather than getting caught up in hype and hysteria about current events and newspaper headlines, are you looking beyond the commotion of this world with the realization that you could soon meet Christ face-to-face, and are you preparing your heart and soul for that? Instead of despairing, as some do, over how long Christ has delayed His coming, are you filled with hope and expectation? Are you eager and watching, knowing that the time still draws nigh? That is the attitude Scripture calls us to.

The Second Coming is not supposed to make us stop what we're doing to wait for the Lord's return. And neither should it motivate us to focus all our attention on the events and political developments of this world. Instead, it should direct our hearts toward Christ, whose coming we await—and it should prompt us to purify ourselves as He is pure.

13

THE SEVEN LAST SAYINGS OF CHRIST[1]

Therefore My Father loves Me, because I lay down My life that I may take it again. No one takes it from Me, but I lay it down of Myself. I have power to lay it down, and I have power to take it again. This command I have received from My Father.

JOHN 10:17–18 (NKJV)

Because of the physical rigors of crucifixion, Christ spoke only with great difficulty during His final hours on the cross. Scripture records only seven brief sayings from the Savior on the cross, but every one of them reveals that Christ remained sovereignly in control, even as He died. And each of His sayings was rich with significance.

A PLEA FOR FORGIVENESS

The first was a plea for mercy on behalf of His tormentors. Luke records that shortly after the cross was raised on Calvary—while the soldiers were still gambling for His clothing—He prayed to God for forgiveness on their behalf: "And when they had come to the place called Calvary, there they crucified Him, and the criminals, one on the right hand and the other on the left. Then Jesus said, 'Father, forgive them, for they do not know what they do'" (Luke 23:33–34 NKJV).

J. C. Ryle wrote, "These words were probably spoken while our Lord was being nailed to the cross, or as soon as the cross was reared up on end. It is worthy of remark that as soon as the blood of the Great Sacrifice began to flow, the Great High Priest began to intercede."[2] While others were mocking Him— just as the taunting and jeering reached a fever pitch—Christ responded in precisely the opposite way most men would have. Instead of threatening, lashing back, or cursing His enemies, He prayed to God on their behalf.

As we have seen with so many of the details surrounding Jesus' death, this priestly intercession on behalf of His own killers was done in fulfillment of Old Testament prophecy: "He poured out His soul unto death, and He was numbered with the transgressors, and He bore the sin of many, *and made intercession for the transgressors*" (Isa. 53:12 NKJV, emphasis added). The whole meaning of the cross is summed up in this one act of intercession. "For God did not send His Son into the world to condemn the world, but that the world through Him might be saved" (John 3:17 NKJV). Certainly any mortal man would have desired only to curse or revile his killers under these circumstances. One might even think that God incarnate would wish to call down some thunderous blast of judgment against men acting so wickedly. But Christ was on a mission of mercy. He was dying to purchase forgiveness for sins. And even at the very height of His agony, compassion was what filled His heart.

The phrase "for they do not know what they do" does not suggest that they were unaware that they were sinning. Ignorance does not absolve anyone from sin. These people were behaving wickedly, and they knew it. Most were fully aware of the *fact* of their wrongdoing. Pilate himself had testified of Jesus' innocence. The Sanhedrin were fully aware that no legitimate charges could be brought against Him. The soldiers and the crowd could easily see that a great injustice was being done, and yet they all gleefully participated. Many of the taunting spectators at Calvary had heard Christ teach and seen Him do miracles. They could not have really believed in their hearts that He deserved to die this way. Their ignorance itself was inexcusable, and it certainly did not absolve them of guilt for what they were doing.

But they were ignorant of the *enormity* of their crime. They were blinded to the full reality of whom they were crucifying. They were spiritually insensitive, because they loved darkness rather than light. Therefore they did not recognize that the one they were putting to death was the Light of the World. "Had they known, they would not have crucified the Lord of glory" (1 Cor. 2:8 NKJV).

How was Jesus' prayer answered? In innumerable ways. The first answer came with the conversion of one of the thieves on the cross next to Jesus (Luke 23:40–43). Another followed immediately, with the conversion of a centurion, one of the soldiers who had crucified Christ (v. 47). Other answers to the prayer came in the weeks and months that followed the crucifixion—particularly at Pentecost—as untold numbers of people in Jerusalem were converted to Christ.

No doubt many of them were the same people who had clamored for Jesus' death and railed at Him from the foot of the cross.

It is important to understand that Jesus' plea for His killers' forgiveness did not guarantee the immediate and unconditional forgiveness of everyone who participated in the crucifixion. He was interceding on behalf of all who would repent and turn to Him as Lord and Savior. His prayer was that when they finally realized the enormity of what they had done and sought the heavenly Father's forgiveness for their sin, He would not hold the murder of His beloved Son against them. Divine forgiveness is never granted to people who remain in unbelief and sin. Those who clung to their hatred of Jesus were by no means automatically absolved from their crime by Jesus' prayer. But those who, like the centurion or the thief on the cross, repented and sought forgiveness would find abundant mercy in answer to Christ's petition on their behalf.

The prayer was a token of mercy offered to all who heard. He prayed aloud for their sakes (cf. John 11:42). Their sin was so unfathomably heinous that if witnesses had not actually heard Him pray for His killers' forgiveness, most might have assumed they had committed an unpardonable offense.

The forgiveness Christ prayed for is freely offered to all (Rev. 22:17). In fact, God is *eager* to forgive repentant sinners. (The prodigal son's father pictures God's eagerness to forgive.) He pleads for every sinner to be reconciled to Him (2 Cor. 5:20; Ezek. 18:23–32; Acts 17:30). Those who do, He promises to lavish freely with forgiveness. And that offer was extended even to those who personally participated in the murder of Jesus.

A PROMISE OF SALVATION

Christ's second utterance from the cross marks the first glorious fulfillment of His prayer for His killers' forgiveness, and it shows how generously that forgiveness was bestowed, even on the most unlikely of recipients.

As the hours of agony passed on the cross, one of the two thieves who had mocked Christ earlier now had a change of heart. What prompted the change is not mentioned. Perhaps the thief heard and was touched by Jesus' prayer for mercy, realizing that it applied to him. Whatever prompted his turnaround, it was a tremendous miracle.

The man was undoubtedly one of the most thoroughly degenerate people on the scene. He and his confederate were career criminals whose lives had been devoted to thievery and mayhem. The deep-down bad-to-the-bone wickedness of their character was shown by the fact that they used their dying strength to join in the taunting of Christ. They obviously knew of His innocence, because the repentant thief finally rebuked his cohort, saying, "This Man has done nothing wrong" (Luke 23:41 NKJV). Yet until one of them repented, they both were heaping ridicule and scorn on Him anyway.

But there came a point when one thief's taunting turned to silence, and the silence turned to repentance, and the thief's heart was utterly changed. As He studied Jesus, suffering all that abuse so patiently—never reviling or insulting His tormentors—the thief began to see that this Man on the center cross was indeed who He claimed to be. The proof of his repentance is seen in his immediate change of behavior, as his derisive insults turned to words of praise for Christ.

First he rebuked his partner in crime: "Do you not even fear God, seeing you are under the same condemnation? And we indeed justly, for we receive the due reward of our deeds; but this Man has done nothing wrong" (vv. 40–41 NKJV). In saying that much, he confessed his own guilt, and he also acknowledged the justice of the penalty he had been given. He affirmed the innocence of Christ as well.

Then he turned to Jesus and confessed Him as Lord: "Lord, remember me when You come into Your kingdom" (v. 42 NKJV).

That confession was immediately followed by the second of Jesus' seven last sayings: "And Jesus said to him, 'Assuredly, I say to you, today you will be with Me in Paradise'" (Luke 23:43 NKJV).

No sinner was ever given more explicit assurance of salvation. This most unlikely of saints was received immediately and unconditionally into the Savior's kingdom. The incident is one of the greatest biblical illustrations of the truth of justification by faith. This man had done nothing to *merit* salvation. Indeed, he was in no position to do anything meritorious. Already gasping in the throes of his own death agonies, he had no hope of ever *earning* Christ's favor. But realizing that he was in an utterly hopeless situation, the thief sought only a modest token of mercy from Christ: "Remember me."

His request was a final, desperate, end-of-his-rope plea for a small mercy he knew he did not deserve. It echoes the plaintive cry of the publican, who "would not so much as raise his eyes to heaven, but beat his breast, saying, 'God, be merciful to me a sinner!'" (Luke 18:13 NKJV). For either man to be granted eternal life and received into the kingdom, it had to be on the merits of another. And yet in both cases, Jesus gave full and immediate assurance of complete forgiveness and eternal life. Those are classic proofs that justification is by faith alone.

Jesus' words to the dying thief conveyed to him an unqualified promise of full forgiveness, covering every evil deed he had ever done. He wasn't expected to atone for his own sins, do penance, or perform any ritual. He wasn't consigned to purgatory—though if there really were such a place, and if the doctrines that invariably accompany belief in purgatory were true, this man would have been assured a long stay there. But instead, his forgiveness was full, and free, and immediate: *"Today* you will be with Me in Paradise."

That was all Christ said to him. But it was all the thief needed to hear. He was still suffering unspeakable physical torment, but the misery in his soul was now gone. For the first time in his life, he was free from the burden of his sin. The Savior, at his side, was bearing that sin for him. And the thief was now clothed in Christ's perfect righteousness. Soon they would be in Paradise together. The thief had Christ's own word on it.

A PROVISION FOR HIS MOTHER

Jesus' enemies were not the only spectators at the cross. As word got around Jerusalem that morning that Christ was under arrest and had been condemned to death by the Sanhedrin, some of His closest loved ones came to be near Him. John 19:25 describes the scene: "Now there stood by the cross of Jesus His mother, and His mother's sister, Mary the wife of Clopas, and Mary Magdalene" (NKJV). Some interpreters believe John mentions only three women, and that "His mother's sister" is the same person as "Mary the wife of Clopas." But that would mean these two sisters were both named Mary, and that seems highly unlikely. Instead, it seems John was saying there were three women named Mary present (Jesus' mother, Mrs. Clopas, and Mary Magdalene), as well as a fourth woman (Mary's sister) whose name is not given—but she might have been Salome, the mother of James and John. John also indicates in verse 26 that he himself was present, referring to himself the way he always did in his gospel, as "the disciple whom [Jesus] loved" (NKJV, cf. John 21:20–24).

The pain of watching Jesus die must have been agonizing for Jesus' loved ones. But for no one was it more difficult than Mary, His earthly mother. Years before, at his birth, the elderly prophet Simeon had told her, "Behold, this Child is destined for the fall and rising of many in Israel, and for a sign which will be spoken against *(yes, a sword will pierce through your own soul also),* that the thoughts of many hearts may be revealed" (Luke 2:34–35 NKJV, emphasis added). The sword Simeon spoke of was now piercing her heart, as she watched her firstborn Son die.

She had raised Him from childhood. She knew His utter perfection better than anyone. And yet as she watched, crowds of people poured contempt on her Son, cruelly mocking and abusing Him. His bleeding, emaciated form hung helplessly on the cross, and all she could do was watch His agony. The sorrow and pain such a sight would cause His mother is unfathomable. And yet instead of shrieking and crumpling in hysteria, turning and fleeing in terror, or falling into a faint at the horrible sight, she stood. She is the very model of courage.

Jesus saw her standing and grieving there, and His third saying from the cross reflects the tender love of a Son for his mother. "When Jesus therefore saw His mother, and the disciple whom He loved standing by, He said to His mother, 'Woman, behold your son!' Then He said to the disciple, 'Behold your mother!' And from that hour that disciple took her to his own home" (John 19:26–27 NKJV). When Jesus said, "Behold your son," He was not referring to Himself. He probably nodded at John. He was making a gracious provision for Mary in the years to come. He was delegating to John the responsibility to care for Mary in her old age.

This was a beautiful gesture, and it says a lot about the personal nature of Jesus' love. Although He was dying under the most excruciating kind of anguish, Jesus, the King of love, selflessly turned aside to care for the earthly needs of those who stood by His side. Although He was occupied with the most important event in the history of redemption, He remembered to make provision for the needs of one woman, His mother.

He addresses her as "Woman." Nowhere in the gospels does He ever call her "Mother"; only "Woman." The expression conveys no disrespect. But it does underscore the fact that Christ was much more to Mary than a son. He was her *Savior* too (cf. Luke 1:47). Mary was no sinless co-redemptrix. She was as dependent on divine grace as the lowliest of sinners, and after Christ reached adulthood, her relationship to Him was the same as that of any obedient believer to the Lord. She was a disciple; He was the Master.

Christ Himself rebuked those who wanted to elevate Mary to a place of extraordinary veneration: "A certain woman from the crowd raised her voice and said to Him, 'Blessed is the womb that bore You, and the breasts which nursed You!' But He said, 'More than that, blessed are those who hear the word of God and keep it!'" (Luke 11:27–28 NKJV). Mary was blessed because she was obedient to the Word of God—the same as any other believer. Her position as Christ's mother did not carry with it any special titles such as Co-mediatrix, Queen of heaven, or any of the other forms of deification medieval superstition has attached to the popular concept of Mary.

Let's be perfectly clear: it is a form of idolatry to bestow on Mary honor, titles, or attributes that in effect give her a coequal status in the redemptive work of her Son or elevate her as a special object of veneration.

Nonetheless, Christ loved and honored His mother *as a mother.* He fulfilled the fifth commandment as perfectly as He fulfilled them all. And part of the responsibility of honoring one's parents is the duty to see that they are cared for in their old age. Christ did not neglect that duty.

It is perhaps significant that Jesus did not commit Mary to the care of His own half brothers. Mary was evidently a widow by now. Nothing is said of Joseph after the gospel narratives about Jesus' birth and childhood. Apparently he had died by the time Jesus began His public ministry. But Scripture suggests that after Jesus' birth Mary and Joseph had a marital relationship that was in every sense normal (Matt. 1:25). Despite the claims of the Roman Catholic Church, Scripture does not allow us to believe Mary remained perpetually a virgin. On the contrary, the gospels clearly state that Jesus had brothers (Mark 3:31–35; John 2:12; Luke 8:19–21). Matthew even names them: "James, Joses, Simon, and Judas" (Matt. 13:55). They would have in fact been half brothers, as the natural offspring of Mary and Joseph.

Why didn't Jesus appoint one of His own brothers to look after Mary? Because, according to John 7:5, "His brothers did not believe in Him" (NKJV). They *became* believers when Jesus rose from the dead, and therefore Acts 1:14 records that they were among the group meeting for prayer in the Upper Room when the Holy Spirit came at Pentecost: "These all continued with one accord in prayer and supplication, with the women and Mary the mother of Jesus, *and with His brothers*" (NKJV; emphasis added). But they were evidently not believers yet when Jesus died. So as He was dying on the cross, He committed His mother to the care of His beloved disciple.

A PETITION TO THE FATHER

Christ's fourth saying from the cross is by far the most rich with mystery and meaning. Matthew writes, "Now from the sixth hour until the ninth hour there was darkness over all the land. And about the ninth hour Jesus cried out with a loud voice, saying, 'Eli, Eli, lama sabachthani?' that is, 'My God, My God, why have You forsaken Me?'" (Matt. 27:45–46 NKJV).

It might seem at first glance that Christ was merely reciting the words of Psalm 22:1 ("My God, My God, why have You forsaken Me? Why are You so far from helping Me, and from the words of My groaning?"). But given the fact that all of Psalm 22 is an extended prophecy about the crucifixion, it might be better to see the psalm as a prophetic anticipation of the cry of Jesus' heart as He bore the sins of the world on the cross. It was no mere recitation.

Some commentators have gone to great lengths to explain why Jesus would utter such words. To them, it seems unthinkable that Jesus would actually feel abandoned on the cross—and even more unthinkable to surmise that God in any sense abandoned His beloved Son. And so they insist that Jesus was merely reciting Scripture, not expressing what He truly felt in His heart.

But that betrays a serious misunderstanding of what was taking place on the cross. As Christ hung there, He was bearing the sins of the world. He was dying as a substitute for others. He was carrying the guilt of their sins and suffering the punishment for that sin on their behalf. And part of that punishment was the outpouring of God's wrath against sinners. In some mysterious way during those awful hours on the cross, the Father poured out the full measure of His wrath against sin, and the recipient of that wrath was God's own beloved Son!

In this lies the true meaning of the cross. Those who try to explain the atoning work of Christ in any other terms inevitably end up nullifying the truth of Christ's atonement altogether. Christ was not merely providing an example for us to follow. He was no mere martyr being sacrificed to the wickedness of the men who crucified Him. He wasn't merely making a public display so that people would see the awfulness of sin. He wasn't offering a ransom price to Satan—or any of the other various explanations religious liberals, cultists, and pseudo-Christian religionists have tried to suggest over the years.

Here's what was happening on the cross: God was punishing His own Son as if He had committed every wicked deed done by every sinner who will ever believe. And He did it so that He could forgive and treat those redeemed ones as if they had lived Christ's perfect life of righteousness.

Scripture teaches this explicitly: "He made Him who knew no sin to be sin for us, that we might become the righteousness of God in Him" (2 Cor. 5:21 NKJV).

> Surely He has borne our griefs
> And carried our sorrows;
> Yet we esteemed Him stricken,
> Smitten by God, and afflicted.
> But He was wounded for our transgressions,
> He was bruised for our iniquities;
> The chastisement for our peace was upon Him,
> And by His stripes we are healed. (Isaiah 53:4–5 NKJV)

"He had done no violence, nor was any deceit in His mouth. Yet it pleased the LORD to bruise Him; He has put Him to grief [in order to] make His soul an offering for sin" (vv. 9–10 NKJV). "Messiah shall be cut off, but not for Himself" (Dan. 9:26 NKJV). "What the law could not do in that it was weak through the flesh, God did by sending His own Son in the likeness of sinful flesh, on account of sin: He condemned sin in the flesh" (Rom. 8:3 NKJV). "Christ has redeemed us from the curse of the law, having become a curse for us (for it is written, 'Cursed is everyone who hangs on a tree')" (Gal. 3:13 NKJV). "Christ also suffered once for sins, the just for the unjust, that He might bring us to God, being put to death in the flesh" (1 Peter 3:18 NKJV). "He Himself is the propitiation for our sins" (1 John 2:2 NKJV).

That word "propitiation" speaks of an offering made to satisfy God. Christ's death was a satisfaction rendered to God on behalf of those whom He redeemed. "It *pleased* the LORD to bruise Him" (Isa. 53:10 NKJV, emphasis added). God the Father saw the travail of His Son's soul, and He was "satisfied" (v. 11). Christ made propitiation by shedding His blood (Rom. 3:25; Heb. 2:17).

It was God's own wrath against sin, God's own righteousness, and God's own sense of justice, that Christ satisfied on the cross. The shedding of His blood was a sin offering rendered to God. His death was *not* merely a satisfaction of public justice, or a ransom paid to Satan. Neither Satan nor anyone else had any right to claim a ransom from God for sinners. But when Christ ransomed the elect from sin (1 Tim. 2:6), the ransom price was paid to God. Christ died in our place and in our stead—and He received the very same outpouring of divine wrath in all its fury that *we* deserved for our sin. It was a punishment so severe that a mortal man could spend all eternity in the torments of hell, and still he would not have begun to exhaust the divine wrath that was heaped on Christ at the cross.

This was the true measure of Christ's sufferings on the cross. The physical pains of crucifixion—dreadful as they were—were nothing compared to the wrath of the Father against Him. The anticipation of *this* was what had caused Him to sweat blood in the garden. This was why He had looked ahead to the cross with such horror. We cannot begin to fathom all that was involved in paying the price of our sin. It's sufficient to understand that all our worst fears about the horrors of hell—and more—were realized by Him as He received the due penalty of others' wrongdoing.

And in that awful, sacred hour, it was as if the Father abandoned Him. Though there was surely no interruption in the Father's love for Him *as a Son,* God nonetheless turned away from Him and forsook Him *as our Substitute.*

The fact that Christ—suffering from exhaustion, blood loss, asphyxia, and all the physical anguish of the cross—nonetheless made this cry "with a loud voice" proves it was no mere recitation of a psalm. This was the outcry of His soul; it was the very thing the psalm foretold. And all nature groaned with Him.

A PLEADING FOR RELIEF

"After this, Jesus, knowing that all things were now accomplished, that the Scripture might be fulfilled, said, 'I thirst!'" (John 19:28 NKJV). This was Christ's fifth utterance from the cross. As the end neared, Christ uttered a final plea for physical relief. Earlier He had spat out the vinegar mixed with painkiller that had been offered Him. Now, when He asked for relief from the horrible thirst of dehydration, He was given only a sponge saturated with pure vinegar. John writes, "Now a vessel full of sour wine was sitting there; and they filled a sponge with sour wine, put it on hyssop, and put it to His mouth" (v. 29 NKJV).

In His thirst we see the true humanity of Christ. Although He was God incarnate, in His physical body, He experienced all the normal human limitations of real human flesh. And none was more vivid than this moment of agonizing thirst after hours of hanging on the cross. He suffered bodily to an extent few have ever suffered. And—again, so that the Scriptures might be fulfilled—all He was given to salve His fiery thirst was vinegar. "They also gave me gall for my food, And for my thirst they gave me vinegar to drink" (Ps. 69:21 NKJV).

A PROCLAMATION OF VICTORY

John's account of the crucifixion continues: "So when Jesus had received the sour wine, He said, 'It is finished!'" (John 19:30 NKJV). In the Greek text, this sixth utterance of Jesus from the cross is a single word: *Tetelestai!*

It was a triumphant outcry, full of rich meaning. He did not mean merely that His earthly life was over. He meant that the work the Father had given Him to do was now complete. As He hung there, looking every bit like a pathetic, wasted victim, He nonetheless celebrated the greatest triumph in the history of the universe. Christ's atoning work was finished, and He was triumphant.

The work of redemption was now done. Christ had fulfilled on behalf of sinners everything the law of God required of them. Full atonement had been made. Everything the ceremonial law foreshadowed had been accomplished. God's justice was satisfied. The ransom for sin was paid in full. The wages of sin were about to be settled forever. All that remained was for Christ to die so that He might rise again.

That is why nothing can be added to the work of Christ for salvation. No religious ritual—neither baptism, nor penance, nor any other human work—needs to be added to make His work effectual. No supplemental human works could ever augment or improve the atonement He purchased on the cross. The sinner is required to contribute nothing to earn forgiveness or a right standing with God; the merit of Christ alone is sufficient for our full salvation. *Tetelestai!* His atoning work is done. All of it. "For by grace you have been saved through faith, and that not of yourselves; it is the gift of God, not of works, lest anyone should boast" (Eph. 2:8–9 NKJV).

A PRAYER OF CONSUMMATION

Christ's final saying from the cross was a prayer that expressed the unqualified submission that had been in His heart from the very beginning. Luke records those final words: "And when Jesus had cried out with a loud voice, He said, 'Father, into Your hands I commit My spirit.' Having said this, He breathed His last" (Luke 23:46 NKJV).

Christ died as no other man has ever died. In one sense He was murdered by the hands of wicked men (Acts 2:23). In another sense it was the Father who sent Him to the cross and bruised Him there, putting Him to grief—and it pleased the Father to do so (Isa. 53:10). Yet in still another sense, no one took Christ's life. He gave it up willingly for those whom He loved (John 10:17–18).

When He finally expired on the cross, it was not with a wrenching struggle against His killers. He did not display any frenzied death throes. His final passage into death—like every other aspect of the crucifixion drama—was a deliberate act of His own sovereign will, showing that to the very end, He was sovereignly in control of all that was happening. John says, "Bowing His head, He gave up His spirit" (John 19:30 NKJV). Quietly, submissively, He simply gave up His life.

Everything had come to pass exactly as He said it would. Not only Jesus, but also His killers and the mocking crowd, together with Pilate, and Herod, and the Sanhedrin—all had perfectly fulfilled the determined purpose and foreknowledge of God to the letter.

And thus Christ calmly and majestically displayed His utter sovereignty to the end. It seemed to all who loved Him—and even many who cared little for Him—like a supreme tragedy. But it was the greatest moment of victory in the history of redemption, and Christ would make that fact gloriously clear when He burst triumphantly from the grave just days later.

14

How Did Creation Happen?[1]

Scripture clearly teaches that God created the universe out of *nothing*. He spoke it into existence by His Word. In fact, one of the unique features of the creation account in Genesis is a repeated stress on divine creation by *fiat*—meaning that a simple decree from God brings the created thing into being—*ex nihilo*—out of nothing. It's one of the fundamental tenets of true faith: "By faith we understand that the worlds were framed by the word of God, so that the things which are seen were *not made of things which are visible*" (Heb. 11:3 NKJV, emphasis added).

Evolution teaches the exact opposite. Evolution turns the creation event into a process that spanned billions of years and is still not complete. Evolutionists further insist that neither life itself nor any of the various species of living creatures came into being by immediate creation from nothing, but that they all emerged first from inanimate matter and then from preexisting life forms through a series of slow changes and genetic mutations that took some twenty billion years (or longer)—and that everything is still evolving. The modern scientific community has demanded and received almost universal acceptance of these basic principles of evolutionary theory.

Of course, time is the hero of all the evolutionists' theories. If the universe is not billions and billions of years old, we can discard evolutionary theory from the outset. On the other hand, if we accept the evolutionists' theory that the universe has existed for countless epochs, we must adjust our interpretation of Scripture to accommodate an old earth and thereby capitulate to one of evolution's most essential dogmas. Unfortunately, many Christian leaders today are advocating the latter approach.

EARTH SHAPED BY CONSTANCY OR CATASTROPHE?

The hypothesis that the earth is billions of years old is rooted in the unbiblical premise that what is happening now is just what has always happened. This idea is known as *uniformitarianism.* It is the theory that natural and geological phenomena are for the most part the results of forces that have operated continuously, with uniformity, and without interruption, over billions and billions of years. Uniformitarians assume that the forces at work in nature are essentially fixed and constant. Scientists who hold this view explain nearly all geological phenomena in terms of processes that are still occurring. The uniformitarian sees sedimentary rock strata, for example, and assumes that the sediments that formed them resulted from the natural, slow settling of particles in water over several million years' time. A uniformitarian observes the Grand Canyon and assumes the natural flow of the Colorado River carved that immense chasm over many ages with a steady (though constantly decreasing) stream.

Uniformitarianism was first proposed around the beginning of the nineteenth century by two British geologists, James Hutton and his best-known disciple, Charles Lyell. Lyell's work, *Principles of Geology,* was an explicit rejection of Creation- and Flood-based explanations for geological formulations. Lyell insisted that all the features of earth's geology must be explainable by natural, rather than supernatural, processes. He regarded all biblical or supernatural explanations as inherently unscientific and therefore false. In other words, he began with the presupposition that Scripture itself is untrue. And his work essentially canonized atheistic naturalism as the basis for "scientific" research.

Naturalism itself is a religious belief. The conviction that nothing happens supernaturally is a tenet of faith, not a fact that can be verified by any scientific means. Indeed, an *a priori* rejection of everything supernatural involves a giant, irrational leap of faith. So the presuppositions of atheistic naturalism are actually no more "scientific" than the beliefs of biblical Christianity. That obvious fact seems to have escaped Lyell and many who have followed him.

Nonetheless, Lyell's uniformitarian theory was enormously influential on other scientists of his age. (Darwin even took a copy of Lyell's work with him when he sailed on the *Beagle* in 1831.) And from the first publication of Lyell's work until today, the hypothesis that the earth is ages old has dominated secular science. The theory of evolution itself was the predictable and nearly immediate result of Lyell's uniformitarian hypothesis.

Of course, modern scientists have expanded their estimates of the age of the earth beyond anything Lyell himself ever imagined. But the basic theory of uniformitarianism first emerged from his antibiblical belief system.

The opposite of uniformitarianism is *catastrophism,* the view that dramatic geological changes have occurred in sudden, violent, or unusual events. A catastrophist observing sedimentary rock formations or large canyons is more likely (and more accurately) to interpret them as the result of massive flooding. Of course, this yields a much younger time frame for the development of earth's geological features. (A sudden flood, for example, can produce a thick layer of sediment in a few hours' time. That means a large stratum of sedimentary rock, which a uniformitarian might assume took millions of years to form, could actually be the result of a single flash flood.) Catastrophism therefore poses a major challenge to the evolutionary timetable, eliminating the multiple billions of years demanded to make the evolutionary hypothesis work. And for that reason it is rejected out of hand by most evolutionists.

But a moment's reflection will reveal that the fossil record is impossible to explain by any uniformitarian scheme. For a living creature to become fossilized (rather than decay and turn to dust—Job 34:15), it must be buried immediately under a great weight of sediment. Apart from a catastrophic deluge on a scale unlike any observed in recent history, how can we explain the existence of massive fossil beds (such as the Karoo formation fossil field in Africa, which is thought to hold 800 billion vertebrate fossils)? Natural sedimentation over several ages' time cannot explain how so many fossils came to be concentrated in one place. And every inhabited continent contains large fossil beds where millions of fossilized species are found together in large concentrations, as if all these creatures were destroyed and buried together by massive flooding. Fossils of sea creatures are even found on many of the world's highest mountaintops. How do uniformitarians explain such phenomena? The only way they can: they constantly increase their estimate of the age of the earth.

Scripture expressly condemns uniformitarianism in 2 Peter 3:4. Peter prophesied that this erroneous view would be adopted in the last days by scoffers—men walking after their own lusts—who imagine that "all things continue as they were from the beginning of creation" (NKJV). The apostle Peter goes on to write, "For this they willfully forget: that by the word of God the heavens were of old, and the earth standing out of water and in the water, by which the world that then existed perished, being flooded with water" (vv. 5–6 NKJV).

In other words, the plain teaching of Scripture is that this world's history has *not* been one of uniform natural and geological processes from the beginning. But according to the Bible, there have been at least two global cataclysmic events: Creation itself, and a catastrophic worldwide flood in Noah's time. These would sufficiently explain virtually all the geological and hydrological features of the earth as we know it.[3]

In fact, large-scale catastrophic forces are the only really plausible explanation for some geological features. Not far from where I live is an area known as Vasquez Rocks. It has the appearance of a rugged moonscape (and is a familiar site in science-fiction films, where it is often employed as a setting for scenes depicting exotic planets). Its main features are massive shards of jagged rock strata, broken sharply and thrusting out of the ground to great heights. Whatever force stood those rocks on end was obviously sudden and violent, not slow and gradual. The entire region is filled with similar evidences of catastrophe. Not far away is the infamous San Andreas Fault. There, where the roadway has been cut into the hillside, travelers may observe violently twisted rock strata. These features are mute evidence to extraordinary forces that have shaped the topography of Southern California—far exceeding the power of any known earthquake. Such phenomena are what we might expect, given the historicity of the biblical record. Scripture says, for example, that when the Flood began, "all the fountains of the great deep were broken up" (Gen. 7:11 NKJV). No doubt the Flood was accompanied by volcanic activity, massive geological movements, and the shifting of the earth's tectonic plates. Such a catastrophe would not only explain twisted and upthrust rock strata, but it would also easily explain why so many of the earth's mountain ranges give evidence of having once been under the sea. Uniformitarians cannot agree on any feasible explanation for features like these.

A massive flood would also explain the formation of the Grand Canyon. In fact, it would be a better explanation of how the canyon came to be than any uniformitarian hypothesis. The features of the canyon itself (extremely deep gorges with level plateaus at the rims) suggest that it was formed by rapid erosion. A strikingly similar formation is Providence Canyon, near Lumpkin, Georgia—a spectacular canyon that covers more than eleven hundred acres. In the early 1800s the entire area was flat farmland. By the mid-1800s, farmers had completely cleared the area of trees and their root systems, leaving the area susceptible to erosion. In 1846, heavy rainfall began forming small gullies and crevices. These expanded with every successive rainfall. By the 1940s, nearby buildings and towns had to be moved to accommodate the growing canyon. Today the canyon comprises sixteen fingers, some more than a mile in length. At places the distance from the canyon floor to the rim is as high as a fifteen-story building. Today it is a scenic area, lush with trees and wildlife, often called "Georgia's Little Grand Canyon." Its features are indistinguishable from canyons geologists claim took billions of years to form.[4]

Douglas Kelley writes,

The uniformitarian assumption that millions of years of geological work (extrapolating from present, slow, natural processes) would be required to explain structures such as the American Grand Canyon for instance, is called into serious question by the explosion of Mount St. Helens in the state of Washington on the 18th of May 1980. Massive energy equivalent to 20 million tons of TNT destroyed 400 square kilometers of forest in six minutes, changing the face of the mountain and digging out depths of earth and rock, leaving formations not unlike parts of the larger Grand Canyon. Recent studies of the Mount St. Helens phenomenon indicate that if attempts were made to date these structures (which were formed in 1980) on the basis of uniformitarian theory, millions of years of formation time would be necessarily postulated.[5]

Christians who reinterpret the biblical text to try to accommodate the uniformitarians' old-earth hypotheses do so unnecessarily. To imagine that the earth was formed by natural processes over billions and billions of years through slow and steady evolution is to deny the very essence of what Scripture teaches about the earth's creation. It is to reject the clear account of God Himself that He created the earth and all its life in six days.

WHICH CAME FIRST—THE CHICKEN OR THE EGG?

One rather obvious fact ignored by many is that the universe was mature when it was created. God created it with the *appearance* of age. When He created trees and animals, for example, He created them as mature, fully developed organisms. According to the biblical account, He did not create just seeds and cells. He certainly did not plant a single cell programmed to evolve itself into a variety of creatures. He made trees with already mature fruit (Gen. 1:11). He didn't merely create an egg; He made chickens already full grown. (Thus Genesis 1:21 plainly answers the familiar conundrum.) He created Adam full grown and fully capable of marriage and procreation.

Did Adam have a navel? It's worth noting that some modern creationists, including Ken Ham (whose work I have the utmost respect for), believe the answer is no, because the navel is a scar left from the umbilical cord, and a created being would have no use for such a scar.[6]

The question of whether Adam had a navel may sound frivolous, but in medieval and Renaissance times it was often the subject of intense debate. Artists who depicted Adam and Eve in the garden were faced with a theological dilemma: should our first parents be portrayed with navels, or not? Not a few artists solved the problem by painting fig leaves large enough to extend above where the navel would be. But in his famous painting that is the centerpiece of the Sistine Chapel's ceiling, Michelangelo gave Adam an impressive belly button. And he was fiercely criticized for it by some of the sterner theologians of his day.

But is it really so far-fetched to think that God would have created Adam with a navel? After all, the navel is an integral part of normal human anatomy. The structure of our abdominal muscles and vascular system is designed to accommodate the navel. I know of no necessary theological or biblical reason to *insist* that Adam and Eve could not have had them. Our first parents surely appeared like normal adults in every respect. They were probably given calluses to protect the soles of their feet like any normal adult, and the edges of their teeth were no doubt smooth, as if from normal use, rather than sharp, as if they had never been used.

Of course, the whole question of whether Adam and Eve had belly buttons (or calluses or smooth edges on their teeth) is purely speculative. Scripture simply does not address the issue. So while the question itself is intriguing, there's no need to revive a trivial debate with medieval intensity.

But the fact remains that Adam certainly had many features associated with maturity. He wasn't created as an embryo or an infant. Rather, he was a fully grown man. There is no reason to doubt that he had normal adult features; he certainly would have had fully developed muscles; and we know he was created with enough knowledge to tend the garden, name the animals, and talk with God. Without any growth, history, or experience, he was still a mature adult man.

Suppose a modern scientist could travel back in time and arrive in the garden moments after Adam's creation. If he examined Adam, he would see adult features (perhaps a navel, calluses, or smooth edges on his teeth—or at the very least, an adult frame and musculature). If he could converse with Adam, he would find a man with adult knowledge and fully formed language skills. But if he interpreted those things as conclusive proof that Adam was more than one hour old, he would simply be wrong. When we're dealing with things created *ex nihilo*, evidences of maturity or signs of age do not constitute proof of antiquity.

And what if that same time-traveling scientist did a botanical study of a newly created oak tree? He would observe the size of the tree, note the tree's fruit (acorns), and probably conclude that the tree itself was many years old.

What if he cut down one of the trees to examine its growth rings? Would he find growth rings inside, indicating that the tree had been there for many seasons? Why not? Those rings of xylem and phloem are not only signs of the tree's age, but they also compose the tree's vascular system. They are essential to the strength of a large tree as well. But if our imaginary scientist concluded on the basis of tree rings that the tree was ninety years old, he would be wrong again. The garden itself was created mature, fully functional, and therefore with the appearance of age.

The garden was no doubt filled with creatures that had every appearance of age. On day seven, when the Lord rested from His labor, everything was fully mature and fully functional. The eagles soaring overhead might have appeared to be thirty years old, but they were less than a week old. Elephants roaming around might have had full tusks and appeared to be fifty years old, but they were merely one *day* old. Any mountains, rivers, or other geological features probably also appeared to have been there for some time. There were no doubt beautiful waterfalls and canyons and other features that the typical geologist would surmise had been formed by several ages of wind and water or volcanic eruptions and earthquakes. But the fact is that they were all made in one day. And when Adam looked up into the heavens and saw that incredible expanse with millions of bright stars, he was seeing light from millions of light years away—even though those stars had all had been there less than four days. The light he saw was itself part of God's creation.

All those marks of age and maturity are part of every creative miracle. When Jesus turned water to wine, for example, He utterly bypassed the fermentation and aging process. He made wine instantly from water, and those who tasted it testified that it was the best wine of all (John 2:10)—meaning it was mature and well seasoned already, even though it was an instantaneous creation. When He multiplied the loaves and fishes, He created bread and fish that were already cooked and ready to eat.

We certainly expect people who reject Scripture and despise God to accept the notion that the universe has existed for aeons and aeons. For obvious reasons, they want to eliminate every supernatural explanation for the origin of humanity. They don't want any binding moral law or omnipotent Judge to whom they must be accountable. So of course they embrace the naturalistic theories of evolution and an ancient earth with great enthusiasm.

But it is shocking and disturbing to see how the idea that the earth is billions of years old has begun to dominate even the evangelical Christian community. In recent years a number of leading evangelical theologians, Bible commentators, and apologists have begun arguing that it is now necessary to go beyond the plain meaning of the creation account in Genesis and try to adapt our understanding of creation as closely as possible to the theories currently in vogue in secular science. If we insist on a literal six-day creation and a young age for the universe, they claim, we will sacrifice our academic credibility and weaken our testimony to those educated in the theory of evolution.

SHOULD WE APPRAISE SCRIPTURE BY SCIENCE, OR VICE VERSA?

Perhaps the leading evangelical figure in the effort to harmonize Genesis with current scientific theories is Hugh Ross, a former astrophysicist who is now a full-time apologist and advocate for old-earth creationism. (Dr. Ross employs the term "progressive creationism" to describe his views.)

Ross, to his credit, says he affirms without reservation the absolute authority and inerrancy of Scripture. He accepts the biblical testimony that God created each species of living creature individually. He does not believe that lower life forms evolved into higher ones, or that humans evolved from animal species. In fact, he regards Adam and Eve as historical figures, the literal parents of the entire human race. In all these ways, the views advocated by Hugh Ross are far superior to those of "theistic evolutionists" or other professing Christians who imbibe evolutionary theory and conclude that the early chapters of Genesis are merely myth or error. Unlike them, Hugh Ross is an evangelical. The doctrinal statement his ministry publishes is a straightforward statement of basic evangelical convictions. His books are endorsed by a Who's Who of evangelical leaders.

So what's the problem? Simply this: Hugh Ross has embraced selected theories of "big bang" cosmology, which he regards as undisputed fact—including the notion that the universe and the earth are billions of years old—and he employs those theories as lenses through which to interpret Scripture. In effect, he makes Scripture subservient to "science"—and he does so without carefully separating scientific fact from scientific theory.

Hugh Ross is convinced modern scientific theories can give us a superior understanding of the basic facts related to the origin of the universe. All Ross's books therefore argue, in effect, that the findings of modern science are *necessary* to interpret the Bible's true meaning. According to Ross, our generation—thanks to the evolutionists' big-bang theory—is now able to understand the true meaning of the biblical creation narratives in a way no previous generation ever could. In effect, he believes the modern scientific opinion about the age and origin of the universe is *essential* to explain what Scripture really meant all along. He is therefore convinced that Scripture aims to teach us that creation was a process that took billions of years, not just one week, to complete. And that means all past generations from Moses through the late twentieth century have been clueless as to the true meaning of Genesis.

Obviously, Ross himself does not accept *all* the claims of evolutionists. But if his views are correct, we should be able to separate what is "factual" from what is theoretical in modern science, and use the *facts* of science as a guideline for interpreting the biblical creation account. This approach, he insists, yields an understanding of Genesis that perfectly harmonizes with modern cosmology's belief that the universe is some twenty billion years old.

Unfortunately, Ross himself seems to use a completely arbitrary method to determine which doctrines of modern science should be regarded as fact and which are mere theory.

For example, the big-bang theory itself is still highly controversial, even among Ross's fellow astronomers. It is only the latest in a long line of "scientific" explanations of how the universe came to be. Big-bang cosmology itself is in constant flux. (For example, scientists once believed that the entire universe emerged when an unimaginably enormous mass of matter exploded, but the theory currently in vogue is that all the matter of the universe emerged from a particle that was infinitesimally small.) Yet despite all the uncertainty surrounding the big bang, Hugh Ross regards it as an "unshakably established" fact,[7] and he insists that it sheds necessary light on the true meaning of Scripture.

Ross also advocates a scheme of long paleontological eras which he claims harmonizes perfectly with the six days of Scripture. In order to maintain his view, he is forced to ignore or dismiss in a facile way some rather obvious difficulties. For example, plant life appears on day three in the biblical account, but the sun, essential to sustaining those plants, doesn't appear until day four. And insects aren't created until day six, which would be millions of years after the appearance of plant life, if Ross's view of the "days" is correct. Of course, the paleontological sequence Ross proposes is by no means universally accepted by scientists; it is merely one of several popular theories.[8] But Ross treats it as authoritative fact and lets it dictate his whole understanding of the Bible's six days of creation.

Ross treats many similarly questionable theories as indisputable facts. He believes, for example, that science has proven irrefutably that the Flood of Noah's era could not really have been the sort of worldwide deluge a literal reading of Genesis 7:19–24 would clearly indicate. He apparently believes science has established with absolute certainty the existence of pre-Adamic hominids—

subhuman creatures who were perfectly manlike in appearance. He states as a matter of fact that "bipedal, tool-using, large-brained hominids roamed the earth at least as long ago as one million years"[9]—long ages before he believes Adam appeared on the scene. And in order to explain how species like that arose and disappeared in the long ages before Adam's creation Ross also insists that the world was filled with bloodshed, death, violence, and decay for countless millennia—even prior to the fall of Adam and the curse of Genesis 3:14–19.

Reading through Ross's books, one is at a complete loss to discover *how* he determines which modern scientific ideas are facts and which ones are mere theories. He constantly cites "the latest research findings"; "recent studies"; "current estimates"; "newer data"—while acting as if he were citing matters of well-established, universally accepted fact. Dr. Ross's tendency to treat questionable theories as if they were irrefutable fact is well documented.[10] The conclusion is inescapable that his own arbitrary judgment is the main standard by which he determines which scientific ideas are established facts and which are mere theory.

But the question of whether a scientific doctrine is truly fact or merely theory is not one that can be brushed aside if one accepts Dr. Ross's views, because his entire system is built on the idea that Scripture and the facts of science are *equal* in authority.

According to Ross, *general revelation* (the display of divine glory that is evident in creation) is every bit as essential and as authoritative as *special revelation* (the truth God has revealed in Scripture). Indeed, Ross would be perfectly happy to give science a place in the canon. "God's revelation is not limited exclusively to the Bible's words," he says. *"The facts of nature may be likened to a sixty-seventh book of the Bible."*[11]

Ross seems to try to back away from the implications of that statement, but he cannot:

> Some readers might fear I am implying that God's revelation through nature is somehow on an equal footing with His revelation through the words of the Bible. Let me simply state that truth, by definition, is information that is perfectly free of contradiction and error. Just as it is absurd to speak of some entity as more perfect than another, so also one revelation of God's truth cannot be held as inferior or superior to another.[12]

In other words, Ross clearly *does* believe "that God's revelation through nature is . . . on an equal footing with His revelation through the words of the Bible." No other sensible conclusion may be drawn from his words. If the facts of nature might as well be written down and stitched into the Bible as a "sixty-seventh book," then there is no reason to subjugate science to Scripture, rather than vice versa.

After all, if the voice of nature really *does* speak with the same clarity and authority as the inspired words of Scripture, who could argue with Ross's approach?

IS GENERAL REVELATION EQUAL TO
SPECIAL REVELATION?

But how much and what kind of truth does God reveal through nature? Hugh Ross seems to believe that general revelation alone is sufficient to tell us all we need to know about God and Creation. "God reveals himself faithfully through the 'voice' of nature as well as through the inspired words of scripture," Ross writes.[13] What about the truth of the gospel? Is it discernable to someone who observes only nature and the cosmos apart from Scripture? Ross seems to suggest that it is, and in support he cites Colossians 1:23, where we are told that the gospel "has been proclaimed to every creature under heaven" (NIV).[14] Thus Ross implies that nature, like Scripture, is a *sufficient* revelation, able to make people wise unto salvation and thoroughly equip them for every good work (cf. 2 Tim. 3:15–17).

Ross claims the classic evangelical view of a literal six-day creation and a young earth is rooted in a faulty "single revelational theology," which he defines as "the belief that the Bible is the only authoritative source of truth."[15] He refers to his own view as "dual revelation theology"—and in support of his view he supplies a list of Scripture references that establish the doctrine of general revelation—chiefly Psalm 19:1–4 and Romans 1:19–20.

Reading Ross's treatment of the subject, one might get the impression that young-earth creationists deny general revelation altogether. But the reality is that *all* evangelical theologians recognize the legitimate place of general revelation. In the passages Ross cites, Scripture plainly states that "The heavens declare the glory of God" (Ps. 19:1 NKJV). The revelation of God and His glory through nature is obvious enough so that anyone who rejects the God of the Bible is "without excuse" (Rom. 1:19–20 NKJV). The Romans 1 passage even says the evidence of creation reveals to everyone certain "invisible attributes" of God, namely "His eternal power and Godhead" (i.e., His divinity).

But those passages do not teach what Dr. Ross claims they teach. They certainly do not put nature on an equal footing with Scripture. In fact, Jesus

Himself expressly debunked the notion that nature and Scripture are equivalent forms of revelation when He said, "Heaven and earth will pass away, but My words will by no means pass away" (Matt. 24:35 NKJV; cf. Mark 13:31).

Furthermore, nothing in Scripture suggests that *everything* we need to know about God is revealed to us in nature. On the contrary, the whole point of Psalm 19 is to underscore the necessity, the absolute sufficiency, and the preeminence of *special* revelation—Scripture. Nature simply puts God's glory on display in a mute testimony that declares His majesty, power, divinity, and existence to all— and leaves them without excuse if they ignore or reject the God of the Bible. In other words, natural revelation is sufficient to condemn sinners but not to save them. Scripture, on the other hand, is perfect, sure, right, pure, clean, and altogether true (vv. 7–9). Unlike the general revelation available to us in nature, the truth of Scripture converts the soul, makes wise the simple, enlightens the eyes, and endures forever (vv. 7–9). So the psalm plainly underscores the *superiority* of Scripture. Its whole point is that the revelation of God in nature is not as powerful, as enduring, as reliable, as clear, or as authoritative as Scripture. Scripture is a *sufficient* revelation; nature is not. Scripture is clear and complete; nature is not. Scripture therefore speaks with more authority than nature and should be used to assess scientific opinion, not vice versa.

Unlike nature, Scripture is *perspicuous;* its meaning is clear and easy to understand. Not all Scripture is *equally* perspicuous, of course. Some portions are notoriously hard to understand (2 Peter 3:16), and even the simplest passage of Scripture must be correctly interpreted in order to yield its true meaning. But the perspicuity and the comprehensiveness of Scripture are vastly superior to that of nature. And therefore Scripture should be the rule by which we measure science, rather than the reverse approach.

Hugh Ross places *too much* stress on the value of general revelation. He errs in making general revelation and special revelation exact parallels—as if everything Scripture says about its own authority and sufficiency were true of nature as well. Worse, his view of "the facts of nature" is framed by current scientific hypotheses about the age and origin of the universe. So Ross is actually suggesting that evolutionists' theories (or at least some of them) ought to be esteemed as highly as biblical revelation. In practice, however, he and other progressive creationists have made scientific theories a *superior* authority, because they employ those theories as a rule by which they interpret the statements of the Bible. Current scientific theory has thus become an interpretive grid through which progressive creationists read and explain Scripture. They have made science the interpreter of Scripture in a manner that is completely unwarranted. In effect, they have simply borrowed ideas from modern scientific theory and imported those thoughts *into* the text of Scripture. The actual language of the text is thus obscured or overturned in favor of an unbiblical idea that has been imposed on it. Such a method naturally yields an interpretation that is utterly disconnected from and often flatly contrary to the actual words of Scripture. And frankly, that is the only way anyone could ever read the testimony of Scripture and conclude that the universe is billions of years old.

IS THE UNIVERSE YOUNG OR OLD?

In fact, it is virtually impossible to begin with a straightforward reading of Genesis and arrive at the opinion that the universe is older than a few thousand years.

Take the age of the human race, for example. Hugh Ross believes, on the basis of the fossil record, that the creation of Adam may have occurred as much as fifty thousand years ago.[16] But Genesis contains a detailed genealogy that traces the development of the human race from Adam to Abraham and beyond. The genealogy includes a chronology with the exact ages of individuals when their offspring were born. Archbishop James Ussher did a careful analysis of the genealogies in the seventeenth century and concluded that the date for Adam's creation was 4004 B.C. Some scholars have suggested that there may be gaps in the genealogy, where a generation or two is skipped and the name of a grandson or great-grandson is substituted for the name of a son. Such gaps can be demonstrated in some biblical genealogies. (In Matthew 1:8, for instance, Matthew skips three generations from Joram to Uzziah, apparently to maintain a symmetry in the genealogy.) No such gaps can be proven in the detailed genealogies of Genesis 5 and 11. But even allowing for some possible gaps, it's inconceivable that the date for Adam's creation could be much more than ten thousand years ago. As Henry Morris has written, "At the outside, it would seem impossible to insert gaps totaling more than about five thousand years in these chapters without rendering the record irrelevant and absurd. Consequently, the Bible will not support a date for the creation of man earlier than about 10,000 B.C."[17]

What about the notion that the "days" of creation were long epochs? Nothing in the immediate context suggests that these early chapters of Genesis are to be interpreted figuratively. Jesus treated the biblical creation account as history (Matt. 19:4), as did the apostles Paul (2 Cor. 4:6) and Peter (2 Peter 3:5). It is presented as straightforward history. Indeed, the *only* reason for interpreting the six days of Genesis as long epochs is for the sake of harmonizing Genesis with recent scientific theories. As Edward J. Young observed,

What strikes one immediately [about such an approach] is the low esti-mate of the Bible which it entails. Whenever "science" and the Bible are in conflict, it is always the Bible that, in one manner or another, must give way. We are not told that "science" should correct its answers in the light of Scripture. Always it is the other way round. Yet this is really sur-prising, for the answers which scientists have provided have frequently changed with the passing of time. The "authoritative" answers of pre-Copernican scientists are no longer acceptable; nor, for that matter, are many of the views of twenty-five years ago.[18]

But the order of creation itself rules out the possibility that the "days" of Genesis 1 were really long ages. For example, plant life was created on day three, includ-ing flowering plants and seed-producing trees (1:12). But birds didn't appear until the fifth day (v. 21), and earthbound animal creatures—including insects ("creeping thing[s]," v. 24)—were not created until the sixth day. As every gar-dener knows, there is a necessary symbiosis between most flowering plants and the insect kingdom that utterly rules out the existence of one apart from the other. All these different, interdependent life forms could not have evolved together simultaneously; neither could the flowering plants have been created thousands of years before the insects and birds.

Scripture says *all* these creatures were made in a week's time. Life did not appear slowly and gradually on the earth, in increasing degrees of complexity, and over many ages of time. That is what evolution teaches. The Bible stresses the sudden and immediate *ex nihilo* creation of everything in the universe. It was all created in a very short time, despite its incredible vastness and complexity.

Obviously, the mind steeped in modern science and its antisupernatural bias struggles to fathom how so much could occur in so short a time. But there's no reason a Christian should doubt that God could have created everything fully mature in a nanosecond if He chose to do so. There's *certainly* no reason a Christian should balk at believing that God created everything in six days. After all, that is what a straightforward reading of Scripture plainly teaches.

Nonetheless, Hugh Ross evidently thinks the intricacy and perfection of cre-ation is an argument against a young earth. After listing several scientific "proofs" that the universe is billions of years old, he writes,

One further consideration from an altogether different perspective con-cerns the nature of creativity itself. Observe any skilled sculptor, painter, or poet, a craftsman of any kind. Observe the painstaking yet joyful labor poured into each object of his design. Examine the creation on any scale, from a massive galaxy to the interior of an atom, from a whale to an amoeba. The splendor of each item, its beauty of form as well as of function, speaks not of instantaneous mass production, but rather of time and attention to detail, of infinite care and delight.[19]

The argument seems to suggest that God could not possibly have created such an intricate universe in only six days' time. Yet the whole point of Genesis 1–2 is that God's creative power, like the universe itself, is unfathomable to the human mind. With His infinite power and wisdom, He had no need of aeons to design and perfect His creation. He simply spoke the word and brought forth out of nothing everything we see. And Scripture says He did it in six days' time.

Absolutely nothing in the text of Genesis 1:1–2:3 speaks of evolution or long geological ages in the creation process. The text itself is in fact a straightforward refutation of all evolutionary principles. Theistic evolution, billion-year-old-earth theories, and "progressive creationism" are all refuted if we simply take the statements of Genesis at face value. Only by denying key expressions or interpreting them in a nonliteral sense can the Christian read any degree of evolution or "progressive creation" into the Genesis account.

Consequently, it's a very difficult task for any commentator or exegete to impose old-earth theories on the biblical creation account. In order to attempt it at all, they must begin by obscuring the obvious historical sense of the passage and turn instead to literary devices such as allegory, myth, legend, or poetic expressions.

And in doing so, they are attempting to make the Word of God bow the knee to godless naturalism and its ever-changing theories. We ought rather to allow the unchanging, ever-authoritative Word of God to inform our understanding, and let science bow the knee to Scripture.

Dr. Ross remains an evangelical who believes in the historicity of Adam and Eve precisely because at some juncture he decided to accept the revealed truth of Scripture *instead of* the theories of modern science. It would be much better to recognize the superiority of Scripture up-front and make Scripture the authority whereby *all* scientific theory is evaluated. That is the historic principle of *sola Scriptura*. Christians who hold to the authority of Scripture over scientific theory will not be ashamed when all the true facts come in. Remember, Christ Himself said, "Heaven and earth will pass away, but My words will by no means pass away" (Matt. 24:35 NKJV). The Word of God still stands unchanged after thousands of years, while the theories of secular science change dramatically with every new generation.

Heaven and earth *will* pass away. The universe will one day dissolve as quickly as it came into being (2 Peter 3:10–12), only to be replaced immediately by a new heaven and new earth (Rev. 21:1–5). And the biblical account of the first creation will be fully vindicated.

15

COMMON MEN, UNCOMMON CALLING[1]

For you see your calling, brethren, that not many wise according to the flesh, not many mighty, not many noble, are called. But God has chosen the foolish things of the world to put to shame the wise, and God has chosen the weak things of the world to put to shame the things which are mighty; and the base things of the world and the things which are despised God has chosen, and the things which are not, to bring to nothing the things that are, that no flesh should glory in His presence.

1 CORINTHIANS 1:26–29 (NKJV)

From the time Jesus began His public ministry in His hometown of Nazareth, He was enormously controversial. The people from His own hometown literally tried to kill Him immediately after His first public message in the local synagogue. "All those in the synagogue, when they heard these things, were filled with wrath, and rose up and thrust Him out of the city; and they led Him to the brow of the hill on which their city was built, that they might throw Him down over the cliff. Then passing through the midst of them, He went His way" (Luke 4:28–30 NKJV).

Ironically, Jesus became tremendously popular among the people of the larger Galilee region. As word of His miracles began to circulate throughout the district, massive hordes of people came out to see Him and hear Him speak. Luke 5:1 records how "the multitude pressed about Him to hear the word of God" (NKJV). One day, the crowds were so thick and so aggressive that He got into a boat, pushed it offshore far enough to get away from the press of people, and taught the multitudes from there. (Not by mere happenstance, the boat Jesus chose belonged to Simon. Jesus would rename him Peter, and he would become the dominant person in Jesus' closest inner circle of disciples.)

Some might imagine that if Christ had wanted His message to have maximum impact, He could have played off His popularity more effectively. Modern conventional wisdom would suggest that Jesus ought to have done everything possible to exploit His fame, tone down the controversies that arose out of His teaching, and employ whatever strategies He could use to maximize the crowds around Him. But He did not do that. In fact, He did precisely the opposite. Instead of taking the populist route and exploiting His fame, He began to emphasize the very things that made His message so controversial. At about the time the crowds reached their peak, He preached a message so boldly confrontational and so offensive in its content that the multitude melted away, leaving only the most devoted few (John 6:66–67).

Among those who stayed with Christ were the Twelve, whom He had personally selected and appointed to represent Him. They were twelve perfectly ordinary, unexceptional men. But Christ's strategy for advancing His kingdom hinged on those twelve men rather than on the clamoring multitudes. He chose to work through the instrumentality of those few fallible individuals rather than advance His agenda through mob force, military might, personal popularity, or a public-relations campaign. From a human perspective, the future of the church and the long-term success of the gospel depended entirely on the faithfulness of that handful of disciples. There was no plan B if they failed.

The strategy Jesus chose typified the character of the kingdom itself. "The kingdom of God does not come with observation; nor will they say, 'See here!' or 'See there!' For indeed, the kingdom of God is within you" (Luke 17:20–21 NKJV). The kingdom advances "'not by might nor by power, but by My Spirit,' says the LORD of hosts" (Zech. 4:6 NKJV). Eleven men under the power of the Holy Spirit are a more potent force than the teeming masses whose initial enthusiasm for Jesus was apparently provoked by little more than sheer curiosity.

Christ personally chose the Twelve and invested most of His energies in them. He chose them before they chose Him (John 15:16). The process of choosing and calling them happened in distinct stages. Careless readers of Scripture sometimes imagine that John 1:35–51; Luke 5:3–11; and the formal calling of the Twelve in Luke 6:12–16 are contradictory accounts of how Christ called His apostles. But there is no contradiction. The passages are simply describing different stages of the apostles' calling.

In John 1:35–51, for example, Andrew, John, Peter, Philip, and Nathanael encounter Jesus for the first time. This event occurs near the beginning of Jesus' ministry, in the wilderness near the Jordan River, where John the Baptist was ministering. Andrew, John, and the others were there because they were already disciples of John the Baptist. But when they heard their teacher single out Jesus and say, "Behold the Lamb of God!" they followed Jesus.

That was phase one of their calling. It was a calling to *conversion*. It illustrates how every disciple is called first to salvation. We must recognize Jesus as the true Lamb of God and Lord of all and embrace Him by faith. That stage of the disciples' call did not involve full-time discipleship. The gospel narratives suggest that although they followed Jesus in the sense that they gladly heard His teaching and submitted to Him as their Teacher, they remained at their full-time jobs, earning a living through regular employment. That is why from this point until Jesus called them to full-time ministry, we often see them fishing and mending their nets.

Phase two of their calling was a call to *ministry*. Luke 5 describes the event in detail. This was the occasion when Jesus pushed out from shore to escape the press of the multitudes and taught from Peter's boat. After He finished teaching, He instructed Peter to launch out to the deep water and put in his nets. Peter did so, even though the timing was wrong (fish were easier to catch at night when the water was cooler and the fish surfaced to feed); the place was wrong (fish normally fed in shallower waters and were easier to catch there); and Peter was exhausted (having fished all night without any success). He told Jesus, "Master, we have toiled all night and caught nothing; nevertheless at Your word I will let down the net" (Luke 5:5 NKJV). The resulting catch of fish overwhelmed their nets and nearly sank two of their fishing boats! (vv. 6–7).

It was on the heels of that miracle that Jesus said, "Follow Me, and I will make you fishers of men" (Matt. 4:19 NKJV). Scripture says it was at this point that "they forsook all and followed Him" (Luke 5:11 NKJV). According to Matthew, Andrew and Peter "immediately left their nets and followed Him" (Matt. 4:20 NKJV). And James and John "immediately . . . left the boat and their father, and followed Him" (v. 22 NKJV). From that point on, they were inseparable from the Lord.

Matthew 10:1–4 and Luke 6:12–16 describe a third phase of their calling. This was their calling to *apostleship*. It was at this point that Christ selected and appointed twelve men in particular and made them His apostles. Here is Luke's account of the incident:

> Now it came to pass in those days that He went out to the mountain to pray, and continued all night in prayer to God. And when it was day, He called His disciples to Himself; and from them He chose twelve whom He also named apostles: Simon, whom He also named Peter, and Andrew

his brother; James and John; Philip and Bartholomew; Matthew and Thomas; James the son of Alphaeus, and Simon called the Zealot; Judas the son of James, and Judas Iscariot who also became a traitor. (NKJV)

This marks the beginning of a kind of internship. Christ sends them out. Mark 6:7 says they were sent out two by two. At this stage they were not quite ready to go out alone, so Christ teamed them in pairs, so that they would offer one another mutual support.

Throughout this phase of their training, the Lord Himself stuck closely with them. He was like a mother eagle, watching the eaglets as they began to fly. They were always checking back with Him, reporting on how things were going (cf. Luke 9:10; 10:17). And after a couple of seasons of evangelistic labor, they returned to the Lord and remained with Him for an extended time of teaching, ministry, fellowship, and rest (Mark 6:30–34).

There was a fourth phase of their calling, which occurred after Jesus' resurrection. Judas was now missing from the group, having hanged himself after his betrayal of Christ. Jesus appeared to the remaining eleven in His resurrection body and sent them into all the world, commanding them to disciple the nations. This was, in effect, a call to *martyrdom*. Each of them ultimately gave his life for the sake of the gospel. History records that all but one of them were killed for their testimony. Only John is said to have lived to old age, and he was severely persecuted for the sake of the gospel, then exiled to the tiny island of Patmos.

Despite the obstacles they faced, they triumphed. In the midst of great persecution and even martyrdom, they fulfilled their task. Against all odds, they entered victorious into glory. And the continuing witness of the gospel—spanning two thousand years' time, and reaching into virtually every corner of the world—is a testimony to the wisdom of the divine strategy. No wonder we are fascinated by these men.

Let's begin our study of the Twelve by looking carefully at phase three of their calling—their selection and appointment to apostleship. Notice the details as Luke gives them to us.

THE TIMING

First, the timing of this event is significant. Luke notes this with his opening phrase in Luke 6:12: "Now it came to pass in those days" (NKJV). The New American Standard Bible renders the phrase this way: "And it was at this time." Luke is not talking about clock time, or the specific days of a specific month. "At this time" and "in those days" refers to a period of time; a season; a distinct phase in Jesus' ministry. It was an interval in His ministry when the opposition to Him peaked.

"In those days" refers back to the immediately preceding account. This section of Luke's gospel records the vicious opposition Christ was beginning to receive from the scribes and Pharisees. Luke 5:17 is Luke's first mention of the Pharisees, and verse 21 is his first use of the word "scribes." (The scribes are mentioned alongside the Pharisees as "teachers of the law" in verse 17.)

So we are first introduced to Jesus' chief adversaries in Luke 5:17, and Luke's account of their opposition fills the text through the end of chapter 5 and well into chapter 6. Luke is describing the escalating conflict between Jesus and the religious leaders of Judaism. They opposed Him when He healed a paralytic and forgave his sins (5:17–26). They opposed Him for eating and drinking with tax collectors and sinners (5:27–32). They opposed Him when He permitted His disciples to pluck heads of grain and eat them on the Sabbath (6:1–5). And they opposed Him for healing a man with a withered hand on the Sabbath (6:6–11). One after another, Luke recounts those incidents and highlights the growing opposition of the religious leaders.

The conflict reaches a high point in Luke 6:11. The scribes and Pharisees "were filled with rage, and discussed with one another what they might do to Jesus" (NKJV). Both Mark and Matthew are even more graphic. They report that the religious leaders wanted to destroy Jesus (Matt. 12:14; Mark 3:6). Mark says the religious leaders even got the Herodians involved in their plot. The Herodians were a political faction that supported the dynasty of the Herods. They were not normally allied with the Pharisees, but the two groups joined together in collusion against Jesus. They were already hatching plans to murder Him.

It is at this precise point that Luke interjects his account of how the Twelve were chosen and appointed to be apostles. "It came to pass *in those days*"—when the hostility against Christ had escalated to a murderous fever pitch. Hatred for Him among the religious elite had reached its apex. Jesus could already feel the heat of His coming death. The crucifixion was now less than two years away. He already knew that He would suffer death on the cross, that He would rise from the dead, and that after forty days He would ascend to His Father. He therefore also knew that His earthly work would have to be handed off to someone else.

It was now time to select and prepare His official representatives. Jesus—knowing the hatred of the religious leaders; fully aware of the hostility against Him; seeing the inevitability of His execution—therefore chooses twelve key men to carry on the proclamation of His gospel for the salvation of Israel and the establishment of the church. Time is now of the essence. There aren't many days left (about eighteen months, by most estimates) before His earthly ministry would end. Now was the time to choose His apostles. Their most intensive training would begin immediately and be complete within a matter of months.

The focus of Christ's ministry therefore turned at this point from the multitudes to the few. Clearly, it was the looming reality of His death at the hands of His adversaries that signaled the turning point.

There's another striking reality in this. When Jesus chose the Twelve to be His official representatives—preachers of the gospel who would carry both His message and His authority—He didn't choose a single rabbi. He didn't choose a scribe. He didn't choose a Pharisee. He didn't choose a Sadducee. He didn't choose a priest. Not one of the men He chose came from the religious establishment. The choosing of the twelve apostles was a judgment against institutionalized Judaism. It was a renunciation of those men and their organizations, which had become totally corrupt. That is why the Lord didn't choose one recognized religious leader. He chose instead men who were not theologically trained—fishermen, a tax collector, and other common men.

Jesus had long been at war with those who saw themselves as the religious nobility of Israel. They resented Him. They rejected Him and His message. They hated Him. The gospel of John puts it this way: "He came to His own, and His own did not receive Him" (John 1:11 NKJV). The religious leaders of Judaism constituted the core of those who rejected Him.

Nearly a year and a half before this, in one of the first official acts of Jesus' ministry, He had challenged members of Israel's religious establishment on their own turf in Jerusalem during the Passover—the one time of year when the city was most populated with pilgrims coming to offer sacrifices. Jesus went to the temple mount, made a whip of small cords, drove the thieving money changers out of the temple, poured out their money, overturned their tables, and chased their animals away (John 2:13–16). In doing that, He struck a devastating blow at institutionalized Judaism. He unmasked the religious nobility as thieves and hypocrites. He condemned their spiritual bankruptcy. He exposed their apostasy. He publicly rebuked their sin. He indicted them for gross corruption. He denounced their deception. That is how He *began* His ministry. It was an all-out assault on the religion of the Jewish establishment.

Now, many months later, at the height of Jesus' Galilean ministry, far removed from Jerusalem, the resentment that must have been inaugurated at that first event had reached a fever pitch. The religious leaders were now blood-thirsty. And they began to devise a scheme to execute Him.

Their rejection of Him was complete. They were hostile to the gospel He preached. They despised the doctrines of grace He stood for, spurned the repentance He demanded, looked with disdain upon the forgiveness He offered, and repudiated the faith He epitomized. In spite of the many miracles that proved His messianic credentials—despite actually seeing Him cast out demons and heal every conceivable sickness—they would not accept the fact that He was God in human flesh. They hated Him. They hated His message. He was a threat to their power. And they desperately wanted to see Him dead.

So when it was time for Jesus to select twelve apostles, He naturally did not choose people from the establishment that was so determined to destroy Him. He turned instead to His own humble followers and selected twelve simple, ordinary working-class men.

THE TWELVE

If you've ever visited the great cathedrals in Europe, you might assume that the apostles were larger-than-life stained-glass saints with shining halos who represented an exalted degree of spirituality. The fact of the matter is that they were very, very common men.

It's a shame they have so often been put on pedestals as magnificent marble figures or portrayed in paintings like some kind of Roman gods. That dehumanizes them. They were just twelve completely ordinary men—perfectly human in every way. We mustn't lose touch with who they really were.

I recently read a biography of William Tyndale, who pioneered the translation of Scripture into English. He thought it wrong that common people heard the Bible only in Latin and not in their own language. The church leaders of his day, incredibly, did not want the Bible in the language of the people because (like the Pharisees of Jesus' day) they feared losing their ecclesiastical power. But against their opposition, Tyndale translated the New Testament into English and had it published. For his efforts he was rewarded with exile, poverty, and persecution. Finally, in 1536, he was strangled and burned at the stake.

One of the main things that motivated Tyndale to translate Scripture into the common language was a survey of English clergy that revealed most of them did not even know who the twelve apostles were. Only a few of them could name more than four or five of the leading apostles. Church leaders and Christians of today might fare just as poorly on the test. The way the institutional church has canonized these men has actually dehumanized them and made them seem remote and otherworldly. It is a strange irony, because when Jesus chose them, He selected them not for any extraordinary abilities or spiritual superiority. He seems to have deliberately chosen men who were notable only for their ordinariness.

What qualified these men to be apostles? Obviously it was not any intrinsic ability or outstanding talent of their own. They were Galileans. They were not the elite. Galileans were deemed low-class, rural, uneducated people. They were commoners—nobodies. But again, they were not selected because they were any more distinguished or more talented than others in Israel at the time.

Certainly, there *are* some rather clear moral and spiritual qualifications that have to be met by men who would fill this or any other kind of leadership role in the church. In fact, the standard for spiritual leadership in the church is extremely *high*. Consider, for example, the qualifications for being an elder or a pastor, listed in 1 Timothy 3:2–7:

[He] must be blameless, the husband of one wife, temperate, sober-minded, of good behavior, hospitable, able to teach; not given to wine, not violent, not greedy for money, but gentle, not quarrelsome, not covetous; one who rules his own house well, having his children in submission with all reverence (for if a man does not know how to rule his own house, how will he take care of the church of God?); not a novice, lest being puffed up with pride he fall into the same condemnation as the devil. Moreover he must have a good testimony among those who are outside, lest he fall into reproach and the snare of the devil. (NKJV)

Titus 1:6–9 gives a similar list. Hebrews 13:7 also suggests that church leaders must be exemplary moral and spiritual examples, because their faith must be the kind others can follow, and they will be required to give an account to God for how they conduct themselves. These are very, very high standards.

By the way, the standard is no lower for the rest of the church. Leaders are examples for everyone else. There's no acceptable "lower" standard for rank-and-file church members. In fact, in Matthew 5:48, Jesus said to *all* believers, "Be perfect, just as your Father in heaven is perfect" (NKJV).

Frankly, no one meets such a standard. Humanly speaking, no one "qualifies" when the standard is utter perfection. No one is fit to be in God's kingdom, and no one is inherently worthy to be in God's service. All have sinned and fall short of God's glory (Rom. 3:23). There is none righteous, no not one (Rom. 3:10).

Remember, it was the mature apostle Paul who confessed, "I know that in me (that is, in my flesh) nothing good dwells" (Rom. 7:18 NKJV). In 1 Timothy 1:15 he called himself the chief of sinners.

So there are no intrinsically qualified people. God Himself must save sinners, sanctify them, and then transform them unqualified into instruments He can use.

The twelve were like the rest of us; they were selected from the unworthy and the unqualified. They were, like Elijah, men "with a nature like ours" (James 5:17 NKJV). They did not rise to the highest usefulness because they were somehow *different* from us. Their transformation into vessels of honor was solely the work of the Potter.

Many Christians become discouraged and disheartened when their spiritual lives and witness suffer because of sin or failure. We tend to think we're worthless nobodies—and left to ourselves, that would be true! But worthless nobodies are just the kind of people God uses, because that is all He has to work with.

Satan may even attempt to convince us that our shortcomings render us useless to God and to His church. But Christ's choice of the apostles testifies to the fact that God can use the unworthy and the unqualified. He can use nobodies. They turned the world upside down, these twelve (Acts 17:6). It was not because they had extraordinary talents, unusual intellectual abilities, powerful political influence, or some special social status. They turned the world upside down because God worked in them to do it.

God chooses the humble, the lowly, the meek, and the weak so that there's never any question about the source of power when their lives change the world. It's not the man; it's the truth of God and the power of God *in* the man. (We need to remind some preachers today of this. It's not their cleverness, or their personalities. The power is in the Word—the truth that we preach—not in us.) And apart from one Person—one extraordinary human being who was God's Son incarnate, the Lord Jesus Christ—the history of God's work on earth is the story of His using the unworthy and molding them for His use the same careful way a potter fashions clay. The Twelve were no exception to that.

The apostles properly hold an exalted place in redemptive history, of course. They are certainly worthy of being regarded as heroes of the faith. The book of Revelation describes how their names will adorn the twelve gates of the heavenly city, the New Jerusalem. So heaven itself features an eternal tribute to them. But that doesn't diminish the truth that they were as ordinary as you and me. We need to remember them not from their stained-glass images, but from the down-to-earth way the Bible presents them to us. We need to lift them out of their otherworldly obscurity and get to know them as real people. We need to think of them as real men, and not as some kind of exalted figures from the pantheon of religious ritualism.

Let's not, however, underestimate the importance of their office. Upon their selection, the twelve apostles in effect became the true spiritual leaders of Israel. The religious elite of *apostate* Israel were symbolically set aside when Jesus chose them. The apostles became the first preachers of the new covenant. They were the ones to whom the Christian gospel was first entrusted. They represented the true Israel of God—a genuinely repentant and believing Israel. They also became the foundation stones of the church, with Jesus Himself as the chief cornerstone (Eph. 2:20). Those truths are heightened, not diminished, by the fact that these men were so ordinary.

Again, that is perfectly consistent with the way the Lord always works. In 1 Corinthians 1:20–21 we read, "Where is the wise? Where is the scribe? Where is the disputer of this age? Has not God made foolish the wisdom of this world? For since, in the wisdom of God, the world through wisdom did not know God, it pleased God through the foolishness of the message preached to save those who believe" (NKJV). That is the very reason there were no philosophers, no brilliant writers, no famous debaters, no distinguished teachers, and no men who had ever distinguished themselves as great orators among the twelve Christ chose. They *became* great spiritual leaders and great preachers under the power of the Holy Spirit, but it was not because of any innate oratorical skill, leadership abilities, or academic qualifications these men had. Their influence is owing to one thing and one thing only: the power of the message they preached.

On a human level, the gospel was thought a foolish message and the apostles were deemed unsophisticated preachers. Their teaching was beneath the elite. They were mere fishermen and working-class nobodies. Peons. Rabble. That was the assessment of their contemporaries. (The same thing has been true of the genuine church of Christ throughout history. It is true in the evangelical world today. Where are the impressive intellects, the great writers, and the great orators esteemed by the world? They're not found, for the most part, in the church.) "For you see your calling, brethren, that not many wise according to the flesh, not many mighty, not many noble, are called" (v. 26 NKJV).

> But God has chosen the foolish things of the world to put to shame the
> wise, and God has chosen the weak things of the world to put to shame
> the things which are mighty; and the base things of the world and the
> things which are despised God has chosen, and the things which are not,

to bring to nothing the things that are, that no flesh should glory in His presence. (vv. 27–29 NKJV)

God's favorite instruments are nobodies, so that no man can boast before God. In other words, God chooses whom He chooses in order that *He* might receive the glory. He chooses weak instruments so that no one will attribute the power to human instruments rather than to God, who wields those instruments. Such a strategy is unacceptable to those whose whole pursuit in life is aimed toward the goal of human glory.

With the notable exception of Judas, these men were not like that. They certainly struggled with pride and arrogance like every fallen human being. But the driving passion of their lives became the glory of Christ. And it was that passion, subjected to the influence of the Holy Spirit—not any innate skill or human talent—that explains why they left such an indelible impact on the world.

THE TEACHER

Bear in mind, then, that the selection of the Twelve took place at a time when Jesus was faced with the reality of His impending death. He had experienced the rising hostility of the religious leaders. He knew His earthly mission would soon culminate in His death, resurrection, and ascension. And so from this point on, the whole character of His ministry changed. It became His top priority to train the men who would be the chief spokesmen for the gospel after He was gone.

How did He choose them? He first went off to commune with His Father. "He went out to the mountain to pray, and continued all night in prayer to God" (Luke 6:12 NKJV).

Throughout the first five chapters of his gospel, Luke has already made clear that prayer was a pattern in the life of Jesus. Luke 5:16 says, "He Himself often withdrew into the wilderness and prayed" (NKJV). It was His habit to slip away in solitude to talk to His Father. He was always under pressure from the massive multitudes when He was in the towns and villages of Galilee. The wilderness and the mountain regions afforded solitude where He could pray.

We don't know *which* mountain this was. If it mattered, Scripture would tell us. There are lots of hills and mountains around the northern Galilee area. This one was probably in close walking distance to Capernaum, which was a sort of home base for Jesus' ministry. He went there and spent the entire night in prayer.

We often see Him praying in anticipation of crucial events in His ministry. (Remember, that is what He was doing on the night of His betrayal—praying in a garden where He found some solitude from the hectic atmosphere in Jerusalem. Judas knew he would find Jesus there because according to Luke 22:39 it was His *habit* to go there and pray.)

Here is Jesus in His true humanity. He was standing in a very volatile situation. The brewing hostility against Him was already threatening to bring about His death. He had a very brief amount of time remaining to train the men who would carry the gospel to the world after His departure. And the chilling reality of those matters drove Him to the top of a mountain so He could pray to God in total solitude. He had made Himself of no reputation and taken the form of a bond servant, coming to earth as a man. The time was now approaching when He would further humble Himself unto death—even the death of the cross. And thus He goes to God as a man would go, to seek God's face in prayer and to commune with the Father about the men whom He would choose for this vital office.

Notice that He spent the entire night in prayer. If He went to the mountain before dark, that was probably around seven or eight o'clock in the evening. If He came back down after dawn, that would have been around six in the morning. In other words, He prayed for at least ten hours straight.

To say He spent the whole night requires several words in English. It's only one word in the Greek: *dianuktereuo*. The word is significant. It speaks of enduring at a task through the night. The word could not be used of sleeping all night. It's not an expression you would use if you wanted to say it was dark all night. It has the sense of toiling through the night, staying at a task all night. It suggests that He remained awake through the darkness until morning, and that He was persevering all that time in prayer with an immense weight of duty upon Him.

Another interesting note comes through in the Greek language although we don't see it in the English. Our English version says that He "continued all night in prayer *to* God." Actually, the Greek expression means that He spent the whole night in the prayer *of* God. Whenever He prayed, it was quite literally the prayer of God. He was engaged in intertrinitarian communion. The prayer being offered was the very prayer of God. The members of the Trinity were communing with one another. His prayers were all perfectly consistent with the mind and the will of God—for He Himself *is* God. And therein do we see the incredible mystery of His humanity and His deity brought together. Jesus in His humanity needed to pray all night, and Jesus in His deity was praying the very prayer of God.

Don't miss the point: the choice Christ would soon make was of such monumental importance that it required ten or twelve hours of prayer in preparation. What was He praying for? Clarity in the matter of *whom* to choose? I don't think so. As omniscient God incarnate, He knew the divine will—it was no mystery. He was no doubt praying for the men He would soon appoint, communing with the Father about the absolute wisdom of His choice, and acting in His capacity as Mediator on their behalf.

When the night of prayer was over, He returned to where His disciples were and summoned them. ("And when it was day, He called His disciples to Himself"—Luke 6:13 NKJV). It was not only the Twelve whom He summoned. The word "disciple" in this context speaks of His followers in a broad sense. The word itself means "student, learner." There must have been numerous disciples, and from them, He would choose twelve to fill the office of an apostle.

It was common, both in the Greek culture and the Jewish culture of Jesus' day, for a prominent rabbi or philosopher to attract students. Their teaching venue was not necessarily a classroom or an auditorium. Most were peripatetic instructors whose disciples simply followed them through the normal course of everyday life. That is the kind of ministry Jesus maintained with His followers. He was an itinerant Teacher. He simply went from place to place, and as He taught, He attracted followers, who followed His movements. We get a picture of this back in verse 1: "Now it happened on the second Sabbath after the first that He went through the grainfields. And His disciples plucked the heads of grain and ate them, rubbing them in their hands" (NKJV). They were walking with Him, following Him from place to place as He taught, gleaning grain for food as they walked.

We don't know how many disciples Jesus had. At one point, He sent seventy out in pairs to evangelize in communities where He was preparing to visit (Luke 10:1). But the total number of His followers was undoubtedly far more than seventy. Scripture indicates that multitudes followed Him. And why not? His teaching was absolutely unlike anything anyone had ever heard in its clarity and obvious, inherent authority; He had the ability to heal diseases, cast out demons, and work miracles; He was full of grace and truth. It's not amazing that He drew so many disciples. What is amazing is that anyone rejected Him. But reject Him they did, mainly because His message was more than they could bear.

We see something of the dynamics of this in John 6. At the beginning of the chapter, He feeds more than five thousand people who had come out to see Him. (John 6:10 says the men alone numbered five thousand. Counting women and children, the crowd might have easily been double that number or more.) It was an amazing day. Many of those people were already following Him as disciples; many others were no doubt prepared to do so. John writes, "Then those men, when they had seen the sign that Jesus did, said, 'This is truly the Prophet who is to come into the world'" (v. 14 NKJV). Who was this Man who could produce food out of nothing? *They* spent most of their lives farming, harvesting, raising animals, and preparing meals. *Jesus* could just create food! That would change their lives. They must have had visions of leisure and free food, already prepared. This was the kind of Messiah they had hoped for! According to John, "They were about to come and take Him by force to make Him king" (v. 15 NKJV). He escaped by a series of supernatural events that culminated in His walking on the water.

The next day the people found Him in Capernaum, on the other side of the lake. Crowds of them had come looking for Him, obviously hoping He would give them more food. He chided them for following Him out of wrong motives: "You seek Me, not because you saw the signs, but because you ate of the loaves and were filled" (v. 26 NKJV). When they continued to ask for more food, He told them, "I am the living bread which came down from heaven. If anyone eats of this bread, he will live forever; and the bread that I shall give is My flesh, which I shall give for the life of the world" (v. 51 NKJV). The saying was so hard for them to understand that they pressed Him to explain. He continued:

> "Most assuredly, I say to you, unless you eat the flesh of the Son of Man and drink His blood, you have no life in you. Whoever eats My flesh and drinks My blood has eternal life, and I will raise him up at the last day. For My flesh is food indeed, and My blood is drink indeed. He who eats My flesh and drinks My blood abides in Me, and I in him. As the living Father sent Me, and I live because of the Father, so he who feeds on Me will live because of Me. This is the bread which came down from heaven—not as your fathers ate the manna, and are dead. He who eats this bread will live forever." These things He said in the synagogue as He taught in Capernaum. (vv. 53–59 NKJV)

This was so offensive that even many of His disciples began to have second thoughts about following Him. John writes, "From that time many of His disciples went back and walked with Him no more" (v. 66 NKJV).

So disciples were coming and going. People were attracted, then disillusioned. And on that particular occasion described in John 6, Jesus even said to the Twelve, "Do you also want to go away?" (v. 67 NKJV). Peter spoke for the group when he answered, "Lord, to whom shall we go? You have the words of eternal life. Also we have come to believe and know that You are the Christ, the Son of the living God" (vv. 68–69 NKJV).

Those who stayed were people whom God had sovereignly drawn to His own Son (v. 44). Jesus had also drawn them to Himself in particular. He told them, "You did not choose Me, but I chose you and appointed you that you should go and bear fruit, and that your fruit should remain" (John 15:16 NKJV). He sovereignly selected them, and (with the exception of Judas, whom Christ knew would betray Him) He sovereignly worked in them and through them to guarantee that they would persevere with Him, that they would bear fruit, and that their fruit would remain. Here we see the principle of God's electing grace at work.

The sovereignty of His choice is seen in an extraordinary way by the selection of the Twelve. Out of the larger group of disciples, perhaps hundreds of them, He chooses twelve men in particular and appoints them to the apostolic office. It was not a job for which applicants or volunteers were sought. Christ *chose* them sovereignly and appointed them, in the presence of the larger group.

This was a very special moment for those twelve. Up to this point, Peter, James, John, Andrew, Nathanael, Matthew, and the others were just part of the crowd. They were learners like everyone else in the group. They had been following and listening and observing and absorbing His teaching. But they didn't yet have any official role of leadership. They had not yet been appointed to any role that set them apart from the others. They were faces in the crowd until Christ selected them and made twelve of them apostles.

Why twelve? Why not eight? Why not twenty-four? The number twelve was filled with symbolic importance. There were twelve tribes in Israel. But Israel was apostate. The Judaism of Jesus' time represented a corruption of the faith of the Old Testament. Israel had abandoned divine grace in favor of works-religion. Their religion was legalistic. It was shot through with hypocrisy, self-righteous works, man-made regulations, and meaningless ceremonies. It was heretical. It was based on physical descent from Abraham rather than the *faith* of Abraham. In choosing twelve apostles, Christ was in effect appointing new leadership for the new covenant. And the apostles represented the new leaders of the true Israel of God—consisting of people who believed the gospel and were following the faith of Abraham (cf. Rom. 4:16). In other words, the twelve apostles symbolized judgment against the twelve tribes of Old Testament Israel.

Jesus Himself made the connection plainly. In Luke 22:29–30, He told the apostles, "I bestow upon you a kingdom, just as My Father bestowed one upon Me, that you may eat and drink at My table in My kingdom, and sit on thrones judging the twelve tribes of Israel" (NKJV).

The significance of the number twelve would have been immediately obvious to almost every Israelite. Jesus' messianic claims were clear to all who listened to His teaching. He constantly spoke of His coming kingdom. Meanwhile, throughout Israel, expectation was running high that the Messiah would very soon appear and establish His kingdom. Some had thought John the Baptist would be that Messiah, but John pointed them to Christ (cf. John 1:19–27). They knew very well that Christ had all the messianic credentials (John 10:41–42). He wasn't the kind of political leader they expected, so they were slow to believe (John 10:24–25). But they surely understood the claims He was making, and they were filled with anticipation.

So when He publicly appointed twelve men to be His apostles, the significance of that number was loud and clear. The apostles represented a whole new Israel, under the new covenant. And their appointment—bypassing the religious establishment of official Judaism—signified a message of judgment against national Israel. Clearly, these twelve ordinary men were not destined for an ordinary role. They stood in the place of the heads of twelve tribes. They were living proof that the kingdom Jesus was about to establish was altogether different from the kingdom most Israelites anticipated.

Luke 6:13 says, "He chose twelve whom He also named apostles" (NKJV). The title alone was significant. The Greek verb *apostello* means "to send out." The noun form, *apostolos,* means "one who is sent." The English word "apostle" is a transliteration, rather than a translation, of the Greek word. The apostles were "sent ones." But they were not mere messengers. The Greek word for "messenger" was *angelos,* from which we get our word "angel." An *apostolos* was something more significant than a courier or a herald; *apostolos* conveyed the idea of an ambassador, a delegate—an official representative.

The word has an exact parallel in Aramaic—*shaliah.* (Remember that the common language in Israel in Jesus' time—the language Jesus Himself spoke—was not Hebrew, but Aramaic.) In that first-century Jewish culture, the *shaliah* was an official representative of the Sanhedrin, the ruling council of Israel. A *shaliah* exercised the full rights of the Sanhedrin. He spoke for them, and when he spoke, he spoke with their authority. He was owed the same respect and deference as the council itself. But he never delivered his own message; his task was to deliver the message of the group whom he represented. The office of a *shaliah* was well known. *Shaliah* were sent out to settle legal or religious disputes, and they acted with the full authority of the whole council. Some prominent rabbis also had their *shaliah,* "sent ones" who taught their message and represented them with their full authority. Even the Jewish Mishnah (a collection of oral traditions originally conceived as a commentary on the Law) recognized the role

COMMON MEN, UNCOMMON CALLING

of the *shaliah*. It says, "The one sent by the man is as the man himself." So the nature of the office was well known to the Jewish people.

Thus when Jesus appointed apostles, He was saying something very familiar to people in that culture. These were His delegates. They were His trusted *shaliah*. They spoke with His authority, delivered His message, and exercised His authority.

THE TASK

The familiar role of the *shaliah* in that culture virtually defined the task of the apostles. Obviously, Christ would delegate His authority to these twelve and send them out with His message. They would represent Him as official delegates. Virtually everyone in that culture would have instantly understood the nature of the office: these twelve men, commissioned as Jesus' apostles, would speak and act with the same authority as the one who sent them. "Apostle" was therefore a title of great respect and privilege.

Mark 3:14 records this same event: "Then He appointed twelve, that they might be with Him and that He might send them out to preach" (NKJV). Notice the two-step process. Before they could be sent out to preach, they had to be pulled in. It was absolutely critical that they be with Jesus before they be sent out. In fact, it isn't until Luke 9:1 that Jesus calls the Twelve together and gives them authority over the demons and power to heal diseases. At that point, He literally delegates to them His miracle power. So in Luke 6, He identifies and appoints them and brings them under His direct and personal tutelage ("that they might be with Him"). In Luke 9, several months later, He gives them power to work miracles and cast out demons. Not until then did He "send them out to preach."

Up to this point, Jesus was speaking to huge crowds most of the time. With the calling of the Twelve in Luke 6, His teaching ministry becomes more intimate, focused primarily on them. He would still draw large crowds and teach them, but His focus was on the disciples and their training.

Notice the natural progression in their training program. At first, they simply followed Jesus, gleaning from His sermons to the multitudes and listening to His instructions along with a larger group of disciples. They apparently did not do this full time, but as opportunity allowed in the course of their regular lives. Next (as recorded in Matt. 4), He called them to leave everything and follow Him exclusively. Now (in the incident recorded in Luke 6 and Matt. 10), He selects twelve men out of that group of full-time disciples, identifies them as apostles, and begins to focus most of His energies on their personal instruction.

Later, He will gift them with authority and miracle power. Finally, He will send them out. At first, they go on short-term mission assignments, but they keep coming back. But when He leaves to return to the Father, they will go out for good on their own. There's a clear progression in their training and entry into full-time ministry.

No longer just disciples, they are now apostles—*shaliah.* They occupy an important office. Luke uses the word "apostles" six times in his gospel and about thirty times in the book of Acts. Their role in the gospels pertains primarily to taking the gospel to Israel. In Acts, they are engaged in the founding of the church.

Although they were common men, theirs was an uncommon calling. In other words, the task they were called to, and not anything about the men per se, is what makes them so important. Consider how unique their role was to be.

Not only would they found the church and play a pivotal leadership role as the early church grew and branched out, but they also became the channels through which most of the New Testament would be given. They received truth from God by divine revelation. Ephesians 3:5 is very explicit. Paul says that the mystery of Christ, which in earlier ages was not made known, "has now been revealed by the Spirit to His holy apostles and prophets" (NKJV). They did not preach a human message. The truth was given to them by direct revelation.

They were therefore the source of all true church doctrine. Acts 2:42 describes the activities of the early church in these terms: "They continued stead-fastly in the apostles' doctrine and fellowship, in the breaking of bread, and in prayers" (NKJV). Before the New Testament was complete, the apostles' teaching was the *only* source of truth about Christ and church doctrine. And their teaching was received with the same authority as the written Word. In fact, the written New Testament is nothing other than the Spirit-inspired, "inscripturated" record of the apostles' teaching.

In short, the apostles were given to edify the church. Ephesians 4:11–12 says Christ gave the apostles "for the equipping of the saints for the work of ministry, for the edifying of the body of Christ" (NKJV). They were the original Christian teachers and preachers. Their teaching, as recorded in the New Testament, is the only rule by which sound doctrine can be tested, even today.

They were also examples of virtue. Ephesians 3:5 calls them "holy apostles" (NKJV). They set a standard for godliness and true spirituality. They were the first examples for believers to emulate. They were men of character and integrity, and they set the standard for all who would subsequently become leaders in the church.

They had unique power to perform miracles that confirmed their message. Hebrews 2:3–4 says that the gospel "first began to be spoken by the Lord, and was confirmed to us by those who heard Him, God also bearing witness both with signs and wonders, with various miracles, and gifts of the Holy Spirit" (NKJV). In other words, God confirmed His Word through the apostles by the miracles that they were able to do. The New Testament indicates that *only* the apostles and those who were closely associated with them had the power to do miracles. That is why 2 Corinthians 12:12 speaks of such miracles as "the signs of an apostle" (NKJV).

As a result of all this, the disciples were greatly blessed and held in high esteem by the people of God. Jesus' expectations for them were met through their faithful perseverance. And His promise to them was fulfilled in the growth and expansion of the church. You may recall that in Luke 18:28, Peter said to Jesus, "See, we have left all and followed You" (NKJV). The disciples were apparently concerned about the way things were going and what might happen to them. Peter's words were actually a plea. It is as if he was saying, on behalf of the others, "What's going to happen to us?"

Jesus replied, "Assuredly, I say to you, there is no one who has left house or parents or brothers or wife or children, for the sake of the kingdom of God, who shall not receive many times more in this present time, and in the age to come eternal life" (v. 30 NKJV). They had not left anything that He would not more than make up to them. And God *did* bless them in this life (even though, as we discover when we examine each life, most of them were martyred). God blessed them in this life through the founding and growth of the church. They not only gained influence, respect, and honor among the people of God; but as for their homes and families, they gained multitudes of spiritual children and brethren as the church grew and believers multiplied. And they will be greatly honored in the age to come as well.

THE TRAINING

All of that might have seemed remote and uncertain on the morning Jesus summoned His disciples and appointed the Twelve. They still needed to be taught. All their shortcomings and human failings seemed to overshadow their potential. Time was short. They had already left whatever vocations they were expert in. They had abandoned their nets, forsaken their fields, left the tax tables behind. They had relinquished everything they knew, in order to be trained for something for which they had no natural aptitude.

But when they forsook their jobs they by no means became idle. They became full-time students, learners—*disciples*. Now the next eighteen months of their lives would be filled with even more intensive training—the best seminary education ever. They had the example of Christ perpetually before them. They could listen to His teaching; ask Him questions; watch how He dealt with people; and enjoy intimate fellowship with Him in every kind of setting. He gave them ministry opportunities, instructing them and sending them out on special assignments. He graciously encouraged them, lovingly corrected them, and patiently instructed them. That is how the best learning always occurs. It isn't just information passed on; it's one life invested in another.

But it was not an *easy* process. The Twelve could be amazingly thickheaded. There was a reason they weren't the academic elite. Jesus Himself often said things like, "Are you also still without understanding? Do you not yet understand?" (Matth. 15:16–17 NKJV; cf. 16:9). "O foolish ones, and slow of heart to believe" (Luke 24:25 NKJV). It is significant that Scripture doesn't cover their defects. The point is not to portray them as superholy luminaries or to elevate them above mere mortals. If that were the aim, there would be no reason to record their character flaws. But instead of whitewashing the blemishes, Scripture seems to make a great deal of their human weaknesses. It's a brilliant reminder that "[our] faith should not be in the wisdom of men but in the power of God" (1 Cor. 2:5 NKJV).

Why was the learning process so difficult for the apostles? First of all, they lacked spiritual understanding. They were slow to hear and slow to understand. They were at various times thick, dull, stupid, and blind. All those terms or their equivalents are used to describe them in the New Testament. So how did Jesus remedy their lack of spiritual understanding? He just kept teaching. Even after His resurrection, He stayed forty days on earth. Acts 1:3 says that during that time He was "speaking of the things pertaining to the kingdom of God" (NKJV). He was still persistently teaching them until the moment He ascended into heaven.

A second problem that made the learning process difficult for the disciples is that they lacked humility. They were self-absorbed, self-centered, self-promoting, and proud. They spent an enormous amount of time arguing about who would be the greatest among them (Matt. 20:20–28; Mark 9:33–37; Luke 9:46). How did Jesus overcome their lack of humility? By being an example of humility to them. He washed their feet. He modeled servanthood. He humbled Himself, even unto the death of the cross.

Third, not only did they lack understanding and humility; they lacked faith. Four times in the gospel of Matthew alone Jesus says to them, "O you of little faith" (6:30; 8:26; 14:31; 16:8 NKJV). In Mark 4:40, He asked them, "How is it that you have no faith?" (NKJV). At the end of Mark's gospel, after they had spent months in intensive training with Jesus—even after He had risen from the dead—Mark writes, "He rebuked their unbelief and hardness of heart" (Mark 16:14 NKJV). What remedy did Jesus have for their lack of faith? He kept doing miracles and wonderful works. The miracles were not primarily for the benefit of unbelievers; most of His miracles were deliberately done "in the presence of His disciples" so that *their* faith could be strengthened (John 20:30 NKJV).

Fourth, they lacked commitment. While the crowds were cheering and the miracles were being multiplied, they were thrilled. But as soon as the soldiers came into the garden to arrest Jesus, they all forsook Him and fled (Mark 14:50). Their leader ends up denying Jesus and swearing he doesn't even know the man. How did Jesus remedy their proneness to defection? By interceding for them in prayer. John 17 records how Jesus prayed that they would remain ultimately faithful and that the Father would bring them to heaven (John 17:11–26).

Fifth, they lacked power. On their own, they were weak and helpless, especially when confronted with the enemy. There were times when they tried but could not cast out demons. Their faithlessness left them unable to harness the power that was available to them. What did Jesus do to remedy their weakness? On the day of pentecost He sent the Holy Spirit to indwell and empower them. This was His promise to them: "You shall receive power when the Holy Spirit has come upon you; and you shall be witnesses to Me in Jerusalem, and in all Judea and Samaria, and to the end of the earth" (Acts 1:8 NKJV). That promise was mightily fulfilled.

We're inclined to look at this group with all their weaknesses and wonder why Jesus did not simply pick a different group of men. Why would He single out men with no understanding, no humility, no faith, no commitment, and no power? Simply this: His strength is made perfect in weakness (2 Cor. 12:9). Again we see how He chooses the weak things of this world to confound the mighty. No one could ever examine this group of men and conclude that they did what they did because of their own innate abilities. There is no human explanation for the influence of the apostles. The glory goes to God alone.

Acts 4:13 says this about how the people of Jerusalem perceived the apostles: "Now when they saw the boldness of Peter and John, and perceived that they were uneducated and untrained men, they marveled. And they realized that they had been with Jesus" (NKJV). The Greek text says people perceived that they were *"aggramatoi . . . idiotai"*—literally, "illiterate ignoramuses." And that was true from a worldly viewpoint. But it was obvious that they had been with Jesus. The same thing should be said of every true disciple. Luke 6:40 says, "A disciple is not above his teacher, but everyone who is perfectly trained will be like his teacher" (NKJV).

The apostles' relatively brief time of training with Jesus bore eternal fruit. At first, it might have seemed that everything would be for naught. The night Jesus was betrayed, they were scattered like sheep whose shepherd had been smitten (Matt. 26:31). Even after the Resurrection, they seemed timid, full of remorse over their failure, and too aware of their own weaknesses to minister with confidence.

But after Jesus ascended to heaven, the Holy Spirit came, infused them with power, and enabled them to do what Christ had trained them to do. The book of Acts records how the church was launched, and the rest is history. Those eleven men, through the legacy of New Testament Scripture and the testimony they left, are still changing the world even today.

NOTES

CHAPTER 1

1. From John MacArthur, *Our Sufficiency in Christ* (Dallas: Word, 1991), 75–90.
2. Albert Barnes, *Notes on the Old Testament: Psalms,* vol. 1 (Grand Rapids, Mich.: Baker, 1974), 171.
3. Samuel Cox, cited in Marvin Vincent, *World Studies in the New Testament: II Peter* (Grand Rapids, Mich.: Eerdmans, 1980), 687.
4. Priscilla Slagle, *The Way Up from Down* (New York: Random House, 1987), 218–27.

CHAPTER 2

1. From John MacArthur, *The Ultimate Priority* (Chicago: Moody, 1983), 73–86.
2. C. S. Lewis, *The Lion, the Witch, and the Wardrobe* (New York: Macmillan, 1950), 75–76.

CHAPTER 3

1. From John MacArthur, *The Gospel According to Jesus* (Grand Rapids: Zondervan, 1988), 196–202.
2. Cf. Zane C. Hodges, *The Hungry Inherit* (Portland: Multnomah, 1980), 83–84, where Hodges writes, "How fortunate that one's entrance into the kingdom of God [does] not depend on his discipleship. If it did, how few would ever enter that kingdom!" Yet didn't Jesus Himself explicitly teach that "few" would enter? Wasn't that the whole point of His warning about the small gate and the narrow road? "*Few are those who find it*" (Matt. 7:14).
3. It is also apparent, however, that not every disciple is necessarily a true Christian (cf. John 6:66). The term "disciple" is sometimes used in Scripture in a general sense, to describe those who, like Judas, outwardly followed Christ. It certainly is not restricted to some higher level of believers. The disciple in Matthew 8:21–22, for example, was anything but committed.
4. John R. W. Stott, *Basic Christianity* (London: Inter-Varsity, 1958), 108.
5. Notice that in this same verse our Lord says the one who *does* look back is unfit for the kingdom of God.

CHAPTER 4

1. From John MacArthur, *Faith Works* (Dallas: Word, 1993), 87–104.
2. R. C. Sproul, "Works or Faith?" *Tabletalk* (May 1991), 6.
3. Cited in Roland Bainton, *Here I Stand* (New York: Abingdon, 1950), 65.
4. Ibid.
5. Henry Bettenson, ed., *Documents of the Christian Church* (New York: Oxford, 1963), 263.
6. Philip Schaff, ed., *The Creeds of Christendom,* 3 vols., reprint (Grand Rapids, Mich.: Baker, 1983), 3:94.
7. Earl Radmacher, "First Response to 'Faith According to the Apostle James' by John F. MacArthur, Jr.," *Journal of the Evangelical Theological Society* 33 (March 1990): 40.
8. John Calvin, *Institutes of the Christian Religion* 3:16:1, trans. Henry Beveridge, (Grand Rapids: Eerdmans, 1966 reprint), 2:99.

9. Ibid., 2:115.

10. Martin Luther, *Table Talk,* in Helmut T. Lehman, ed., *Luther's Works,* 55 vols., trans. Theodore G. Tappert (Philadelphia: Fortress, 1967), 54:248.

11. Ibid., 54:289–90.

12. Ibid., 54:290.

13. Schaff, *The Creeds of Christendom,* 3:117–118.

14. Ibid., 3:118 (emphasis added).

15. Ibid., 3:119.

16. Cited in Augustus H. Strong, *Systematic Theology* (Philadelphia: Judson, 1907), 875.

17. J. Kevin Butcher, "A Critique of *The Gospel According to Jesus," Journal of the Grace Evangelical Society,* vol. 2, no.1 (Spring 1989): 28. Butcher believes that by describing Chafer, Ryrie, and Hodges as antinomian I am implying "that these men (as well as the view they represent) are only concerned with populating heaven, showing a disdain for holiness and a consistent Christian walk." But that is not what the term *antinomian* means, as the discussion on these pages shows.

18. Zane Hodges, "Calvinism Ex Cathedra," *Journal of the Grace Evangelical Society,* vol. 4, no. 2 (Autumn 1991): 68.

19. Ibid., 69.

20. Charles C. Ryrie, *Balancing the Christian Life* (Chicago: Moody, 1969), 35. The context of this quotation is a section arguing that believers have two natures. Ryrie suggests that carnality can be a continued state of existence for the Christian (Ibid., 170–173). When he speaks of those who "choose to leave God out and live according to the old nature" he is clearly speaking of something more than temporary failure.

21. There are many parallels between modern no-lordship theology and the other forms of antinomianism that have emerged from time to time in church history. These include, for example, the teachings of Johann Agricola, whom Luther condemned, and the Sandemanian cult that flourished in Scotland in the 1700s.

22. Charles Ryrie, *So Great Salvation* (Wheaton, Ill.: Victor 1989), 45.

23. Hodges, "Calvinism Ex Cathedra," 67. In a footnote Hodges implies that he expressed this same view in *Absolutely Free!* (Grand Rapids, Mich.: Zondervan, 1989), 213–15. But in *Absolutely Free!,* Hodges never made such an assertion. Turning to the section of *Absolutely Free!* Hodges cites, we find that ironically, he begins by condemning me for writing, "Obedience is the inevitable manifestation of saving faith" (*AF* 213). He concludes incongruously by stating, "We must add that there is no need to quarrel with the Reformers' view that where there is justifying faith, works will undoubtedly exist too" (*AF* 215). But that is precisely the view Hodges *is* arguing against! Hodges concludes that it is only "a reasonable assumption" that works will follow faith. And such works might be invisible to a human observer: "God alone may be able to detect the fruits of regeneration in some of His children" (p. 215).

24. Ryrie, *So Great Salvation,* 45.

25. Ibid., 150.

26. Ibid., 151.

27. Ibid., 141.

28. In my reading of *Absolutely Free!* I could not find a single occurrence of the words "sanctify" or "sanctification," except in one quotation from my book. Nor is sanctification dealt with in either of Hodges's other major works on the lordship issue, *The Gospel Under Siege* (Dallas: Redención Viva, 1981) and *Grace in Eclipse,* (Dallas: Redención Viva, 1985). Hodges evidently views practical holiness and growth in grace as purely the *believer's* work (*AF* 117–126).

29. R. T. Kendall, whom Hodges frequently cites for support, is explicit about this: "It is true that sanctification was not a prerequisite for glorification, or Paul would have placed it in line with 'calling' and 'justification' (Romans 8:30)." R. T. Kendall, *Once Saved, Always Saved* (Chicago: Moody, 1983), 134. Note the similarity between Kendall's statement and the paragraph quoted above from Ryrie (*SGS* 150).

CHAPTER 5

1. From John MacArthur, *Charismatic Chaos* (Grand Rapids: Zondervan, 1992), 264–290.
2. Kenneth E. Hagin, "How to Write Your Own Ticket with God" (Tulsa: Faith Library, 1979).
3. Kenneth E. Hagin, "Godliness Is Profitable" (Tulsa: Faith Library, 1982).
4. Kenneth Copeland, *The Laws of Prosperity* (Fort Worth: Kenneth Copeland, 1974).
5. Charles Capps, "God's Creative Power Will Work for You" (Tulsa: Harrison House, 1976).
6. Charles Capps, *Releasing the Ability of God Through Prayer* (Tulsa: Harrison House, 1978).
7. Oral Roberts, *God's Formula for Success and Prosperity* (Tulsa: Healing Waters, 1955).
8. Gordon Lindsay, *God's Master Key to Prosperity* (Dallas: Christ for the Nations, 1960).
9. Jerry Savelle, *Living in Divine Prosperity* (Tulsa: Harrison House, 1982).
10. Most Word Faith advocates would affirm the personality of the Holy Spirit. In effect, however, their teachings depersonalize Him by consistently speaking of Him as a power to be drawn upon rather than understanding the biblical truth that it is *we* who are to be *His* instruments.
11. Cf. Hagin, "How to Write Your Own Ticket," 3, where Hagin sees a vision of Jesus and says to Him, "Dear Lord, I have two sermons I preach concerning the woman who touched Your clothes and was healed when You were on earth. *I received both of these sermons by inspiration*" (emphasis added). Later, Hagin quotes what Jesus told him in reply: "You are correct. My Spirit, the Holy Spirit, has endeavored to get another sermon into your spirit, but you have failed to pick it up. While I am here, I will do what you ask. I will give you that sermon outline. Now get your pencil and paper and write it down" (p. 4).

    Hagin claims to have received numerous visions, as well as eight personal visitations from Jesus. Hagin has written, "The Lord Himself taught me about prosperity. I never read about it in a book. I got it directly from heaven." (Kenneth E. Hagin, "How God Taught Me About Prosperity" [Tulsa: Faith Library, 1985], 1.) That claim, as we shall see, is a lie (see note 79).
12. Kenneth E. Hagin develops this point in his book *The Authority of the Believer* (Tulsa: Faith Library, 1979), long sections of which were taken verbatim from others' writings (see note 79).
13. Robert Tilton, *God's Miracle Plan for Man* (Dallas: Robert Tilton, 1987), 36.
14. Charles Capps, *The Tongue: A Creative Force* (Tulsa: Harrison House, 1976), 78.
15. Ibid., 79.
16. Ibid., 79–80 (emphasis in original).
17. Ibid., 136–137 (emphasis in original).
18. Norvel Hayes, "Prostitute Faith" (Tulsa: Harrison House, 1988), 22–23.
19. Norvel Hayes, *Putting Your Angels to Work* (Tulsa: Harrison House, 1989), 8.
20. Ibid.
21. Kenneth Copeland, "The Force of Love" (Fort Worth: Kenneth Copeland Ministries, n.d.), cassette tape #02–0028.
22. Ibid.
23. Ibid.
24. Kenneth Copeland, *The Believer's Voice of Victory* broadcast, 9 July 1987.
25. *Praise the Lord* broadcast on the Trinity Broadcasting Network, 7 July 1986.
26. *Praise the Lord* broadcast on the Trinity Broadcasting Network, November 15, 1990.
27. Charles Capps, "Seedtime and Harvest" (Tulsa: Harrison House, 1986), 7 (emphasis in original).
28. Earl Paulk, *Satan Unmasked* (Atlanta: Kingdom, 1985), 97.
29. Robert Tilton, *God's Laws of Success* (Dallas: Word of Faith, 1983), 170.
30. *Praise the Lord* broadcast on the Trinity Broadcasting Network, 6 January 1988.
31. "Praise-a-thon" broadcast on the Trinity Broadcasting Network, November 1990.
32. Benny Hinn, "Our Position in Christ" (Orlando: Orlando Christian Center, 1990), cassette tape #A031190.
33. Kenneth E. Hagin, "As Christ Is—So are We" (Tulsa: Rhema), cassette tape #44H06.

34. Walter Martin, "Ye Shall Be As Gods," *The Agony of Deceit,* ed. Michael A. Horton (Chicago: Moody, 1990), 97.
35. Kenneth Copeland, *Believer's Voice of Victory* magazine, 8 August 1988, 8.
36. Ibid. The idea that Jesus emptied Himself of His deity during His incarnation (known as kenotic theology) is a heretical teaching promoted by nineteenth-century liberal theology. Conservative theology has always maintained that Christ's self-emptying (cf. Phil. 2:7) means that He laid aside the independent use of His divine attributes, not that He ceased to be God. His immutability makes that impossible: "Jesus Christ is the same yesterday and today, yes and forever" (Heb. 13:8; cf. Mal. 3:6; James 1:17).
37. Kenneth Copeland, "Substitution and Identification" (Fort Worth: Kenneth Copeland Ministries, n.d.), cassette tape #00–0202.
38. Christ alone could atone for our sins (1 Peter 1:18–19). He is the *only* begotten Son of God (John 1:14; 3:16). One of the key messages of the New Testament book of Hebrews is the utter supremacy of Christ and the uniqueness of His priesthood (7:22–28; 9:11–15, 26–28; 12:2).
39. Kenneth Copeland, "What Happened from the Cross to the Throne?" (Fort Worth: Kenneth Copeland Ministries, n.d.), cassette tape #02–0017.
40. Ibid.
41. Frederick K. C. Price, "The Ever Increasing Faith Messenger" (ministry newsletter, June 1980).
42. Kenneth Copeland, "What Satan Saw on the Day of Pentecost" (Fort Worth: Kenneth Copeland Ministries, n.d.), cassette tape #02–0022.
43. Kenneth E. Hagin, "How Jesus Obtained His Name" (Tulsa: Rhema), cassette tape #44H01.
44. Pat Robertson, *Answers to 200 of Life's Most Probing Questions* (Nashville: Nelson, 1984), 271.
45. Capps, *The Tongue,* 8–9.
46. Hagin, "How to Write Your Own Ticket," 8 (emphasis in original). Hagin's supposedly inspired four-point sermon is: Say it, do it, receive it, and tell it. Hagin claims Jesus told him, "If anybody, anywhere, will take these four steps or put these four principles into operation, he will always have whatever he wants from Me or God the Father" (p. 5).
47. Ibid., 10. Hagin evidently misses a key passage in Mark 9, where Jesus healed a boy whose father had prayed, "I do believe; help me overcome my unbelief!" (v. 24 NIV) Hagin and other Word Faith teachers would no doubt label such a prayer "negative confession." But Jesus honored it as the honest expression of that man's heart.
48. Capps, *The Tongue,* 91 (emphasis in original).
49. This is a clearly superstitious fear, closely akin to the Hindu idea of karma or the pagan view of "bad luck."
50. Kenneth E. Hagin, "Words" (Tulsa: Faith Library, 1979), 20–21 (emphasis added).
51. Bruce Barron, *The Health and Wealth Gospel* (Downers Grove, Ill.: InterVarsity, 1987), 128.
52. Ibid., 131.
53. Kenneth E. Hagin, "Praying to Get Results" (Tulsa: Faith Library, 1983), 5–6.
54. Ibid., 5. Hagin claims the woman had begun to rise supernaturally out of the wheelchair and into the air. Fearful, she pulled herself back into the chair. That was when Hagin castigated her.
55. Kenneth E. Hagin, "Having Faith in Your Faith" (Tulsa: Faith Library, 1980), 4.
56. Ibid., 4–5 (emphasis added).
57. In a chapter titled "Pleading the Blood," Hagin tells of how he once overheard a missionary rebuke a scorpion bite with the words, "In the Name of Jesus, I plead the blood against this!" He writes, "So I picked up that phrase, 'In the Name of Jesus, I plead the blood' . . . and all through these years I've always pled the blood in the Name of Jesus. *There's power in the blood,* glory to God! It's worked for me, and it'll work for you, too." Kenneth E. Hagin, "The Precious Blood of Jesus" (Tulsa: Faith Library, 1984), 30–31. The notion that repeating a phrase can work miracles is pure superstition (cf. Matt. 6:7).

58. Kenneth E. Hagin, "You Can Have What You Say" (Tulsa: Faith Library, 1979), 14 (emphasis in original).
59. *Praise the Lord* broadcast on the Trinity Broadcasting Network, 15 September 1988.
60. Ibid.
61. *Believer's Voice of Victory* broadcast on the Trinity Broadcasting Network, 20 January 1991.
62. *Success in Life* broadcast on the Trinity Broadcasting Network, 2 December 1990.
63. *Success in Life* broadcast on the Trinity Broadcasting Network, 5 December 1990.
64. Ibid.
65. Ibid.
66. *Success in Life* broadcast on the Trinity Broadcasting Network, 14 February 1991.
67. Kenneth L. Woodward and Frank Gibney Jr., "Saving Souls—or a Ministry?" *Newsweek*, 13 July 1987, 53.
68. Ibid.
69. Tilton berates listeners who don't pay their vows to his ministry. One of the biggest problems his ministry faces is how to deal with people who make vows, then cannot pay when the promised results don't materialize. Cf. *Success in Life*, 5 April 1991.
70. *Praise the Lord* broadcast on the Trinity Broadcasting Network, 21 September 1990.
71. Kenneth E. Hagin, "How Jesus Obtained His Name" (Tulsa: Rhema), cassette tape #44H01.
72. Kenneth E. Hagin, *Exceedingly Growing Faith* (Tulsa: Faith Library, 1983), 10.
73. God allegedly once told Charles Capps that "you are under an attack of the evil one and I can't do anything about it. You have bound me by the words of your own mouth" (Capps, *The Tongue*, 67).
74. It would appear that many of the heroes of faith named in Hebrews 11 did not really have strong faith after all—if the Word Faith definition of faith is valid. Certainly those who experienced scourgings, chains, and imprisonment (v. 36); who went about in shabby clothes, destitute, afflicted and ill-treated (v. 37); who lived in the deserts, mountains, caves and holes in the ground (v. 38) must not have been very adept at creating their own reality. Yet they gained approval from God for their faith (v. 39). That's because Hebrews 11 teaches that real faith has to do with our obeying God, not His giving us material things.
75. Capps, *The Tongue*, 27 (emphasis in original).
76. Ibid., 43.
77. D. R. McConnell, *A Different Gospel* (Peabody, Mass.: Hendrickson, 1988).
78. Ibid., 3–14.
79. Ibid., 8–12. McConnell also states that Hagin plagiarized the writings of a Christian and Missionary Alliance minister named John A. MacMillan.

W. R. Scott gives solid evidence that these accusations are true as well. Specifically, it seems incontrovertible that Hagin lifted at least three-quarters of his book *The Authority of the Believer* verbatim from MacMillan's magazine article of the same title. (W. R. Scott, "What's Wrong with the Faith Movement?" [unpublished paper, n. d.], Appendix B, 2–10.) Scott also documents Hagin's plagiarism of Finis Jennings Dake, *God's Plan for Man* [Lawrenceville, Ga.: Dake Bible Sales, 1949], Appendix A, 1–2.) Dake was a well-known Assembly of God pastor and author of a pentecostal study Bible.

Hagin's pattern of plagiarism would seem to cast doubt on his credibility. It certainly invalidates his many claims that he received these teachings by divine inspiration.
80. Ibid., 15–56.
81. Ibid., 57–76.

CHAPTER 6
1. From John MacArthur, *Reckless Faith* (Wheaton, Ill.: Crossway, 1994), 91–117.
2. Recently republished in four volumes by Baker Books.
3. A detailed account of how this process occurred in one institution is George Marsden's *Reforming Fundamentalism: Fuller Seminary and the New Evangelicalism* (Grand Rapids: Eerdmans, 1987).

4. Foreword to James R. Spencer, *Heresy Hunters: Character Assassination in the Church* (Lafayette, La.: Huntington House, 1993), vii.

5. Ibid.

6. Philip Schaff, *The Creeds of Christendom,* 3 vols. (Grand Rapids: Baker, 1983 reprint), 1:531.

7. Charles Colson, *The Body* (Dallas: Word, 1992).

8. Ibid., 185.

9. Ibid., 104.

10. Ibid.

11. Ibid., 170.

12. Ibid., 171.

13. Ibid., 186.

14. Ibid., 185.

15. Ibid., 186.

16. Ibid., 198–199.

17. Ibid., 104. Note that here Colson formulates his list in a slightly different way, separating the Resurrection from the Second Coming. This makes six points of doctrine, one more than the five in Colson's numbered list on page 186. On pages 108–109 Colson gives an expanded five-point list borrowed from another source, then adds a sixth point—the authority of the inerrant Word. But in each case the core doctrines he lists are essentially the same.

    Of course, there is a world of meaning wrapped up in terms like "atonement" and "the authority of Scripture." If Colson were appealing for faith in Scripture as the Christian's *sole* authority (excluding papal dictums and magisterial traditions), I would be more comfortable with his formula. But throughout his book he makes repeated, explicit appeals for evangelical Christians to open their arms to Catholicism and Eastern Orthodoxy.

    Therefore whatever he means by "the authority of Scripture" cannot be what the Reformers meant when they spoke of *sola Scriptura,* Scripture as our supreme and sufficient authority.

18. *The Fundamentals* included articles defending justification by faith alone, as well as articles titled, "Is Romanism Christianity?" (*No, it is not* was the thrust of the tract), and "Rome, the Antagonist of the Nation."

19. Colson, *The Body,* 186.

20. Schaff, *Creeds of Christendom,* 1:14–23. See also Herman Witsius, *Sacred Dissertations on the Apostles' Creed,* 2 vols. (Phillipsburg, N. J., 1993 reprint), 1:1–15; and William Cunningham, *Historical Theology,* 2 vols. (Edmonton, Alb.: Still Waters, 1991 reprint), 1:79–93.

21. Schaff, *Creeds of Christendom,* 1:19.

22. Ibid., 1:21.

23. Cunningham, *Historical Theology,* 1:89.

24. Witsius, *Sacred Dissertations,* 30–31 (emphasis added).

25. Cunningham, *Historical Theology,* 1:89.

26. Francis Turretin, *Institutes of Elenctic Theology,* vol. 1, trans. George Musgrave Giger (Phillipsburg, N.J.: Presbyterian & Reformed, 1992), 53.

27. Owing to a misunderstanding of this article, one of the great Protestant hymns includes a line about the church's "mystic sweet communion with those whose rest is won." But far from teaching that people on earth can commune with the dead, Scripture condemns in the strongest terms any activity aimed at establishing that sort of communication (Deut. 18:10–12).

28. Cunningham, *Historical Theology,* 1:89.

29. Ibid., 1:90.

30. Colson, *The Body,* 171.

31. Ibid., 112.

32. Ibid.
33. For the section that follows I am largely indebted to Witsius (op cit.), who includes a marvelous treatment of this very subject in volume 1, pages 16–33. It is noteworthy that Witsius spoke of "fundamental articles" at least 250 years before the fundamentalist movement was named.
34. Turretin, *Institutes of Elenctic Theology*, 48.
35. Witsius, *Sacred Dissertations*, 20.
36. Ibid., 21.
37. Ibid., 27–29.
38. Turretin, *Institutes of Elenctic Theology*, 54.
39. Witsius, *Sacred Dissertations*, 29.
40. Ibid., 31.
41. Ibid., 33.

CHAPTER 7

1. From John MacArthur, *Ashamed of the Gospel* (Wheaton: Crossway, 1993), 119–136.
2. Charles H. Spurgeon, "Another Word Concerning the Down-Grade," *The Sword and the Trowel* (August 1887), 398–99.
3. Doug Murren, *The Baby Boomerang* (Ventura, Calif.: Regal, 1990), 217–18.
4. Ibid., 102–103.
5. Douglas D. Webster, *Selling Jesus: What's Wrong with Marketing the Church* (Downers Grove, Ill.: InterVarsity, 1992), 83–84.
6. John MacArthur, *Romans 1–8* (Chicago: Moody Press, 1991).
7. George Barna, *Marketing the Church* (Colorado Springs: Navpress, 1988), 42–43.
8. Bill Hybels, cited in Douglas D. Webster, *Selling Jesus: What's Wrong with Marketing in the Church?* (Downers Grove, Ill.: InterVarsity, 1992), 58.
9. Charles H. Spurgeon, "Paul the Ready," *The Metropolitan Tabernacle Pulpit*, vol. 38 (London: Passmore and Alabaster, 1892), 578.
10. John MacArthur, *The Gospel According to Jesus*, second ed. (Grand Rapids: Zondervan, 1994); *Faith Works: The Gospel According to the Apostles* (Dallas: Word, 1993).
11. Luther, *Table Talk*, 54:308–9.
12. Murren, *Baby Boomerang*, 215–17.
13. Ibid.
14. C. H. Spurgeon, "Attempts at the Impossible," *The Sword and the Trowel* (December 1888), 619.
15. C. H. Spurgeon, "Progressive Theology," *The Sword and the Trowel* (April 1888), 157–58.
16. Quoted in "Notes," *The Sword and the Trowel* (August 1888), 445. Years before, Varley, a butcher turned lay evangelist, had been one of the key men responsible for encouraging D. L. Moody on his first visit to England. A Plymouth Brethren, Varley and Spurgeon were by no means close theological allies. Over the years Spurgeon had been outspoken in his criticism of the Plymouth Brethren and their exclusivist tendencies. But Varley's defense of Spurgeon in this lengthy and eloquent letter to the editor was one of the high points of the Down-Grade Controversy.

CHAPTER 8

1. From John MacArthur, *The Vanishing Conscience* (Dallas: Word, 1994), 145–166.
2. John Owen, *The Works of John Owen*, 16 vols. (Edinburgh: Banner of Truth, 1967 reprint of 1853 edition), 6:177, 6:9.
3. Ibid., 6:8 (emphasis added).
4. D. Martyn Lloyd-Jones, *Romans: An Exposition of Chapter 8:5–17: The Sons of God* (Grand Rapids: Zondervan, 1974), 92 (emphasis added).
5. Owen, *Works of John Owen*, 6:16–17.
6. D. Martyn Lloyd-Jones, *Sanctified Through the Truth: The Assurance of Our Salvation* (Wheaton, Ill.: Crossway, 1989), 54.

7. Owen, *Works of John Owen*, 6:20.
8. Ibid., 6:11.
9. Ibid., 6:12 (emphasis added).
10. Ibid., 6:14.
11. Cited in I. D. E. Thomas, *A Puritan Golden Treasury* (Edinburgh: Banner of Truth, 1977), 264.
12. Owen, *Works of John Owen*, 6:56 (emphasis added).
13. Ibid., 6:55.
14. Lloyd-Jones, *Romans: An Exposition*, 143.

CHAPTER 9
1. From John MacArthur, *The Glory of Heaven* (Wheaton, Ill.: Crossway, 1996), 67–87.
2. Wilbur Smith, *Biblical Doctrine of Heaven* (Chicago: Moody, 1968), 155.

CHAPTER 10
1. From John MacArthur, *The Freedom and Power of Forgiveness* (Wheaton, Ill.: Crossway, 1998), 113–136.
2. Jay Adams, *From Forgiven to Forgiving* (Amityville, N.Y.: Calvary, 1994), 34.
3. Ibid.
4. Jay Adams cites this verse but argues that it calls only for the preparation of the heart for forgiveness. He suggests that the command "forgive" in this verse merely means that the one praying should be "*ready* to forgive" (p. 30)—but Adams believes actual forgiveness does not occur until the offender asks for forgiveness. The person who has "forgiven" in this manner therefore cannot regard the forgiveness as complete until he confronts the offender, obtains that person's repentance, and formally grants forgiveness.
5. Matthew Henry, *Matthew Henry's Commentary*, 6 vols. (Old Tappan, N.J.: Revell, n.d.), 2:586.

CHAPTER 11
1. From John MacArthur, *Successful Christian Parenting* (Nashville: Word, 1998), 3–24.
2. Associated Press, March 30, 1997.
3. *Milwaukee Journal Sentinel*, July 7, 1998.
4. Barbara Boyer, "Grossberg, Peterson Sent to Jail," *Philadelphia Inquirer*, 10 July 1998, 1.
5. Cited in *Washingtonian* magazine, August 1986, and *Vogue*, September 1989.
6. Cited in the *Washington Post*, 13 November 1983.
7. Michael Fox, "Inhumane Society" (pamphlet), Fox Publications, n.d.
8. David Cooper, *The Death of the Family* (New York: Pantheon, 1971).
9. Kate Millet, *Sexual Politics* (New York: Doubleday, 1970).
10. Hillary Rodham Clinton, *It Takes a Village* (New York: Simon & Schuster, 1996).
11. *Pantagraphy*, 20 September 1970.
12. Gore Vidal, *Reflections Upon a Sinking Ship: A Collection of Essays by Gore Vidal* (Boston: Little, Brown, 1969).
13. Matthew Henry, *Matthew Henry's Commentary on the Whole Bible*, 6 vols. (Old Tappan, N.J.: Revell, n.d.), 3:917.
14. Judith Rich Harris, *The Nurture Assumption: Why Children Turn Out the Way They Do* (New York: Free Press, 1998).
15. Cited in the *Boston Herald*, 17 September.

CHAPTER 12
1. From John MacArthur, *The Second Coming* (Wheaton, Ill.: Crossway, 1999), 25–49.
2. The Jesus Seminar's Web site, with a complete description of their conclusions about Scripture, is online at: www.westarinstitute.org.
3. Antony L. Little, *Faith, Reason, and the Reality of God: A Search for Honesty* (Greenwich, Conn.: Empowerment, 1999), 27.
4. The primary reference of Hosea 11:1 is to the Old Testament nation of Israel, called out of Egypt. But Israel herself was a prophetic *type* (a symbolic prefiguring) of Christ—and

therefore typologically, Israel's sojourn in Egypt prophetically foreshadowed the infant Christ's flight into Egypt. Hosea 11:1 is therefore cited as a prophecy of the infant Christ in Matthew 2:15.

5. In modern times, the word *dowry* usually conveys the idea of money or property brought by the bride to her husband at a marriage, but in biblical times the dowry was a gift bestowed by the bridegroom and his family on the bride (cf. Gen. 34:12).

CHAPTER 13

1. From John MacArthur, *The Murder of Jesus* (Nashville: Word, 2000), 209–224.
2. J. C. Ryle, *Expository Thoughts on the Gospels, Luke,* vol. 2 (New York: Baker & Taylor, n.d.), 467.

CHAPTER 14

1. From John MacArthur, *The Battle for the Beginning* (Nashville: W Publishing Group, 2001), 49–65.
2. *Fiat* is a Latin word meaning "Let it be done."
3. A full discussion of the geological evidences for Creation and the Flood is far beyond the scope of this book. But many fine resources outlining those evidences in detail are available from The Institute for Creation Research (http://www.icr.org) and Answers in Genesis (http://www.answersingenesis.org). See also John Woodmorappe, *Studies in Flood Geology* (Santee, Calif.: Institute for Creation Research, 1999); John C. Whitcomb and Henry M. Morris, *The Genesis Flood* (Grand Rapids: Baker, 1961); and John C. Whitcomb, *The World That Perished* (Grand Rapids: Baker, 1990).
4. See Rebecca Gibson, "Canyon Creation," *Creation Ex Nihilo* (September/November 2000), 46–48. (*Creation Ex Nihilo* is a quarterly magazine published in Australia by Answers in Genesis.)
5. Douglas Kelley, *Creation and Change* (Fearn, Ross-Shire, U.K.: Christian Focus, 1997), 164–5.
6. Ken Ham, *Did Adam Have a Belly Button?* (Green Forest, Ark.: Master Books, 1999). See also Gary Parker, "Did Adam Have a Belly-Button?" on the Answers in Genesis Web site (http://www.answersingenesis.org/docs/1260.asp).
7. Hugh Ross, *The Fingerprint of God* (New Kensington, Pa.: Whitaker House, 1989), 96.
8. Mark Van Bebber and Paul S. Taylor, *Creation and Time: A Report on the Progressive Creationist Book by Hugh Ross* (Gilbert, Ariz.: Eden Communications), 86–89.
9. Ross, *Fingerprint of God,* 160.
10. Van Bebber and Taylor, *Creation and Time: A Report,* 105–110. See also Danny Faulkner, "The Dubious Apologetics of Hugh Ross" (http://www.answersingenesis.org/docs/4149.asp) and Dr. Bolton Davidheiser, "A Statement Concerning the Ministry of Dr. Hugh Ross" (http://www.ldolphin.org/bolton.html).
11. Hugh Ross, *Creation and Time* (Colorado Springs: Navpress, 1994), 56 (emphasis added).
12. Ibid., 57.
13. Ross, *Fingerprint of God,* 145.
14. Ibid.
15. Ibid., 143.
16. Ibid.,159.
17. Henry Morris, *The Genesis Record* (Grand Rapids: Baker, 1976), 45.
18. Edward J. Young, *Studies in Genesis One* (Phillipsburg, N.J.: Presbyterian & Reformed, n.d.), 53.
19. Ross, *Fingerprint of God,* 160.

CHAPTER 15

1. From John MacArthur, *Twelve Ordinary Men* (Nashville: W Publishing Group, 2002), 1–27.

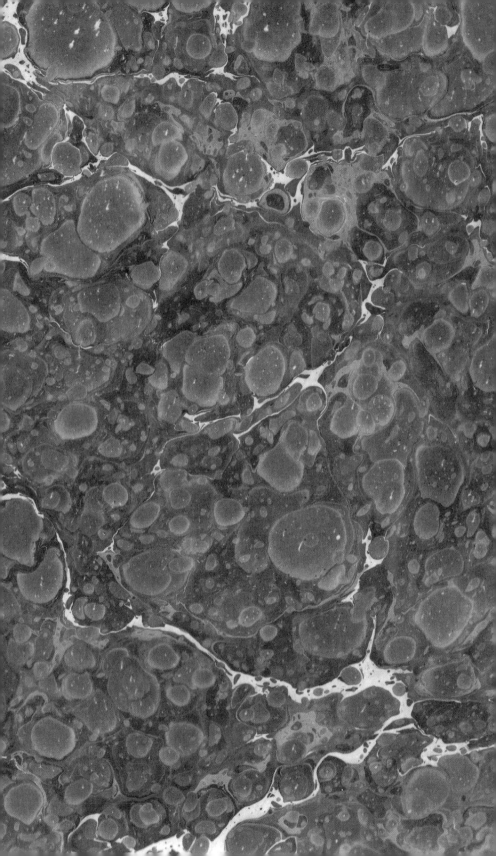

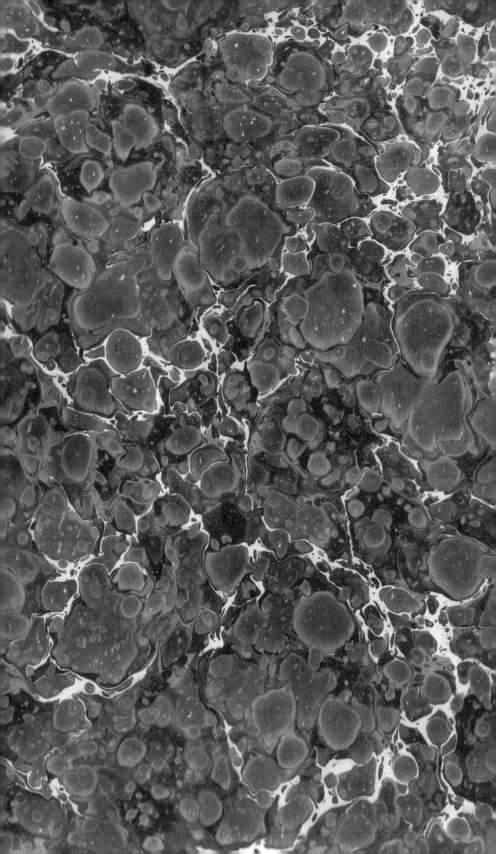